W9-BGD-551

Helping the Obese Patient Find Success

WESTERN® SCHOOLS

By
Wayne C. Miller, PhD

20 contact hours will be awarded upon successful completion of this course.

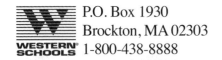
P.O. Box 1930
Brockton, MA 02303
1-800-438-8888

ABOUT THE AUTHOR

Wayne C. Miller, PhD, is a Professor of Exercise Science and Nutrition at the George Washington University Medical Center in Washington, DC. In addition to teaching, Dr. Miller has published more than 65 research articles in the area of obesity and metabolism. He is the author of five books, including *The Non-Diet Diet* and *Negotiated Peace: How to Win the War Over Weight*. Dr. Miller has been the clinical director of three weight loss centers and continues to counsel overweight patients. He was the editor of the *Healthy Weight Journal* and reviews manuscripts for numerous scientific journals. Dr. Miller is an energetic speaker and lectures to scientific and lay audiences on the topics of weight control, exercise, and health behavior.

Wayne C. Miller has disclosed that he has no significant financial or other conflicts of interest pertaining to this course book.

ABOUT THE CONTENT EDITOR

Jessie M. Moore, APRN, MSN, CEN, has more than 25 years of nursing experience, including emergency care, critical care nursing, and health education. She received an Associate's Degree in Nursing in 1979 and a Bachelor of Science in Nursing in 1986, from Mesa College in Grand Junction, Colorado. In 1994, she received a Master of Science in Nursing from the University of Connecticut; and a Post-Master's Certificate as a Family Nurse Practitioner in Primary Care from Fairfield University in 2002. She has held positions in clinical care as well as nursing education.

Ms. Moore is the coordinator for the Center for Obesity Surgery at the Hospital of Saint Raphael in New Haven and provides preoperative and postoperative care and counseling and support as well as nursing education and development related to bariatric care. She is a frequent speaker on bariatric issues regionally and nationally and is involved with legislative efforts related to the access to care for obese patients. Ms. Moore is involved with nursing competency in the care of bariatric patients, and chairs the exam development subcommittee of the Bariatric Nursing Certification Advisory Committee, established by the American Society for Metabolic and Bariatric Surgery.

In addition to editing the content in Chapters 1 through 14, Jessie Moore is the author of Chapter 15.

Jessie Moore has disclosed that she has no significant financial or other conflicts of interest pertaining to this course book.

Nurse Planners: Amy Bernard, MS, BSN, RN-BC and Anne Manton, PhD, APRN, BC, FAAN, FAEN

Amy Bernard and **Anne Manton** have disclosed that they have no significant financial or other conflicts of interest pertaining to this course book.

Copy Editor: Liz Schaeffer

Indexer: Sylvia Coates

Western Schools' courses are designed to provide nursing professionals with the educational information they need to enhance their career development. The information provided within these course materials is the result of research and consultation with prominent nursing and medical authorities and is, to the best of our knowledge, current and accurate. However, the courses and course materials are provided with the understanding that Western Schools is not engaged in offering legal, nursing, medical, or other professional advice.

Western Schools' courses and course materials are not meant to act as a substitute for seeking out professional advice or conducting individual research. When the information provided in the courses and course materials is applied to individual circumstances, all recommendations must be considered in light of the uniqueness pertaining to each situation.

Western Schools' course materials are intended solely for *your* use and *not* for the benefit of providing advice or recommendations to third parties. Western Schools devoids itself of any responsibility for adverse consequences resulting from the failure to seek nursing, medical, or other professional advice. Western Schools further devoids itself of any responsibility for updating or revising any programs or publications presented, published, distributed, or sponsored by Western Schools unless otherwise agreed to as part of an individual purchase contract.

Products (including brand names) mentioned or pictured in Western School's courses are not endorsed by Western Schools, the American Nurses Credentialing Center (ANCC) or any state board.

ISBN: 978-1-57801-326-5

COURSE INSTRUCTIONS
IMPORTANT: Read these instructions *BEFORE* proceeding!

HOW TO EARN CONTACT HOURS

To earn contact hour(s) and receive a certificate of completion, you must read the entire course, pass the final exam with a score of 70% or higher, and complete the course evaluation. **Unless otherwise indicated, contact hours will be awarded for up to 1 year from the date on which this course was purchased.**

FINAL EXAM

Enclosed with your course book you will find a FasTrax Answer Sheet and a FasTrax Instruction Sheet. Use the Answer Sheet to answer all of the final exam questions that appear in this course. FasTrax Answer Sheets are preprinted with your name and address and the course title. If you are completing more than one course, be sure to record your answers on the correct corresponding answer sheet.

Use blue or black ink to completely fill in the circles on the Answer Sheet. The FasTrax grading system will not read pencil. If you make an error, you may use correction fluid (such as Wite-Out®) to correct it. If the course has fewer than 100 questions, leave any remaining answer circles on the Answer Sheet blank.

You must score 70% or higher in order to pass this course. Should you fail to achieve the minimum required score, an additional Answer Sheet will be sent to you so that you may make a second attempt to pass the course. You will be allowed three attempts to pass this course. After three failed attempts, your file will be closed.

COURSE EVALUATIONS

The course evaluation provided in this course book is a required component of the course and must be completed and submitted with your final exam. Responses to evaluation statements should be recorded in the right-hand column of the Answer Sheet, in the section marked "Evaluation." Your evaluation provides Western Schools with vital feedback.

To provide additional feedback regarding this course, our services, or to suggest new course topics, complete the Important Information form found on the back of the Instruction Sheet. Return this completed form to Western Schools with your Answer Sheet.

SUBMITTING THE FINAL EXAM AND EVALUATION

The Instruction Sheet provides detailed steps for submitting your completed Answer Sheet and Important Information form. If you are mailing your Answer Sheet and Important Information form to Western Schools, we recommend that you keep a copy as a back-up.

CHANGE OF ADDRESS?

In the event that your postal or email address changes prior to completing this course, please contact our customer service department at 1-800-618-1670, or customerservice@westernschools.com, so that we may update your file.

WESTERN SCHOOLS GUARANTEES YOUR SATISFACTION

If any continuing education course fails to meet your expectations, or if you are not satisfied for any reason, you may return the course materials for an exchange or a refund (less shipping and handling) within 30 days. Software, video, and audio courses must be returned unopened. Textbooks must not be written in or marked up in any other way. Materials for courses you have already received continuing education credit for will not be accepted.

Thank you for using Western Schools to fulfill your continuing education needs!

WESTERN SCHOOLS
P.O. Box 1930
Brockton, MA 02303
800-438-8888
www.westernschools.com

WESTERN SCHOOLS
STUDY TIME LOG

HELPING THE OBESE PATIENT FIND SUCCESS

INSTRUCTIONS: Use this log sheet to document the amount of time you spend completing this course. Include the time it takes you to read the instructions, read the course book, take the final examination, and complete the evaluation.

Date	Time Spent	
	Hours	Minutes
11/29	4	
~~11/31~~ 12/1	4	
12/2	4	

TOTAL* [   ] [   ]

  Hours   Minutes

***Please use this total study time to answer the final question of the course evaluation.**

iv

WESTERN SCHOOLS
COURSE EVALUATION

HELPING THE OBESE PATIENT FIND SUCCESS

INSTRUCTIONS: Using the scale below, please respond to the following evaluation statements. All responses should be recorded in the right-hand column of the FasTrax answer sheet, in the section marked "Evaluation." Be sure to fill in each corresponding answer circle completely using blue or black ink. Leave any remaining answer circles blank.

A	B	C	D
Agree Strongly	Agree Somewhat	Disagree Somewhat	Disagree Strongly

OBJECTIVES: After completing this course, I am able to

1. Describe obesity and the methods used to measure it in adults and children.
2. Identify health consequences associated with obesity.
3. Discuss factors that contribute to obesity.
4. Describe how to analyze dietary intake and diet composition.
5. Describe techniques used to measure resting metabolic rate (RMR), physical activity, and fitness.
6. Discuss skills needed to help patients recognize and overcome emotional eating.
7. Discuss the most common theories of behavior.
8. Identify communication strategies which foster a therapeutic relationship with the obese patient.
9. Identify sound approaches to dietary modification.
10. Identify necessary components of a successful exercise program for the obese patient.
11. Describe different non-dieting philosophies for obesity management.
12. Describe the clinical application of pharmacotherapy for weight control.
13. Describe bariatric surgery as an effective treatment option for severe obesity.
14. Discuss behavioral factors that enhance weight loss and maintenance.
15. Discuss the issue of weight bias and steps needed to create a sensitive health care environment.

COURSE CONTENT

16. The course materials were presented in a well organized and clearly written manner.
17. The course content was presented in a fair, unbiased and balanced manner.
18. The course expanded my knowledge and enhanced my skills related to the subject matter.
19. I intend to apply the knowledge and skills I've learned to my nursing practice. (Select the appropriate response below.)

    A. Yes   B. Unsure   C. No   D. Not Applicable

ATTESTATION

20. By submitting this answer sheet, I certify that I have read the course materials and personally completed the final examination based on the material presented. Mark "A" for Agree and "B" for Disagree.

continued on next page

COURSE HOURS

21. Choose the response that best represents the total number of clock hours it took to complete this **20 hour** course.

   A. More than 22 hours   B. 18–22 hours   C. Less than 18 hours

Note: To provide additional feedback regarding this course, Western Schools services, or to suggest new course topics, use the space provided on the Important Information form found on the back of the FasTrax instruction sheet included with your course.

CONTENTS

FIGURES AND TABLES

PRETEST

1. Begin this course by taking the pretest. Circle the answers to the questions on this page, or write the answers on a separate sheet of paper. Do not log answers to the pretest questions on the FasTrax test sheet included with the course.

2. Compare your answers to the PRETEST KEY located at the end of the Pretest. The pretest key indicates the page where the content of that question is discussed. Make note of the questions you missed, so that you can focus on those areas as you complete the course.

3. Complete the course by reading the chapters and completing the exam questions at the end of the chapters. Answers to these exam questions should be logged on the FasTrax test sheet included with the course.

Note: Choose the one option that BEST answers each question.

1. The most common measurement of overweight and obesity used worldwide is the

   a. body mass index.
   b. waist circumference.
   c. skinfold measures.
   d. body fat assessment.

2. The most common health problem associated with obesity in the United States is

   a. diabetes.
   b. hypertension.
   c. obstructive sleep apnea.
   d. gastric reflux.

3. Which of the following contributing factors to the development of obesity is generally seen as the most pervasive cause of the current epidemic of overweight?

   a. emotionally triggered eating behavior
   b. genetic predisposition toward obesity
   c. environmental considerations
   d. neurohormonal eating triggers

4. A behavior that is an emotional barrier to healthy eating is

   a. skipping meals.
   b. drinking 6 to 8 glasses of water daily.
   c. eating "fast food."
   d. eating snacks between meals.

5. A patient with a weight that is 50 to 100 lb over the recommended range for age and gender is being seen by a health care provider for a routine physical exam. The term best used by the health professional in initiating a conversation about the patient's weight is

   a. obesity.
   b. fatness.
   c. overweight.
   d. morbid obesity.

6. The dietary modification approach that will achieve the best long-term success for weight loss and maintenance is

   a. a very low-calorie liquid diet.
   b. a commercial weight loss program, such as Weight Watchers.
   c. a low-calorie diet with balanced dietary composition deficits.
   d. a low-carbohydrate, high-protein diet.

7. In order for exercise to contribute to weight loss, it must involve

   a. performance in a setting with available professional supervision.

   b. aerobic activity for at least 60 minutes daily.

   c. lifestyle modification and increased physical activity.

   d. strength training and flexibility activities.

8. A drug that has been approved in a nonprescription form for weight loss is

   a. sibutramine.

   b. orlistat.

   c. phentermine.

   d. metformin.

9. Which patient meets the eligibility criteria for bariatric surgery?

   a. a 36-year-old male with a body mass index (BMI) of 28 and hypertension

   b. a 40-year-old female with a BMI of 36 and type 2 diabetes

   c. a 50-year-old male with a BMI of 38, who is in good health

   d. a 14-year-old female with a BMI of 33 and metabolic syndrome

10. Which situation demonstrates weight bias in the health care setting?

   a. armless chairs in the waiting room

   b. scale located in a public area

   c. use of large patient gowns

   d. floor-mounted toilet available

PRETEST KEY

1.	A	Chapter 1
2.	B	Chapter 2
3.	C	Chapter 3
4.	A	Chapter 6
5.	C	Chapter 8
6.	C	Chapter 9
7.	C	Chapter 10
8.	B	Chapter 12
9.	B	Chapter 13
10.	B	Chapter 15

INTRODUCTION

The prevalence of obesity has reached epidemic proportions in all segments of the population. Two thirds of the adult population in the United States is overweight, with approximately one-third being obese. Obesity carries with it several comorbidities, many of which are life-threatening. Nurses are in a unique position to help the overweight patient adopt and maintain a healthy lifestyle that will reduce and prevent the further development of obesity and its comorbidities.

The objective of this course is to give the nurse the required knowledge and skills to assist the obese patient in meeting weight loss goals. First, a discussion of obesity, its etiology, and the health risks associated with the condition is presented. Following the nursing process, techniques on assessing the patient's specific problems, planning interventions to meet the needs of the patient, and evaluating the results are discussed.

Interventions described help the nurse understand the treatment options available to treat obesity, participate in the prescribed treatment plan, and support the behavior maintenance strategy for the patient. Communication techniques to foster the therapeutic relationship with the patient are also discussed. Throughout the course, information is presented in text format with the addition of participative case studies that demonstrate the concepts being discussed. The final chapter discusses the existence of health care provider bias and the need for sensitivity in the care of the obese patient. Successful holistic care cannot be achieved without an awareness of this aspect.

CHAPTER 1

OBESITY DEFINED

CHAPTER OBJECTIVE

After completing this chapter the learner will be able to describe obesity and the methods used to measure it in adults and children.

LEARNING OBJECTIVES

After completing this chapter, the learner will be able to

1. define obesity conceptually and operationally.

2. describe the methods used to measure adiposity in individuals and populations.

3. list the differences in measuring of overweight children.

INTRODUCTION

The prevalence of obesity has increased dramatically over the past two decades in the United States and in many other countries throughout the world. Worldwide, the number of overweight individuals is equal to the number who are suffering from starvation (Buchwald, 2007). Obesity has been called a modern day global epidemic, and is predicted to number 2.3 billion overweight individuals and 700 million obese citizens worldwide by the year 2015 (World Health Organization, 2008) Obesity presents a problem for several reasons.

- The prevalence of obesity is rising throughout the world.

- Obesity is associated with many types of diseases or medical conditions.

- Obesity has many etiologies and, therefore, is difficult to treat.

- The costs for treating obesity are great.

- Obesity hinders rehabilitation from accidents, injury, and other conditions.

In order to more fully explore the problem, we need to outline the parameters that determine what the term obesity actually means.

CONCEPTUAL AND OPERATIONAL DEFINITIONS OF OBESITY

The accepted conceptual definition of obesity is an excess of body fat that becomes sufficiently large enough to cause reduced health or longevity. How does the conceptual definition of obesity (excess body fat) get translated into an operational definition (something useful, measureable, and medically relevant) for the health care professional? Because there are no ways to directly measure total body fat in freely living individuals, other measures are needed to classify the level of obesity,

Body Mass Index

The World Health Organization and other agencies use the body mass index (BMI) to distinguish among different categories of body weight status for adults. The BMI is a ratio of body weight to height, and is the most common operational definition for obesity. The BMI makes interpreting adiposity guidelines simple and is helpful for cross-comparison of weight recommendations for groups sorted by age, gender, and geographic location. One's BMI is calculated by dividing the individual's body weight by the square of their height, as shown in the following calculation.

$$BMI = \text{weight in kilograms/height in meters}^2$$

OR

$$BMI = \text{weight in pounds/height in inches}^2 \times 703$$

The BMI may produce large standard errors when trying to estimate actual adiposity levels. A BMI value may be misleading for athletic individuals who have an increased weight-to-height ratio because of augmented muscularity. Despite this limitation, it has been widely adopted as the most effective clinical tool for classification of the degree of obesity. Classifications of adult BMI are shown in Table 1-1.

TABLE 1-1: ADULT BODY MASS INDEX CLASSIFICATIONS	
Classification	**BMI**
Underweight	Less than 18.5
Normal Weight	18.5-24.9
Overweight	25.0-29.9
Obesity Class I	30.0-34.9
Obesity Class II	35.0-39.9
Obesity Class III	40.0 or greater
(World Health Organization, 1998)	

Waist and Hip Circumference

Waist-to-hip ratio and the waist circumference are two additional operational definitions for central obesity or abdominal obesity. Abdominal obesity has been shown to strongly correlate with cardiovascular disease, diabetes, metabolic syndrome, and cancer.

There are two general measures of abdominal obesity, the waist circumference and the waist-to-hip ratio (waist centimeters or inches/hip centimeter or inches). Waist circumference is measured just above the upper hip bone (iliac crest), whereas hip circumference is measured at the widest part of the hips. An absolute waist circumference greater than 102 cm (40 in.) in men and 88 cm (35 in.) in women, and a waist-to-hip ratio greater than 0.90 for men and 0.85 for women are both considered the cut points for abdominal obesity (Yusuf et al., 2004).

Waist-to-hip ratio also helps identify body shape. Individuals who have a higher waist than hip circumference are classified as having central obesity. This "apple-shaped" body type has been identified as having a higher risk of cardiac and metabolic disorders than the individual with a higher hip circumference, or "pear-shaped" body.

Predictive Measurements of Body Fat

Although BMI and waist circumference are cost effective methods of defining the degree of obesity, many other methods exist to determine the percentage of fat deposits. These methods have varying degrees of reliability, availability, costs of performing, and practicality of use in the clinical setting. A brief discussion of several of these methods follows.

Circumference Measurements

Circumference measurements (also called girth measurements) taken at certain places on the body have also been used to estimate total body fat content. Anatomical landmarks for common girth measurements used to assess total body fatness follow.

- *Abdomen* – 1.0 in. (2.5 cm) above the umbilicus
- *Hips* – point of maximum protrusion when standing with the heels together
- *Right thigh* – upper thigh just below the buttocks

- *Right upper arm (biceps)* – arm straight, palm facing upward, arm extended in front of the body, measurement taken midway between the shoulder and elbow
- *Right forearm* – arm extended in front of the body, palm up, measure maximum girth
- *Right calf* – measure maximum girth midway between the ankle and knee

The test-retest reliability of girth measurements range from approximately $r = 0.90 - 0.99$, whereas the measurements have a standard error of ~ 2.5% to 4.0%. Mathematical equations for determining body density (and, ultimately, body fat content) are shown in Table 1-2. The ability of the mathematical equations used from circumference measures to determine body fat becomes less accurate for persons who engage in strength training, participate in strenuous sports, or are extremely thin or very fat. Circumference measurements can also be used to determine patterns of fat distribution as well as changes in body size during weight loss/gain. Circumference measures are commonly used as assessment tools in physician offices or health clinics. The major advantage of this technique is that large numbers of subjects can be measured quickly in almost any environment by minimally trained personnel.

Hydrostatic Weighing

Hydrostatic weighing or underwater weighing utilizes the principle that when an object is submerged in water, it will displace a volume of water equal to the object's own volume. Hence, if a person is submerged underwater, the person will displace a volume of water equal to his/her body volume. If body weight is known, then body density can be calculated because density equals weight divided by volume. Body fat content can then be estimated, because the density of fat tissue is different from the density of lean body tissues.

Hydrostatic weighing is often not practical to perform in the clinical setting; however, it has been utilized in scientific study for more than 50 years. This method is rapidly being replaced by more technically advanced body composition analysis systems, such as air displacement plethysmography and dual-energy X-ray absorptiometry.

Bod Pod® or Air Displacement Plethysmography

Modern technology and sensitive instrumentation have allowed scientists to employ air displacement plethysmography as a means for determining body composition. An example of this system is called the Bod Pod (Figure 1-1). In contrast to hydrostatic weighing, the Bod Pod uses air dis-

TABLE 1-2: REGRESSION EQUATIONS FOR PREDICTING BODY DENSITY AND PERCENT BODY FAT IN MEN AND WOMEN USING GIRTH MEASUREMENTS

Sex	Equation
Men	$D_b = -47.371817 + (0.57914807 \times \text{abdomen}) + (0.25189114 \times \text{hips}) + 0.21366088 \times \text{iliac crest}) - (0.35595404 \times \text{weight})$
Women	$D_b = 1.168297 - (0.002824 \times \text{abdomen}) + (0.0000122098 \times \text{abdomen}^2) - (0.000733128 \times \text{hips}) + (0.000510477 \times \text{height}) - (0.000216161 \times \text{age})$

Popular equations for determining % body fat from body density.

Source	Equation
Brozek	% Body Fat = $(457 \div D_b) - 414.2$
Siri	% Body Fat = $(495 \div D_b) - 450$

D_b = body density, which is subsequently converted to % body fat. All girth measurements are made in cm. Weight is recorded in kg. Height is recorded in cm.

placement rather than water displacement to determine body volume and density. Similar to hydrostatic weighing, once body density is determined, standardized equations for calculating body fat are used. Therefore, the only difference between the two methods is how body volume is measured, not how body fat content is calculated.

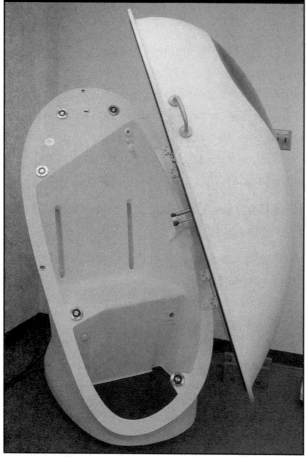

FIGURE 1-1: THE BOD POD® BODY COMPOSITION ASSESSMENT CHAMBER FOR DETERMINING BODY FAT CONTENT

Although research shows that Bod Pod measures correlate with hydrostatic weighing for a heterogeneous subject sample, some studies have revealed that the Bod Pod has some systematic measurement errors for special populations such as college-aged female athletes, young women versus young men, and 10 to 18-year-old boys and girls. Because air-displacement plethysmography is a relatively new technique for determining body composi-

tion, it may just be that population-specific formulas will have to be developed for this technique.

Dual-energy X-ray Absorptiometry

Dual-energy X-ray Absorptiometry (DXA; sometimes abbreviated DEXA) is a technology that has been used for several years to assess bone mineral density. As DXA technology developed, machines were built to perform whole-body scans (Figure 1-2). The DXA can now be used for regional estimates of bone, fat, and lean tissues. Up until 10 years ago, a whole-body DXA scan would take 30 minutes to perform. Now the whole-body scan can be performed in 6 to 10 minutes.

One advantage of the DXA method over other techniques is that analyses can be obtained on various regions of the body simultaneously, making it possible to compare pretest and posttest measures of body fat for targeted areas of the body. A certified DXA technologist or radiologist must perform the test because the DXA scan is actually a low-dose X-ray. The amount of radiation received from a whole-body DXA scan is about 5% of that received in a standard chest X-ray, or equal to the amount of radiation one would receive by flying cross-country in an airplane. The DXA can be used on all people, including children. DXA machines are becoming more popular in hospitals, clinics, physician offices, rehabilitation centers, research institutions, and universities.

Bioelectrical Impedance Analysis

Bioelectrical impedance analysis (BIA) is an easy-to-administer, noninvasive, and safe method of assessing body fatness in almost any setting. With BIA, a small portable instrument is used to pass an electrical current (typically 50 A at 50 kHz) through an extremity. Resistance to the electric current is measured. Lean tissue mass and water are good conductors of electricity, whereas fat tissue is not. The resistance to current flow is therefore inversely related to lean tissue mass and total body water. The accuracy of BIA for determining total

FIGURE 1-2: A DUAL-ENERGY X-RAY ABSORPTIOMETRY MACHINE FOR DETERMINING BODY CONTENT AND BONE DENSITY

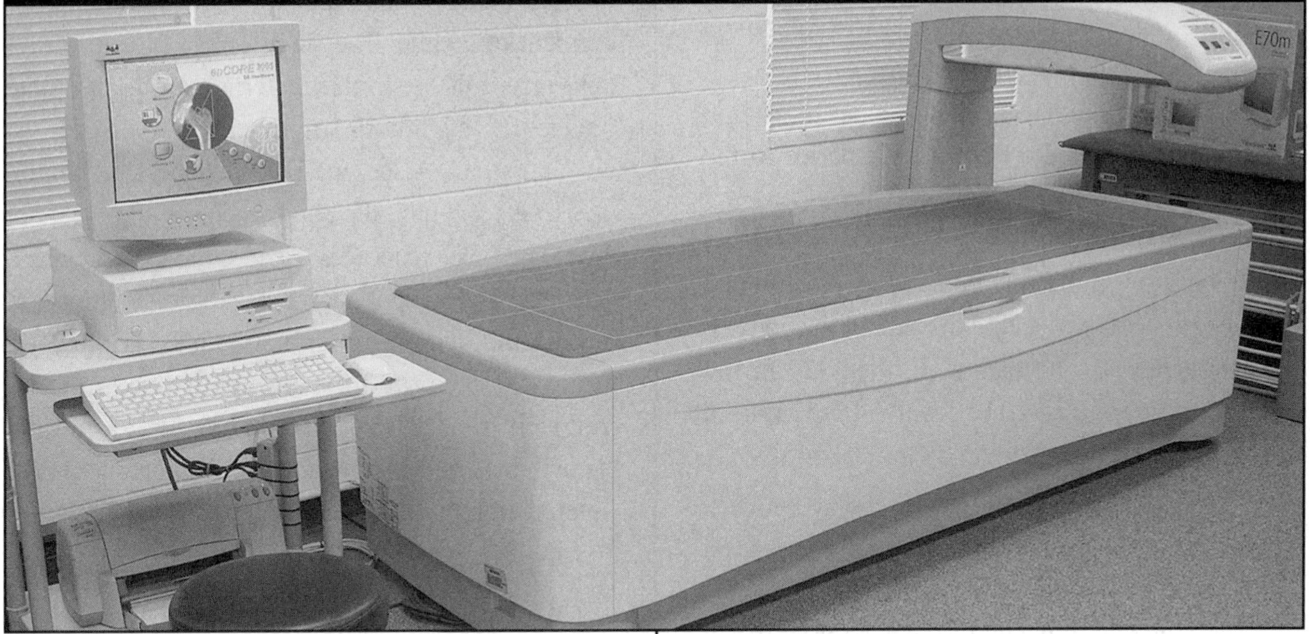

body fat content can be variable, but the reliability of BIA is somewhat questionable. Repeat measures with the same analyzer and comparison measures between analyzers can vary substantially. The reliability of repeated measures for a single person can be affected significantly by their state of hydration, nutritional status, and prior exercise bout. Accuracy can be improved by using a multi-frequency analyzer rather than a single frequency analyzer. Standardized measurement conditions should be used to minimize error, including

- avoidance of eating or drinking immediately before measurement,

- avoidance of exercise or sweating before measurement,

- absence of fluid retention, such as edema, and

- avoiding electrode placement in areas where skin conditions may interfere with electrical transference, such as thickened skin or open lesions (Christensen & Kushner, 2007).

Skinfold Measures

The skinfold method for estimating percent of body fat relies on the relationship between subcutaneous fat and overall body fatness. The skinfold measure is taken by pinching the skin and the underlying fat at certain locations on the body. A caliper is used to measure the thickness of the skinfold pinched. Mathematical equations have been developed to predict the total body fat content from the derived skinfold measures. However, there is a great deal of variability in subcutaneous fat for any degree of body fatness. Hence, more 100 prediction equations have been derived for various subgroups of the population. This abundance of equations creates a problem for the professional who is working with clientele exhibiting varying characteristics.

The selection of the proper prediction equation by a professional depends on how homogeneous or heterogeneous a group of patients are. On the other hand, general equations are derived from populations that are diverse, and can be applied to a heterogeneous sample of patients. A description of the seven most common skinfold sites and measurement procedures follows:

- *Abdominal* – a vertical fold measured 2 cm to the right of the umbilicus

- *Chest* – a diagonal fold measured midway between the anterior axillary line and the nipple for men, or one-third the distance between the anterior axillary line and the nipple for women

- *Subscapular* – a diagonal fold 1 to 2 cm below the inferior angle of the scapula
- *Suprailium* – a diagonal fold along the natural angle of the iliac crest, taken superior to the iliac crest in the anterior axillary line
- *Triceps* – a vertical fold taken midway between the acromion and olecranon processes while the arm is relaxed and to the side of the body
- *Midaxillary* – a vertical fold taken on the midaxillary line at the level of the xiphoid process
- *Thigh* – a vertical fold taken midway between the top of the patella and the inguinal crease on the anterior midline of the thigh

Body fat determination through skinfold measurements compares favorably with hydrostatic weighing; however, a major drawback for the skinfold technique is that the calipers will not fit the obese person, and skinfold measures for the obese are fairly inaccurate. Nonetheless, because the skinfold caliper is relatively inexpensive and small, and the test is easily administered many professionals who do consulting and counseling have added this test to their collection of evaluation tools.

BODY FAT ASSESSMENT IN CHILDREN

The prevalence of overweight continues to rise in children – from a 5% incidence during the period of 1963 to 1970, to a 17% incidence measured during 2003 to 2004. (Krebs et al., 2007) In an attempt to curb the obesity epidemic, many childhood obesity prevention programs have been designed, tested, and implemented. Thus, assessment of childhood adiposity has become a focal point for research and clinical practice.

Body Mass Index in Children

BMI changes throughout the growth and development of a child. The BMI-for-age plots for boys and girls follow similar patterns, but the absolute indices are slightly different between the sexes. At about 2 years of age, the BMI declines and continues to decline until the child reaches 5 to 6 years of age. Then, between ages 4 and 6 the BMI begins a gradual rise and continues to rise throughout most of adulthood. This drop and rise in BMI during a child's growth and development is commonly referred to as adiposity rebound. It is a normal growth pattern for all children, and adults should not interpret this curvilinear growth pattern as abnormal.

The BMI is less accurate in predicting childhood overweight than with adults, because the relationship between weight and height during childhood growth is not linear. However, the BMI can be used as an indicator for tracking body size throughout the life cycle. A child's BMI-for-age is a measure shown to be consistent with the adult BMI. As mentioned earlier, the BMI for children is gender specific and changes throughout growth and development, whereas the BMI for adults is neither gender nor age specific. Figure 1-3 demonstrates a pediatric BMI chart for boys. Recommendations are to classify a child's BMI-for-age at or above the 95th percentile as overweight and between the 85th and 95th percentiles as at risk for overweight. The term overweight rather than obesity is the preferred designation for describing children and adolescents with a BMI-for-age above the 95th percentile.

Childhood Skinfold Measures

Skinfold thickness measurements are accurate as a predictor of total body fat in adolescents and children. The procedure utilizes two skinfold sites, the triceps and calf. The triceps measure is a vertical fold taken midway between the acromion and olecranon on the posterior of the arm with the elbow extended. The calf measure is a vertical fold taken at the place of greatest girth on the inside of

FIGURE 1-3: THE BODY MASS INDEX FOR AGE PERCENTILES FOR BOYS AGE 2 TO 20 YEARS

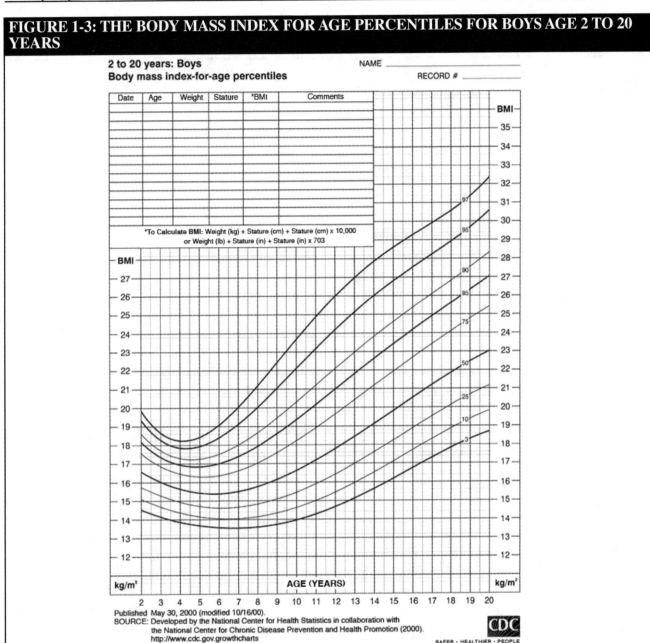

2 to 20 years: Boys
Body mass index-for-age percentiles

Note. From "Overweight and obesity" by Centers for Disease Control and Prevention. Retrieved July 1, 2008, from www.cdc.gov/nccdphp/dnpa/obesity/

the lower leg in line with the medial malleolus. Three measures are taken at each site and the median measure for each site is used for body fat determination. Sum the triceps and calf measurements and convert the sum into percent body fat according to the values presented in Table 1-3.

Despite the accuracy of body fat prediction with this method, experts do not recommend routine use as a screening tool because of the fact that there is a lack of accepted reference data on skinfold thick-

ness in children, and there exists a large potential for measurement error (Krebs et al., 2007).

Waist Circumference

Waist circumference measurement is an evolving area of assessment in pediatrics. It provides a better estimate of visceral adipose tissue and is seen as a more efficient predictor than BMI in identifying risk of serious comorbidities such as early metabolic syndrome. Due to lack of specific clinical guidelines for interpretation of measurements, rou-

TABLE 1-3: BODY COMPOSITION NORMS FOR BOYS AND GIRLS

	Boys		Girls	
	Skinfolds (mm)	*% Fat*	*Skinfolds (mm)*	*% Fat*
Very low	Less than 5	Less than 8	Less than 11	Less than 12
Low	5-10	8-10	11-16	12-15
Normal	11-25	11-20	17-30	16-25
Moderately high	26-32	21-25	31-36	26-30
High	33-40	26-31	37-45	31-38
Very high	Greater than 40	Greater than 31	Greater than 45	Greater than 38

Skinfolds (mm) = the sum of the triceps and calf measurements.

(Lohman, 1987)

tine use has not been established but is expected to continue to develop as a standard measurement (Barlow & Expert Committee, 2007). (See Case Study 1-1.)

THE PREVALENCE OF OBESITY IN THE UNITED STATES

It is well known that the prevalence of overweight and obesity in the United States has risen dramatically over the past two decades. If the BMI of 30 is used as the criteria for obesity, 72 million Americans or 34% of the adult population older than 20 years of age is obese (Centers for Disease Control and Prevention, 2008). This includes 33.3% of the male population and 35.3% of of the female population. The highest prevalence of obesity is found in men (40%) and women (41%) ages 40 to 59. Fortunately, the rising trend in the prevalence of obesity in the United States seems to have leveled off over the past couple of years. The most recent report from the Centers for Disease Control and Prevention states that there was no significant increase in obesity from 2003-2004 to 2005-2006. However, the actual percentages did increase slightly from 2003-2004 when 31.1% of men and 33.2% of women were obese (Centers for Disease Control and Prevention, 2008).

Although obesity pervades all segments of the population, certain ethnic or racial groups present a higher incidence of obesity than others. Obesity is more common among African American and Hispanic women than among Caucasian women. Among African Americans, the proportion of women who are obese is 80% higher than the proportion of men who are obese. The same holds true for Hispanic women and men, but the percentage of Caucasian women and men who are obese is about the same. Approximately 53% of African American women aged 40 to 59 are obese, whereas 51% of Mexican Americans of the same age are obese (Centers for Disease Control and Prevention, 2008).

The term overweight, rather than obesity, is used for children because obesity denotes a disease state; and many overweight children do not present with disease or the comorbidities of obesity. The prevalence of overweight is rising in children as is obesity in adults. The current definition of overweight among children is a statistical definition based on the year 2000 Centers for Disease Control and Prevention growth charts for children in the United States. Overweight is defined as at or above the 95th percentile of BMI. Accordingly, 13.9% of young children are overweight (ages 2 to 5 years), and 18.8% of elementary school-age children (ages 6 to 11 years), and 17.4% of teenagers (ages 12 to 19 years) are overweight (Centers for Disease Control and Prevention, 2008). Race and ethnicity

Case Study 1-1: Body Composition Assessment

You are a nurse practitioner at a bariatric center. Mary, a new patient, is referred to you for a body composition analysis. Mary is concerned with her body fat content and relates to you that 1 month ago she was measured by a skinfold test. She does not believe that the evaluation was accurate. The previous skinfold test measured her at 46% fat. At 5' 4" and 189 lb, she believes this is an unreasonably high body fat content. Mary has not gained or lost weight since her skinfold test. Your clinic has a DXA machine, a Bod Pod, and skinfold calipers. What should you do to rectify the problem?

Intervention/Solution

Mary has a calculated body mass index (BMI) of 32.5, which places her in the obese class I category. You perform a Bod Pod evaluation on Mary, which reveals that Mary's body fat percentage is 38%. You explain to Mary why there was a discrepancy between estimated body fat content between the skinfolds and the Bod Pod.

How does knowledge of Mary's BMI help you solve the problem? What assumption can be made about Mary's body composition considering her weight remains unchanged from the time of the assessment in question? Which of the tests at your disposal are the most reliable and valid for an obese woman?

Resolution

There are several hints or keys that guide you in what to do. First, skinfold tests for obese people are not accurate. The skinfold calipers are not made large enough for obesity testing, and compression of large folds of subcutaneous fat are not accurately measured. So, your first clue leads you to believe that the skinfold test was probably not accurate. The second clue is that you know Mary's weight and height. You can quickly calculate her BMI and find that it is 32.5. Class I obesity, with a BMI of 32.5, is generally not high enough to correlate with a body fat content of 44%. So, you have another indicator that the skinfold test was probably inaccurate. The third clue is that Mary's weight has not changed since the skinfold test. Therefore, you can probably assume that her body composition has not changed either because it has only been a month since she was skinfold tested. This information tells you that you can perform another body composition analysis to compare against the skinfold test done previously.

The key to selecting the Bod Pod for the comparison test is that you only have three re-test choices: DXA, Bod Pod, and skinfolds. You could re-do the skinfold test and compare it with the previous test. However, this approach would only reveal whether the two skinfold tests were highly correlated and not reveal Mary's true body fat content because skinfolds on obese subjects are inaccurate. The DXA is a valid choice because it is highly reliable. However, it does involve low-dose X-ray exposure, and you only desire to know total body fat content, not regional fat content. So, you opt for the Bod Pod, because it is a noninvasive, highly reliable, and valid measurement.

appears to have no influence on childhood overweight until the ages of 12 to 19 years. At this point, more African American and Mexican American children become overweight compared to Caucasian children. The proportion of teenagers from poor households who are overweight is almost twice that of those from middle- and high-income households.

The increase in obesity has led to intense scrutiny and an explosion of suggested solutions and programs dealing with weight loss. Treatment of obesity has become a multimillion dollar industry. Many of these efforts have not been shown to be successful, and some may even be harmful. More research into the causes and contributing factors of the problem and the most effective solutions for specific subgroups within the overall population is needed.

SUMMARY

There are several ways in which obesity can be defined. The most common conceptual definition is an excess of total body fat that increases disease risk and premature mortality. Many methods exist to determine the extent of body fat or to predict the percentage of body fat, though many have limited application in the clinical setting. The most common operational definition of obesity recognized world wide is a BMI greater than 30.

Obesity has reached epidemic proportions in the United States. Over one third of the adult population is obese and childhood obesity has increased substantially over the past 20 years. Research-based solutions are needed to better treat this condition.

EXAM QUESTIONS

CHAPTER 1
Questions 1-3

Note: Choose the one option that BEST answers each question.

1. The operational definition of obesity is most commonly defined in terms of

    a. body mass index.
    b. the waist-to-hip ratio.
    c. total body fat.
    d. essential body fat.

2. A major drawback for the skinfold technique used for determining body fat is that

    a. there are no consistent points at which to measure.
    b. the test is difficult to administer.
    c. calipers typically do not fit the obese person.
    d. the calipers are very expensive.

3. The relationship between weight and height during childhood

    a. is the same for all children between 2 and 18 years old.
    b. accurately predicts overweight in adulthood.
    c. steadily increases from 2 years of age to 20 years of age.
    d. changes throughout growth and development.

REFERENCES

Barlow, S.E. & Expert Committee. (2007). Expert committee recommendations regarding prevention, assessment, and treatment of child and adolescent overweight and obesity: Summary report. *Pediatrics, 120,* 164-192.

Buchwald, H. (2007). Is morbid obesity a surgical disease? *General Surgery News, 6,* 9-15.

Centers for Disease Control and Prevention. (2009). *Overweight and obesity.* Retrieved July 1, 2008, from www.cdc.gov/nccdphp/dnpa/ obesity/

Christenson, K. & Kushner, R. (2007). Measuring body fat in the clinical setting using bioelectrical impedance analysis. *Obesity Management, 3,* 185-186.

Krebs, N.F., Himes, J.H., Jacobson, D., Nicklas, T.A., Guilday, P., & Styne, D. (2007). Assessment of child and adolescent overweight and obesity. *Pediatrics, Supplement, 120,* 193-228.

Lohman, T.G. (1987). The use of skinfolds to estimate body fatness in children and youth. *Journal Physical Education Recreation Dance, 58*(9), 98-101.

World Health Organization. (1998). *Obesity: Preventing and managing the global epidemic: – Report of a WHO consultation on obesity.* Geneva: World Health Organization.

World Health Organization. (2008). *Obesity.* Retrieved February 15, 2009, from www.who.int/ topics/ obesity/en

Yusuf, S., Hawken, S., Ounpuu, S., Dans, T., Avezum, A., Lanas, F., et al. (2004). Effect of potentially modifiable risk factors associated with myocardial infarction in 52 countries (the INTERHEART study): Case-control study. *Lancet, 364:*937-952.

CHAPTER 2

HEALTH RISKS OF OBESITY

CHAPTER OBJECTIVES

After completing this chapter the learner will be able to identify health consequences associated with obesity.

LEARNING OBJECTIVES

After completing this chapter, the learner will be able to

1. identify major health risks associated with obesity.
2. describe health risks of obesity in children and adolescents.
3. state the effect of obesity on mortality rates.
4. describe the elements of a health risk assessment of an obese individual.

INTRODUCTION

Obesity has previously been defined as an excess in body fat that reduces one's health and/or longevity. Obesity is also a medical condition that places a person at risk for other diseases called comorbidities. Understanding of the potential effects of obesity on the health of the individual is essential to all phases of care. Comorbid disease will impact choices of treatment modalities. Ongoing monitoring for improvement of these conditions with weight loss is also necessary.

ENDOCRINE AND METOBOLIC DISORDERS

Central to understanding the metabolic effects on the body is the concept that the fat cell is a type of endocrine cell and adipose tissue functions as an endocrine organ. Whereas waist circumference has been established as a measure of abdominal fat, recent research (Klein & Romijn, 2008) has focused on the differences between subcutaneous abdominal fat and intra-abdominal or visceral fat that is found surrounding abdominal organs. Visceral fat deposition is not yet fully understood; however, it appears to be a consequence of complex neuroendocrine pathway abnormalities. What is clear is this type of fat deposition provides the basis for much of the increased risk of comorbid disease development. Waist circumference does not distinguish between the two, but it does provide a useful assessment of the potential of such deposits and is a useful tool in evaluating potential comorbid disease and risk severity of obesity.

Type 2 Diabetes Mellitus

The increase in obesity has been recognized as a major contributor to a 25% rise in the prevalence of diabetes in the United States over the past 20 years. The risk of diabetes increases in a linear fashion with body mass index (BMI) increase. Data collected in 1998 showed a 2% incidence in individuals with BMIs of 25 to 29.9 (overweight), increasing to 8% for those with BMIs of 30 to 34.9, and 13% in those with BMIs greater than 35 (Klein & Romijn, 2008). As excess fat accumulates in the body, insulin action at the cellular level is impaired, and glucose entrance into the cell is reduced. The pancreas responds by increasing insulin production, and in individuals predisposed to the disease, the B cells of the pancreas begin to fail, and diabetes appears.

Weight loss of 10% to 20% of body weight alone has been shown to reduce the hyperglycemic and hyperinsulinemic state. In addition, physical activity decreases insulin resistance and contributes to better glycemic control.

Dyslipidemia

Although high blood cholesterol is associated with overweight, the increase in incidence is not as significant as other comorbidities. What is significant is alteration in the specific serum lipid abnormalities, including an increase in hypertriglyceridemia, a reduction in high-density lipoprotein cholesterol levels, and an increased fraction of small, dense low-density lipoprotein particles (Pi-Sunyer, 2002). These changes lead to a higher risk of heart disease. Abdominal obesity increases the risk of this disorder.

Metabolic Syndrome

In the past decade, a new classification of comorbid risk factors has emerged. Metabolic syndrome, or Syndrome X, is best described as a cluster of risk factors that place a person at risk for cardiovascular disease and diabetes. The diagnosis of metabolic syndrome is based on the existence of some or all of a cluster of specific health issues, defined as

- insulin resistance,
- hypertension,
- central or abdominal obesity measured by waist circumference,
- decreased high-density lipoprotein cholesterol, and
- elevated triglycerides.

When three or more of these risk factors are present, the individual has metabolic syndrome. A

central cause of this syndrome is visceral fat (NHLBI Obesity Education Initiative Expert Panel on the Identification, Evaluation, and Treatment of Overweight and Obesity in Adults, 1998). Now recognized as a separate health risk, metabolic syndrome is also believed to be a precursor to diabetes.

CARDIOVASCULAR DISORDERS

Hypertension

Hypertension is the most common health condition associated with obesity in the United States (Hellerstein & Parks, 2004), affecting about one third of obese persons with a prevalence more than twice as high as that found in lean subjects. Studies have shown an increase of 3 mm Hg in systolic blood pressure and 2 mm Hg in diastolic blood pressure with every 10-kg rise in body weight (Pi-Sunyer, 2002). Many causes have been theorized. Insulin resistance may influence the condition because insulin enhances the reabsorption of sodium.

Dietary modification alone has been shown to reduce hypertension, and weight loss of 10% can also significantly lower blood pressure (Blackburn, 2002). Increased physical activity also benefits the individual in reducing the level of hypertension and cardiac risk.

Coronary Heart Disease

Increased body mass requires increased blood flow to supply tissues, which can lead to cardiomyopathy, prolonged electrical conduction, and heart failure. Associated risk factors for such conditions include hypertension, dyslipidemia, and diabetes; however, several studies have shown an independent correlation between obesity and heart disease aside from that related to other risk factors (Klein & Romijn, 2008).

As mentioned above, the benefits of weight loss, diet modification and physical activity can greatly reduce this risk. A more gradual approach may be needed to increase physical activity, and heart rate, blood pressure, and any accompanying symptoms should be monitored closely. Reduced-sodium and low-fat diet guidelines are recommended in general therapy as well as weight loss plans. Medications used to treat conditions may reduce heart rate to decrease the workload of the heart, so this parameter may not be as useful for achieving targeted cardiovascular levels of activity.

Cerebrovascular and Thromboembolic Disease

Ischemic stroke risk increases by twofold in obese patients. However, more commonly seen are the problems of venous stasis, deep vein thrombosis, and pulmonary embolism. Increased abdominal obesity plays a factor in this risk by slowing lower extremity venous return as a result of increased abdominal pressure. Insulin resistance causes a prothrombotic state.

Although many of the risks of obesity are well known to the general population, few individuals have awareness of the increased risk of deep vein thrombosis. Avoidance of smoking, and long periods of inactivity as contributing factors are key. Oral contraceptive use in females can also increase risk of thromboembolic events. Weight loss and increased physical activity will have a preventive effect, but patient education of warning signs will help to detect and treat these deadly conditions more quickly.

PULMONARY DISORDERS

Restrictive Lung Disease

Obesity contributes to reduced pulmonary function by increasing the work of breathing and restricting ventilation, particularly in individuals with increased abdominal obesity. Increased weight on the chest wall causes difficulty in breathing. Older individuals are at even higher risk for respiratory insufficiency, given the normal aging changes in the lungs. Although not caused by obesity, asthma symptoms are often worsened by its presence. Additionally, medications used in treatment also can increase heart rate and blood pressure, especially during physical activity, requiring more careful monitoring.

Obstructive Sleep Apnea

Upper airway obstruction caused by excess fatty tissue and relaxation of the pharyngeal and glossal muscles contributes to an increased risk of episodes of apnea and hypoxia during sleep in individuals with a BMI greater than 30 and neck circumference greater than 17 in. in men and 16 in. in women. Daytime sleepiness, excessive snoring, and disrupted sleep are characteristic symptoms. Obstructive sleep apnea affects 10% to 20% of obese individuals (Camden, 2009). Modest weight loss of 9% of initial body weight has been shown to reduce the symptoms of sleep apnea, though research has not yet defined the mechanism of improvement (Blackburn, 2002).

Many cases of sleep apnea are undiagnosed. Individuals with early symptoms should be referred for sleep study evaluation because this condition carries a higher risk of cardiac dysrhythmias during the hypoxic state of sleep.

Obesity Hypoventilation Syndrome

Severe cases of sleep apnea causing persistent hypoxia can result because of the mechanical effects of severe obesity. The most severe form is Pickwickian syndrome, which results in irregular breathing, cyanosis, and polycythemia. Pulmonary hypertension and right ventricular dysfunction are the result. It is usually accompanied by severe obesity and numerous other comorbid conditions. The patient is more likely to benefit from an aggressive weight loss measure, such as bariatric surgery, which is discussed in a later chapter.

GASTROINTESTINAL DISORDERS

Gastroesophageal Reflux Disease

Studies have shown a higher incidence of reflux symptoms, erosive esophagitis, Barrett's esophagus, and esophageal adenocarcinoma (Richter, 2007). A twofold to threefold increase of esophageal symptoms is seen in obese patients. Barrett's esophagus results from severe persistent reflux symptoms, which change the lining of the esophagus, and can be a precursor of esophageal malignancy.

Diet needs in the patient with reflux disease generally include avoidance of foods that trigger symptoms. This factor should not prevent diet modification for weight loss purposes, and may be a motivating factor for the individual who suffers from this problem.

Gallstones

Obesity has long been known to predispose individuals to gallstone formation. Increased cholesterol secretions by the liver as well as decreased motility of the gallbladder contribute to slower emptying. Stones formed increase the tendency of acute and chronic gallbladder inflammation.

Although there is an increase in gallstone formation in obese individuals, the greatest incidence of symptomatic gallstone obstruction occurs during weight loss. Weight loss exceeding 1.5 kg per week has been shown to increase the rate of stone formation. Several sources found that rapid weight loss, such as that occurring in gastric surgery or with a very low-calorie diet (less than 600 kcal/day) increased the incidence of gallstones from 1% to 2% to 25% to 35% (Klein & Romijn, 2008).

Liver Disease

Liver abnormalities related to obesity are commonly referred to collectively as nonalcoholic steatohepatitis. Included in these abnormalities are hepatomegaly, abnormal liver enzymes, steatosis, steatohepatitis, fibrosis, and cirrhosis. The mechanism for such changes is not clear at this time; however, gradual weight loss of 10% usually causes liver enzymes to return to normal and liver size and fat content to decrease. More rapid weight loss can have similar results but also can promote hepatic inflammation and worsening of steatohepatitis. Patient education regarding minimization of other potential insults to the liver, such as drug and alcohol metabolism, and the need for lifetime monitoring of this condition are important aspects of minimizing later complications.

MUSCULOSKELETAL DISORDERS

Osteoarthritis and Gout

Excessive weight causes wear and tear on the weight-bearing joints, particularly the knees, hips, and the spine. Sixty six percent of obese people suffer from osteoarthritis (Camden, 2009). Individuals older than the age of 50 tend to have more limitations related to arthritis. With more severe obesity, gait changes occur as the body adapts to carry the heavier load of body tissues. Musculoskeletal pain often interferes with activities of daily living, and may impact the ability of the individual to perform physical activity recommendations. The challenge of helping the patient find activity that will meet his or her limitations can be difficult. Water activities are much less stressful to weight-bearing joints, but individuals who are obese are commonly self-conscious about being in or even purchasing the swimwear that this type of activity necessitates. Physical therapy can be a good way to introduce such activity and may also stress the importance of this component of weight loss.

Hyperuricemia and gout are associated with obesity, occurring with a higher frequency in males than in females (Pi-Sunyer, 2002). Insulin resistance causes an increase in uric acid, which predisposes the development of gout. High-protein diets, in particular diets containing organ meats, may cause worsening of these symptoms; symptoms will need to be monitored.

GENITOURINARY DISORDERS

Obese woman tend to have irregular menses, polycystic ovarian syndrome, and infertility. These conditions are related to hormonal interactions that are, in part, believed to be as a result of insulin resistance, which as discussed earlier often exists in the obese patient. High insulin levels, in turn, stimulate androgen production, which suppresses ovulation each month, leading to infertility and irregular menses. Increased androgen may also result in hirusitism or male-pattern baldness. Estrogen production and metabolism are also altered in obese women, with increased estrogen production seen with increased weight and body fat. The increased estrogen level is believed to also negatively affect ovulation and fertility (Gambineri, Pelusi, Vicennati, Pagotto, & Pasquali, 2002).

Increased abdominal obesity can also cause urinary stress incontinence. Increased abdominal fat puts extra pressure on the bladder, leading to an increased risk of urine leakage or stress incontinence. These episodes may be triggered by events such as coughing, sneezing, laughing, or even kneeling. This constant abdominal pressure is similar to that which can develop from a traumatic abdominal injury, which can result in abdominal compartment syndrome and increased bladder pressures. In trauma, this condition often requires surgical decompression to prevent bladder damage. Pressure levels in the bladder with abdominal obesity have been shown to be higher than those seen with abdominal compartment syndrome, but they appear to be tolerated without permanent damage because of the more gradual buildup of pressure over time. Weight loss of as little as 10% can

reduce or relieve symptoms, and permanent damage to the bladder is seldom seen once abdominal obesity is reduced (Greenway, 2004).

NEUROLOGICAL DISORDERS

Pseudotumor cerebri, or idiopathic intracranial hypertension, is a condition manifested by frequent headaches, vision abnormalities, and tinnitus. Researchers have found that this disorder can occur with even moderate (5% to 15%) weight gain and can cause vision loss in up to 25% of cases (Daniels et al., 2007). Weight loss will reduce symptoms, and in severe cases, weight loss via bariatric surgery has been more effective than shunting of cerebrospinal fluid (Greenway, 2004). Symptoms may reduce the patient's tolerance of physical activity, requiring individual modification of recommendations.

CANCER

Higher rates of death due to cancer occur in obese individuals, 14% in men, and 20% in women (Klein & Romijn, 2008). It is unclear if this correlation is due to the obesity or in part due to factors contributing to obesity, such as a high-fat, high-calorie diet. In women, higher rates for endometrial, gallbladder, cervical, and ovarian cancers are seen. Increased rates of colorectal and prostate cancer are seen in men. Breast cancer is a higher risk in obese postmenopausal women but is less of a risk to premenopausal women who are obese than in normal weight women. Although the mechanisms are not yet clear, it is felt this particular change may be a result of increased estrogen produced in adipose tissue combined with postmenopausal hormonal changes (Pi-Sunyer, 2002).

PSYCHOLOGICAL ISSUES

The question of weight-related psychological issues is complex and complicated by the lack of research on many aspects of specific disorders. Binge eating is a disorder that has been identified as a subset of the obese population and is characterized by the compulsive nature of eating while feeling out of control. Studies have shown an increased incidence of psychopathology in obese binge eaters, particularly disorders such as depression (Yanovski, 2002). Binge eating may significantly impact the success of weight loss attempts and treatment choices. Even surgical weight loss treatments have had mixed results in binge eaters. Combined treatment to target disordered eating as well as weight loss may be a more effective method. More research is needed to determine best practice in this area.

Body image refers to the individual's perceptions, attitudes, and experiences concerning the body. Dissatisfaction with appearance can produce impaired self-esteem, social anxiety and withdrawal, and depression. These conditions can impact quality of life and can lead to more severe clinical disorders. Weight stigmatization of our society greatly contributes to this problem and is discussed in a later section.

The importance of behavior on weight modification attempts is a key component. Careful screening for repetitive patterns that do not respond to guided self-modification by the health professional should suggest a potential need for a referral for behavioral evaluation and therapy to determine whether other psychopathology is involved.

HEALTH RISKS OF OVERWEIGHT CHILDREN AND ADOLESCENTS

Of great concern is the rapid growth of type 2 diabetes in children and teenagers. Until the past decade, this type of diabetes had been a rare occurrence, but this is not the current situation. The causes of this early onset are undetermined but are associated with obesity, sedentary lifestyles, and specific dietary factors, and these factors may be more prevalent in urban settings (Hellerstein & Parks, 2004). There is little question that this change is of concern to all those dealing with obesity in any age population.

Psychological issues become a prominent issue in discussions of risks to children and adolescents. Obesity carries a well known stigma, which is greater against females than males. This stigma may contribute to the fear of obesity among teenage girls, a phenomenon that may manifest in disordered eating behavior. Binge eating often can appear at this developmental stage. Being severely overweight, being female, and being an adolescent also appear to increase the risk for psychological issues (Dietz, 2002).

Other major health issues in the overweight child or adolescent are sleep apnea and pseudotumor cerebri. Also alarming are recent studies showing that 5% to 10% of overweight children and adolescents have elevated liver enzymes, and liver biopsies have shown steatohepatitis (Dietz, 2002).

Childhood obesity does not often resolve without significant intervention. Approximately 70% of overweight adolescents become obese adults. This trend is becoming of great concern in public health discussions because early manifestations of health consequences in adolescents and children combined with the rise in obesity in this population will produce significant health care challenges for many years to come. More research is needed to identify high risk groups so that strategies can be developed to target these specific groups more effectively.

OBESITY AND MORTALITY

According to studies cited in the 1998 *Clinical Guidelines on the Identification, Evaluation, and Treatment of Overweight and Obesity in*

Adults, mortality begins to increase with BMIs above 25. At BMIs of 30 or above, mortality rate increases from all causes from 30% to 100% above persons with BMIs in the range of 20 to 25. Studies related to older adults and ethnic groups are needed to better identify and address differences that may occur in these subsets.

Three factors appear to affect the risk of death; regional fat distribution, amount of weight gain, and sedentary lifestyle. Several large studies have shown that obese individuals with more android fat distribution (abdominal or central obesity) correlate with higher incidence of diabetes and heart disease. Increasing degrees of weight gain show a graded increase in mortality for heart disease, and a sedentary lifestyle has been found to increase the risk of death at all levels of BMI (Bray, 2004).

ASSESSMENT OF HEALTH RISKS

A thorough assessment of the obese patient should be completed before a treatment plan is implemented. The components of the assessment include: health history, physical examination, and health risk assessment. The health risk assessment will help guide treatment choice as well as areas that will require closer monitoring during treatment.

HEALTH HISTORY

Weight History

A thorough history of the individual's lifetime weight history includes age at onset of obesity, duration of the problem, recent weight changes, and family history of obesity. Previous weight loss attempts, including methods that were most or least successful, will also guide the treatment plans chosen. A thorough dietary and exercise history are also important to obtain, and will be discussed in chapters 4 and 5 in detail.

Associated Medical Conditions

The medical conditions associated with obesity have been detailed previously in this chapter, as well as their influence on potential treatment and results. Other systemic diseases such as hepatic or renal disorders should be noted because they may affect dietary choices, caloric restriction, and the potential use of obesity drugs.

Use of tobacco and alcohol is an important assessment in developing a treatment plan. Smoking cessation commonly results in weight gain, and patients tend to be reluctant to initiate this activity. Reduction of alcohol intake itself can decrease calorie intake. Alcohol also has a known effect of decreasing inhibition, a factor that can affect behavior modification attempts.

Medication History

A complete list of medications including over the counter products is important. Many drugs are associated with increased appetite and weight gain, whereas others have neutral effects or may enhance weight loss to a small degree. Table 2-1 lists drugs known to affect weight.

Drug dosages may need to be monitored as weight loss occurs. Diabetic medications may predispose patients to hypoglycemia, particularly with increased physical activity. Antihypertensive medication dosages often need to be reduced as weight loss is achieved. Medications that are fat-soluble, particularly psychotropic medications may need dosages adjusted downward as fat stores decrease. Patient education should include knowledge about adverse effects of all therapeutic medications in order to detect the need for medication adjustment.

History of previous or current anti-obesity agent use should also be obtained. Any previous use of the drug fenfluramine (*Pondimin*), dexfenfluramine (*Redux*), or combination of fenfluramine/phentermine (Fen-Phen) should trigger a more comprehensive cardiac evaluation because these drugs have been associated with up to a 30% incidence of heart valve problems (Allen, 1997).

TABLE 2-1: DRUGS ASSOCIATED WITH WEIGHT GAIN

The following drugs have been found to have potential weight-related effects in numerous studies. The extent of the impact varies widely among individual patients.

Weight Gain	Weight Neutral Effects
Antipsychotics and Mood Stabilizers	
clozapine (*Clozaril*) olanazapine (*Zyprexa*) quetiapine (*Seroquel*) risperidone (*Risperdal*) chlorpromazine (*Thorazine*) thioridazine (*Mellaril*) lithium	ziprasidone (*Geodon*) aripiprazole (*Abilify*) haloperidol (*Haldol*) (less likely)
Antidepressants	
tricyclic antidepressants monoamine oxidase inhibitors mirtazapine (*Remeron*) selective serotonin reuptake inhibitors	bupropion (*Wellbutrin*) duloxetine (*Cymbalta*) venlafaxine (*Effexor*) citalopram (*Celexa*)
Anticonvulsants	
gabapentin (*Neurontin*) pregabalin (*Lyrica*) valproic acid (*Depakote*, etc.)	carbamazepine (*Tegretol*, etc.) (less likely)
Antidiabetics	

intensive insulin therapy
sulfonylureas
thiazolidinediones: pioglitazone (*Actos*) and
  rosiglitazone (*Avandia*)
meglitinides: nateglinide (*Starlix*) and
  repaglinide (*Prandin*)
	metformin (*Glucophage*)
	pramlintide (*Symlin*) and exenatide (*Byetta*)
	
	Alpha-glucosidase inhibitors, such as acarbose
	  (*Precose*), and miglitol (*Glyset*)

Antihypertensives	
beta blockers, particularly inderol Alpha blockers such as prazosin (*Minipress*)	
Hormone-related therapy	
Corticosteroids Contraceptive therapy, especially medroxyprogesterone injection (*Depo-Provera*)	

Note. From Drugs associated with weight gain. (2007, March). *Prescriber's Letter, 23.* Detail document no. 230212.

PHYSICAL EXAMINATION

Measurements

Baseline measurements will include height, weight, waist circumference, and vital signs of blood pressure, pulse, and respiration. Height should be measured without shoes. Measurement of waist circumference has been described in the previous chapter. An extra large blood pressure cuff is needed to obtain an accurate reading in the patient with large arms. Readings taken with a cuff that is too small will yield falsely high results. Subsequent measurements should be taken under similar conditions to minimize variability.

Measurements of different areas of the body, such as hips, chest, thighs, and arms are useful in establishing a baseline for comparison in future evaluations. They can provide a more complete picture of how body configuration is changing, even during periods when actual weight seems to be slowly decreasing.

Skin

Increased pigmentation in the folds of the neck, axilla, and over the knuckles (acanthosis nigricans) may indicate insulin resistance. A persistent skin rash, intertriginous dermatitis, is commonly found under skin folds in severely obese patients. Purple striation on the abdomen may indicate Cushing syndrome, an endocrine cause of obesity, and this finding requires investigation.

Head and Neck

Neck size should be recorded. A thick neck may be present in obstructive sleep apnea or polycystic ovarian syndrome. Thyroid gland size should be evaluated. Fundoscopic examination may show papilledema in individuals with increased intracranial pressure such as is seen in pseudotumor cerebri.

Chest Examination

Decreased chest expansion and breath sounds in the bases are common in severely obese patients. Wheezing may indicate asthma, and basal crackles may indicate heart failure.

Heart sounds may be difficult to hear, and extra sounds may indicate valvular problems, warranting further cardiac evaluation via echocardiogram. Movement of the point of maximum cardiac impulse laterally or downward may suggest ventricular hypertrophy. Any findings that do not correlate with known patient history should be referred to the appropriate medical provider for further evaluation.

Abdomen

Organomegaly is difficult to ascertain in the obese patient, and examination may be compounded by the presence of ventral or umbilical hernia. Any abnormal findings warrant further evaluation. The history typically provides the most valuable clue to potential comorbid health risk, such as frequent heartburn (indicating gastric reflux and/or hiatal hernia), and intermittent right upper quadrant pain following heavy or fatty meals (indicating a likely gallstone issue). Mild elevations of liver enzymes are common in obese patients; however, fatty liver is often asymptomatic. A history of constipation may indicate a hypothyroid state. Other signs of this disorder include cold intolerance, hair loss, dry skin, brittle nails, hyporeflexia, hypotonia, hypotension, and bradycardia.

Genitourinary System

In women, menstrual history should be evaluated, including any issues related to infertility. Renal disorders are more common in patients with diabetes and hypertension.

Neurological System

Gait abnormalities, neuropathies, and weakness should be noted, and exercise programs need to be adjusted to prevent injury. Patients with a history of headaches should have a fundoscopic examination to look for papilledema.

Musculoskeletal System

Joints should be examined for redness, swelling, and limitations of range of motion. Lower extremity swelling is common, and the extent of edema should be noted. Muscle strength and symmetry should be noted.

HEALTH RISK ASSESSMENT

The health risk assessment is a compilation of all information gathered during various components of the history and physical examination including:

- BMI measurement,

- presence of abdominal obesity using waist circumference measurement,

- previously diagnosed comorbidities,

- suspected comorbidities requiring further investigation, and

- physiologic and behavioral limitations requiring adjustment to therapeutic interventions.

This information will be combined with the diet and physical activity histories and will form the basis for the selection of treatment options. The individual with more severe obesity combined with significant comorbidities may need a more drastic intervention. Tables 2-2 and 2-3 illustrate the level of risk associated with BMI and the recommended treatment options, which will be discussed in depth in subsequent chapters.

SUMMARY

The presence of comorbid diseases impacts the recommendations and guidelines for treatment in many individuals. Adaptations of diet, physical activity, and pharmacotherapy may be required. Comorbid conditions occur in all populations. The *Clinical Guidelines on the Identification, Evaluation, and Treatment of Overweight and Obesity in Adults* (1998; No. 984083) NIH publication recommend that successful treatment should focus more on health improvement than on the amount of weight loss, thus a thorough understanding of weight-related health risks is a requirement in developing an effective treatment plan.

TABLE 2-2: CLASSIFICATION OF BODY MASS INDEX AND ASSOCIATED DISEASE RISK

Description	BMI (kg/m²)	Obesity Class	Disease Risk*
Normal	18.5-24.9		
Overweight	25-29.9		Increased
Mild obesity	30-34.9	I	High
Moderate obesity	35-39.9	II	Very High
Morbid obesity	Greater than 40	III	Extremely High

*Disease risk for type 2 diabetes, hypertension, and cardiovascular disease

(NHLBI Obesity Education Initiative Expert Panel on the Identification, Evaluation, and Treatment of Overweight and Obesity in Adults, 2000)

TABLE 2-3: GUIDELINES IN SELECTING TREATMENT STRATEGY

Treatment	BMI (kg/m²)				
	25.0-26.9	27.0-29.9	30.0-34.9	35.0-39.9	Greater than 40.0
Dietary Modification	+	+	+	+	+
Exercise	+	+	+	+	+
Behavioral Modification	+	+	+	+	+
Pharmacotherapy		*	+	+	+
Bariatric Surgery				x	+

+ indicated therapy
* with comorbidities
x with significant comorbidities, including obstructive sleep apnea, diabetes mellitus, coronary artery disease, and uncontrolled hypertension

(NHLBI Obesity Education Initiative Expert Panel on the Identification, Evaluation, and Treatment of Overweight and Obesity in Adults, 2000)

EXAM QUESTIONS

CHAPTER 2
Questions 4-7

Note: Choose the one option that BEST answers each question.

4. Obesity is a major contributing cause to the development of

   a. peptic ulcer disease.

   b. rheumatoid arthritis.

   c. type 2 diabetes mellitus.

   d. bladder cancer.

5. Psychological issues resulting from weight stigma experienced by overweight adolescents may result in

   a. early development of binge eating disorder.

   b. higher rates of suicide in adolescent males.

   c. drug and alcohol abuse leading to liver damage.

   d. increased diet and weight loss motivation.

6. Mortality rates in obese patients have been found to be increased most by

   a. repeated loss and regain of weight over time.

   b. central and peripheral adiposity.

   c. a sedentary lifestyle.

   d. existence of a comorbid disease.

7. The major purpose of a health risk assessment is to

   a. educate the patient about potential health risks of obesity.

   b. assist in selecting the appropriate treatment options.

   c. determine the type of obesity present.

   d. identify all barriers to healthy eating patterns.

REFERENCES

Allen, J. (1997, October). The rise and fall of fenfluramine and dexfenfluramine. *Prescriber's Letter; 4*(10), Detail Document No. 131022.

Blackburn, G.L. (2002). Weight loss and risk factors in adults. In C.G. Fairburn & K.D. Brownell (Eds.), *Eating disorders and obesity* (2nd ed., pp. 484-489). New York: The Guilford Press.

Bray, G.A. (2004). Risks of obesity. In G.A. Bray, *Practical guideline in office management of obesity*. Philadelphia: Saunders.

Camden, S.G. (2009). Obesity: An emerging concern for patients and nurses. *The Online Journal of Issues in Nursing, 14,* 1-9.

Daniels, A.B., Liu, G.T., Volpe, N.J., Galetta, S.L., Moster, M.L., Newman, N.J., et al. (2007). Profiles of obesity, weight gain, and quality of life in idiopathic intracranial hypertension (pseudotumor cerebri), *American Journal of Opthalmology, 143*(4), 635-641.

Dietz, W.H. (2002). Medical consequences of obesity in children and adolescents. In C.G. Fairburn & K.D. Brownell, (Eds.), *Eating disorders and obesity* (2nd ed., pp. 473-6). New York: The Guilford Press.

Drugs associated with weight gain. (2007, March). *Prescriber's Letter, 23.* Detail Document No. 230212.

Gambineri, A., Pelusi, C., Vicennati, V., Pagotto, U., & Pasquali, R. (2002). Obesity and the polycystic ovary syndrome. *International Journal of Obesity, 26*(7), 883-896.

Greenway, F. (2004). Clinical evaluation of the obese patient. In G.A. Bray (Ed.), *Office management of obesity* (pp. 141-156). Philadelphia: Saunders.

Hellerstein, M.K. & Parks, E.J. (2004). Obesity & overweight. In F.S. Greenspan & D.G. Gardner (Eds.), *Basic and clinical endocrinology* (7th ed., pp. 794-813). New York: McGraw Hill Companies.

Klein, S. & Romijn, J.A. (2008). Obesity. In H.M. Kronenberg, S. Melmed, K.S. Polonsky, & P.R. Larsen (Eds.), *Williams textbook of endocrinology* (pp. 1563-1587). New York: Saunders.

Pi-Sunyer, F.X. (2002). Medical complications of obesity. In C.G. Fairburn & K.D. Brownell, (Eds.), *Eating disorders and obesity* (2nd ed., pp. 467-472). New York: The Guilford Press.

Richter, J.E. (2007). The many manifestations of gastroesophageal reflux disease: Presentation, evaluation and treatment. *Gastroenterology Clinics of North America, 36*(3), 581.

Morgan, C.M., Yanovski, S.Z., Nguyen, T.T., McDuffie, J., Sebring, N.G., Jorge, M.R., et al. (2002). Loss of control over eating, adiposity, and psychopathology in overweight children. *International Journal of Eating Disorders, 31*(4): 430-41.

NHLBI Obesity Education Initiative Expert Panel on the Identification, Evaluation, and Treatment of Overweight and Obesity in Adults. (1998). *Clinical guidelines on the identification, evaluation, and treatment of overweight and obesity in adults: The evidence report* (NIH Publication No. 98-4083). Bethesda, MD: U.S. Department of Health and Human Services.

NHLBI Obesity Education Initiative Expert Panel on the Identification, Evaluation, and Treatment of Overweight and Obesity in Adults. (2000). *The practical guide: Identification and treatment of overweight and obesity in adults.* Bethesda, MD: U.S. Department of Health and Human Services (NIH Publication No. 00-4084).

Yanovski, S.Z. (2002). Binge eating in obese persons. In K.D. Brownell & C.G. Fairburn (Eds.), *Eating disorders and obesity: A comprehensive handbook* (2nd ed., pp. 403-407). New York, NY: The Guilford Press.

CHAPTER 3

COMPLEX CAUSES OF OBESITY

CHAPTER OBJECTIVE

After completing this chapter the learner will be able to discuss factors that contribute to obesity.

LEARNING OBJECTIVES

After completing this chapter, the learner will be able to

1. explain how increased food availability, food marketing, and portion size have contributed to the rise in obesity.

2. differentiate between portion size and serving size.

3. list the different components of energy expenditure that contribute to the 24-hour energy expenditure.

4. describe the effects biological messengers on hunger and satiety.

5. discuss the research related to heredity and obesity.

INTRODUCTION

Fluctuations in body weight have long been viewed simplistically in terms of an energy imbalance. If energy intake is greater than energy expenditure over a prolonged period of time, obesity will develop. If energy expendi-ture remains greater than energy intake, adiposity is reduced. If energy intake and expenditure are balanced, body weight remains stable. This principle has given rise to numerous theories about why the rate of obesity has begun to sky-rocket. Many of these theories focus on environmental change: availability of food, changes in portion size, and reduction in daily physical activity. The entire picture has more recently begun to emerge – that both energy intake and expenditure are affected by a complex system of neurohormonal and genetic influences. The aspects of all of these components will be explored further in this chapter.

AVAILABILITY OF FOOD

Obesity can be attributed in part to the low cost of high-fat, highly sweetened foods. These foods are more energy dense (more kcal per gram weight) and less nutrient dense (less vitamins and minerals per gram weight) than fruits, vegetables, and whole grains.

Increasing food availability in the United States is not limited to energy-dense foods. Almost all foods are more available now than they were 20 years ago (Table 3-1). The greatest increases in food availability are found in added fats and oils, candy and confectionery products, and carbonated soft drinks. There is wider availability in all food

TABLE 3-1: FOOD AVAILABILITY IN THE UNITED STATES

Food*	1986	1996	2006	% Change, 1986-2006
Red Meat, Poultry, Fish	184.7	188.6	201.0	+8.8%
All Dairy Products (Milk Equivalents)	591.4	566.2	606.3	+2.5%
Added Fats and Oils	242.8	272.9	299.2	+23.2%
All Fruits	278.1	287.6	269.6	-3.1%
All Vegetables	361.0	416.5	406.4	+12.6%
Flour and Cereal Products	163.9	196.6	192.8	+17.6%
Candy and Confectionery Products	18.7	23.7	22.9	+22.5%
Carbonated Soft Drinks	42.7	51.6	50.6	+18.5%
Kcal Available per Day	3,500	3,700	3,900	+11%

*Food amounts are reported as pounds per capita, except for carbonated soft drinks, which are reported in gallons.

Most recent data available is from 2004. Data extracted from the United States Department of Agriculture. Economic Research Service: The Economics of Food, Farming, Natural Resources, and Rural America. Available at www.ers.usda.gov/data/foodconsumption/foodavailindex.htm

categories except fruit, which shows a small decrease. There is an overall increase of 11% in kcal per day in food availability over the past 20 years.

Controversies exist as to the underlying reasons for the type of food available to individuals with high versus low incomes. Some sources would indicate government subsidies initiated in the last century in order to stabilize crop prices and provide Americans with an affordable, reliable food supply are largely to blame (Fields, 2004). The increasing use of more processed foods or "fast foods" also has contributed to the problem. Regardless of how one looks at the situation, obesity-promoting foods are easily accessible to most of the U.S. population.

There is little question that such availability of energy dense, nutrient poor foods does contribute to the epidemic of obesity. What are more controversial are the underlying reasons for this occurrence. Although some would argue solely that marketing and availability of these products has led to their increased use, especially among low income populations, it does not explain the increased consumption in populations whose income and availability would allow a wider choice of available foods. It is now known that both

genetic and biologic factors play a role in food selection as well as hunger and satiety (Marx, 2003). Taste receptors are a current area of research, with evidence that individuals may tend to select certain types of nutrients based on genetic predisposition. It is likely that both of these rationales are valid, increasing the complexity of resolving the problem.

PORTION SIZE AND SERVING SIZE

In addition to increased food availability, Americans are also consuming larger quantities than in the past. Portion sizes have increased dramatically over the past 20 years (Table 3-2). Portion sizes offered by fast-food restaurants are typically two to five times larger than they were when first introduced (Young & Nestle, 2003). In response to the parallel in larger food portion sizes and rising rates of obesity, the Surgeon General challenged health professionals, the public, and the food industry to address portion size as a factor in weight control by raising consumer awareness of appropriate portion size and providing foods in more appropri-

TABLE 3-2: COMPARISON OF PORTION SIZES FROM THE 1980s WITH TODAY				
Food	**20 years ago**		**Today**	
	Portion Size	*Kcal*	*Portion Size*	*Kcal*
Bagel	3-inch diameter	140	6-inch diameter	350
Cheesecake Slice	3 ounces	260	7.4 ounces	640
Chicken Caesar Salad	1.5 cups	390	3 cups	790
Chicken Stir Fry	2 cups	235	4 cups	865
Chocolate Chip Cookie	1.5-inch diameter	55	3- to 4-inch diameter	275
Coffee	6 ounces	45	16 ounces	350
Fast Food Cheeseburger	1 cheeseburger	333	1 cheeseburger	590
French Fries	2.4 ounces	210	6.9 ounces	610
Movie Popcorn	5 cups	270	Tub	630
Muffin	1.5 ounces	210	5 ounces	500
Pizza (pepperoni)	2 slices	500	2 slices	800
Spaghetti and Meat Balls	1 cup	500	2 cups	1025
Soda	6.5 ounces	85	20 ounces	250
Turkey Sandwich	1 sandwich on sliced bread	320	10-inch sub	850

Data extracted from National Institutes of Health, National Heart, Lung and Blood Institute. (n.d.). *Portion distortion.*
Accessed September 5, 2008, from http://hp2010.nhlbihin.net/portion

ate amounts (U.S. Department of Health and Human Services, 2001).

Confusion exists concerning the terminology of portion size and serving size. The serving size definition used in the Food Pyramid is different from the serving size on nutrition labels, and serving size on a food label is not meant for direct comparison with the Food Pyramid's recommended servings. The unit of measure for a serving size on the Food Pyramid is often different from the unit of measure used for a serving size on a food label. For example, the food label serving size for ready-to-eat cereals is based on a weight measurement (grams), whereas the Food Pyramid serving size measurement is based on volume (cups). So, for a dense cereal, such as granola, the food label serving size is usually one-half cup, whereas for a puffed cereal, the food label size is 2 cups. The Food Pyramid serving size for both types of cereal would be 1 cup.

What makes this topic even more confusing is that food label and Food Pyramid serving sizes are often not equal to realistic portion sizes. Who ever sat down and ate only one half of an apple or one half of a banana? Who would consider one fourth of a bagel an adequate breakfast? What most people think of when they talk about serving size is really portion size. However, most people do not even know that there is a difference in definitions for portion size versus serving size.

Portion size is defined as the amount of food an individual eats at one sitting. Portion sizes also vary among individuals. One person may consider one-half cup ice cream an adequate portion, whereas another person may consider 1½ cups ice cream a normal portion size.

Changes in portion sizes for foods may have contributed substantially to the obesity epidemic. Table 3-3 illustrates how the energy intake for a meal plan for a single day has more than doubled in the past 20 years. Furthermore, if one looks at

TABLE 3-3: HOW CHANGES IN PORTION SIZE COULD HAVE AFFECTED DAILY ENERGY INTAKE AND PROMOTED OBESITY

	20 years ago	Today
	kcals	*kcals*
Breakfast		
Plain bagel	140	350
Coffee (6 oz)	45	130
Lunch		
Fast-food cheeseburger	333	590
French fries	210	610
Soda	85	250
Dinner		
Chicken Caesar salad	390	790
Spaghetti and meatballs	500	1,025
Slice of cheesecake	260	640
Water	0	0
Total kcal intake	1,963	4,385

Caloric values taken from Table 3-2.

the day's meal plan itself the meal plan does not look unreasonable:

Breakfast – plain bagel and coffee

Lunch – cheeseburger, french fries, and soda

Dinner – Caesar salad, spaghetti and meatballs, slice of cheesecake, and water

However, with today's portion sizes, the meal plan totals 4,605 kcal – much beyond the energy intake required for weight control for most people.

Two well-known studies have illustrated how strongly perception of portion size affects food consumption. In the first study, men and women were served lunch for 1 week (Rolls, Morris, & Roe, 2002). The lunch included an entrée of macaroni and cheese consumed freely. At each meal, the subjects were presented with one of four portions: 500, 625, 750, or 1,000 grams. One half of the subjects were served the measured food amount on their plate, whereas the other half were given the measured food amount in a bowl and then allowed to serve themselves. The participants consumed 30%

more energy when presented the largest portion size as compared to the smallest portion size, regardless of whether they were given the food amount on their plate or could serve themselves from a serving bowl.

The second study shows how food consumption is controlled by portion size even when the food quality is poor (Wansink & Kim, 2005). In this study, 158 moviegoers were randomly given a medium (120 g) or a large (240 g) container of free popcorn that was either fresh or 14 days old. Moviegoers ate 45% more of the fresh popcorn when it was given in a large container versus when it was given in a small container. Surprisingly, the moviegoers still ate 34% more of the stale popcorn when eating from a large container than a smaller container.

Portion size has clearly affected energy intake in the American diet. Effective treatment of obesity will need to focus on education related to more accurately reflecting measurement of actual food energy intake.

FOOD MARKETING

The logical sequence of events mandates that if more food is produced (e.g., more food is available), then this food needs to be marketed. The previous discussion on portion sizes infers that part of the success in food marketing has been through promoting increased portion sizes. A big part of portion size marketing is perceived value. Competition to offer greater value to customers has inspired promotions such as the "Big Gulp" soft drink and the "Supersize" fast-food meal. These promotions present the customer an option of larger portion sizes at a minimal additional cost. Most "bargain buys" for consumers are foods that contain concentrated amounts of refined sugar and fat.

Drewnowski (2004) presents this concept another way. He suggests that because water accounts for the bulk of food weight, it contributes more to the level of energy density in foods than does fat or sugar. The most energy-dense foods, such as potato chips, chocolate, or doughnuts are not necessarily those that are the highest in total sugar or fat, but those that are dry. Thus, they are more concentrated in sugar and fat. On the other hand, fruits and vegetables, which may have a high total sugar content, have a low energy density because their high water volume dilutes the sugar concentration.

Marketing of energy-dense foods depends on a reliable and efficient distribution system as well as successful advertising. Viable and efficient food distribution channels have always been the core to economic growth. Modern technology has provided faster and less expensive ways to get food from the farmer to the consumer. Some examples of where development has occurred in food distribution are: less manual labor to harvest crops, better shipment mechanisms, better refrigeration, better packaging, and global retailers. Large global retailers have had a tremendous impact on food marketing in the United States and other countries.

Food Advertising

More than $10 billion is spent each year for all types of food and beverage marketing to children and youth in America (Committee on Food Marketing and the Diets of Children and Youth, 2006). Children and youth spend over $200 billion a year and have an influence on food and beverage purchases they do not make directly. Unfortunately, leading purchase choices of children are candy, carbonated soft drinks, and salty snacks. It is also unfortunate that children do not have the capacity to discriminate commercial from non-commercial content or to attribute persuasive intent to advertising (Committee on Food Marketing and the Diets of Children and Youth, 2006).

Although cause and effect cannot be confirmed, many of the established associations among childhood overweight and television advertising make one very suspicious as to how food advertising has contributed to the problem. It is established that our children and youth are not achieving basic nutritional goals. They are consuming excess kcal, added sugar, and fat while consuming too little whole grains and fiber. The Committee on Food Marketing and the Diets of Children and Youth (2006) has documented evidence that advertising influences children's food and beverage preferences, a child's requests to buy certain foods and beverages, children's food and beverage beliefs, and short-term food and beverage consumption of children ages 2 to 11 years old. There is also strong evidence that exposure to television advertising is associated with adiposity in children ages 2 to 11 and youth ages 12 to 18 years.

Increasing public awareness of food marketing effects is an important component to changing patterns of behavior that lead to obesity. Helping the individual consumer to identify their own marketing sensitivity will help them to develop new patterns of behavior that can avoid or reduce the effects of such pervasive tactics.

From the above discussion, there is little question of the increases in energy intake and its contribution to the rise in obesity, and the reasons for this situation. We must now examine the other side of the equation – that of energy expenditure.

COMPONENTS OF ENERGY EXPENDITURE

The 24-hour total energy expenditure (TEE) can be broken down into three components: the thermic effect of food (TEF), which accounts for approximately 10% of TEE; the resting energy expenditure (REE), accounting for 70% of TEE; and energy expended in daily physical activity, which accounts for 20% of TEE. The TEF is defined as the amount of energy required to digest, absorb, and further process the nutrients in food. REE is defined as the amount of energy expended to take care of normal cellular and organ functions at rest, whereas the energy expended in physical activity includes exercise and nonexercise physical activity, such as maintaining posture, spontaneous muscle contractions, or fidgeting (Klein & Romijn, 2008). A disruption in any one of these energy components will shift the energy balance and potentially affect body weight.

Thermic Effect of Food

The contribution of the TEF to the total 24-hour energy expenditure of an individual is minimal, and averages about 10%. Given a daily energy expenditure of 2,000 kcal, the TEF would be approximately 200 kcal. Because the biochemical pathways for storing calories from excess dietary fat in the body are more efficient than converting excess calories from carbohydrate and protein into their storage forms, the TEF for a high-protein or high-carbohydrate meal is greater than that for a high-fat meal. However, the TEF varies at most by around 40 kcal per day when altering the fat, protein, carbohydrate mix of the diet. Any attempt to reduce body weight by manipulating the diet com-

position alone would not contribute much to reducing body weight in the short term. For example, it would take almost three months for an individual to lose 1 pound by only changing diet composition without altering the caloric intake. Most people attempting weight loss are not patient enough to wait 3 months for a 1-pound loss. Therefore, from an obesity treatment standpoint, dietary manipulations focused on altering the TEF will not produce clinically significant results.

Resting Energy Expenditure

The REE amounts to about 24 kcal·kg^{-1} of body weight per day in the average person. This number accounts for about 70% of the total energy expenditure or a total of about 1,800 kcal per day for the average 75 kg man. The REE varies somewhat among individuals, but it usually stays within a narrow range. The most dramatic differences among individuals are seen with metabolic disorders, such as thyroid malfunction. Other variances in REE occur due to body composition, gender, and race. Diet and exercise also affect REE, and exercise will be discussed in subsequent chapters.

Body Composition

Individual differences in body mass account for most of the variation in REE among individuals. People with more lean body mass have higher REEs than those with less lean body mass. Muscles, organs, bones, and fluids make up most of the lean body mass. The tissues and organs that contribute most are the liver, skeletal muscles, brain, heart, and kidneys. The size of each of these tissues and organs is directly related to body size. Obese people generally have a REE greater than lean people, because the obese have a larger body size and hence more lean body mass overall.

Fat mass adds relatively little to the REE (approximately 2%). Therefore, it is not a significant contributory cause of the increase in REE. Skeletal muscles, on the other hand, add greatly to the REE (approximately 18%). For this reason, exercise professionals consistently promote strength training as a method to increase the REE and combat obesity.

Because fat mass adds very little to the REE, variations within an individual are predominantly attributed to fluctuations in lean body mass. When an obese person loses weight, his or her REE decreases in proportion to the amount of lean body mass that is lost. For this reason, much attention has been given to maintaining lean body mass in obese individuals as they go through weight loss treatment. For example, the purpose of protein-sparing modified fasts is to sustain a high protein intake, in spite of severe calorie restriction, so that muscle mass and other lean tissue mass will be maintained. In addition, research has repeatedly shown that if exercise is incorporated into a diet plan, less lean tissue is lost during weight loss than if there were no exercise.

Maintaining muscular fitness through aging can also help the loss of lean tissue and maintain the REE. However, declining lean body mass and decreased muscularity in older adults do not fully account for the reduction in REE of about 2% per decade that occurs after age 30. The aging process itself causes the organs to become less active metabolically, and this lack of activity is what is thought to contribute to the reduced REE in older adults.

Gender and Race

Differences in REE between men and women are consistent over a wide range of comparable ages and body weights. Women have a REE that is 5% to 10% lower than men of the equal age and body weight. However, this difference should not be interpreted as a true gender difference in metabolic rates of individual tissues or organs. More likely, it reflects a difference in body composition between the genders because women generally possess more body fat and less muscle mass than men of a comparable age, weight, and size.

The prevalence of obesity is higher in African Americans than Caucasians. One possible explanation is that African Americans have a lower REE. Both African American men and women have a REE that is anywhere from 5% to 20% below that of Caucasians (Forman, Miller, Szymanski, & Fernhall, 1998; Sharp et al., 2002), which means that the range of difference over a 24-hour period amounts to 80 to 200 kcal. This metabolic discrepancy cannot be attributed to differences in age, body mass index, body composition, daily activity levels, menstrual cycle phase, or fitness level. It seems to be a true racial difference. A difference of 80 to 200 kcal a day may not seem like much, but over a period of 1 year, this metabolic discrepancy can amount to between 9 and 21 pounds of body fat.

The mechanism underlying this metabolic discrepancy has not yet been identified, and it is still controversial as to whether this difference in REE between races is the cause of the higher prevalence of obesity in African Americans. More importantly, the health professional should be aware that predicting rate of weight loss in obese African Americans by using regression equations and not direct metabolic measurements will be even less accurate than for Caucasians.

Daily Physical Activity

Daily physical activity is the third component of total daily energy expenditure, accounting for 20% of energy expenditure. The contribution of this component is universally recognized, and it has been the target of behavior modification in numerous weight loss and diet modification programs.

There is little question that the increase of transportation and technology has led to a less physically active lifestyle for many Americans. The 1996 Surgeon General's Report on Activity and Health found 60% of American adults do not obtain regular physical activity, and less than one half of adolescents participated in regular vigorous activity. In addition, 25% of adults reported no physical activity at all, and inactivity rates were higher in women, African Americans, Hispanics, and older adults. The rise in television, video game, and Internet usage has contributed to increased sedentary behavior, as has the use of automobiles and other conveniences.

Diet and physical activity act in synergistic ways. Poor diet may affect the energy and the ability of the individual to become active. There is also evidence that physical activity may help with better appetite control. Effective means of weight control need to include both sides of the energy expenditure equation.

PHYSIOLOGICAL SYSTEM EFFECTS

Emerging as a major contributing factor to weight management is the role of biological functions and genetics. Although research continues to find evidence of the presence of certain genes that may make individuals susceptible to obesity, it has yet to establish a direct causative effect in the absence of a bad environment. Research in this area is providing knowledge of how this influence occurs, specifically in the neurohormonal signaling of hunger and satiation, or satisfaction signals (Marx, 2003; Ikramuddin, Leslie, Whitson, & Kellogg, 2007). These complicated feedback systems affect physiological and behavioral systems. They are found in various organ systems of the gut as well as the central nervous system and are concerned with short-term and long-term regulation of energy intake.

News of research related to this area is a weekly occurrence. Members of the lay public will often cite information heard in the media related to obesity research and question its relationship to their specific problem of obesity. A basic understanding of this emerging area of influence will help the nurse to respond to questions that may arise, and will focus efforts on known ways to

modify energy balance – still chiefly through diet and physical activity modification.

Central Nervous System

The arcuate nucleus, located in the hypothalamus of the brain, has become known as the "satiety center." It is the center of control for short- and long-term weight regulatory systems. Neurons in this area can stimulate and inhibit eating and also reduce metabolism. Neuropeptide Y and agouti-related peptide stimulate appetite, whereas Pro-opiomelanocortin (POMC) and cocaine-amphetamine-regulated transcript neurons decrease appetite and increase energy conservation (Ikramuddin et al., 2007). These neurons receive messages from other hormone produced in the digestive system and in adipocyte cells.

Gastrointestinal Messengers

Short-term regulators help control intake by either stimulating appetite or signaling satiety and suppressing it. Two peptide hormones produced in the digestive system, ghrelin and peptide YY, send signals to the brain to indicate hunger. Ghrelin, discovered in 1999, rises and falls in a daily cycle, with peak levels 1 to 2 hours prior to daily meal times of breakfast, lunch, and dinner, and a smaller peak during the night. This potent messenger has rapidly become known as the "hunger hormone." A significant finding of research studies is that ghrelin levels not only are higher in obese subjects, but that they increase even more when the individual loses approximately 15% of weight during dieting (Cummings et al., 2002). The mechanism is thought to occur in order to protect the body from a perceived deprivation related to food supply; however, it acts to sabotage the efforts of the dieter.

Cholecystokinin is a peptide released into the bloodstream by the intestine and appears to be involved with signaling satiety and gallbladder function. In all, over 20 known messengers are produced in the digestive system (Ikramuddin et al., 2007), and more information regarding their complex interactions continues to unfold. Figure 3-1

FIGURE 3-1: APPETITE CONTROLLERS

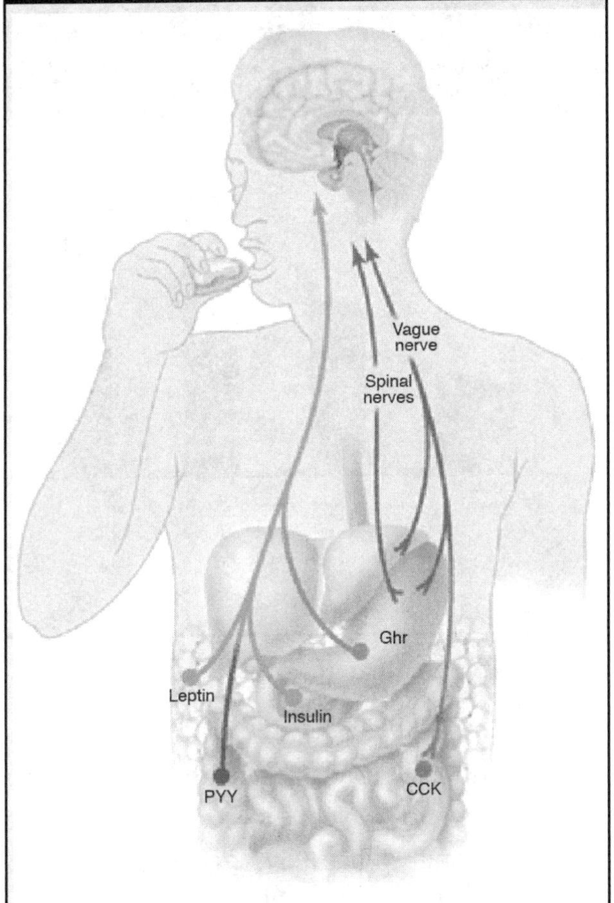

The body produces hormones that act through the brain to regulate short- and long-term appetite and also the body's metabolism. The diagram shows the sources of several of the hormones now under intensive investigation.

Illustration by Katharine Sutliff/*Science*

Note. From Marx, J. (2003). Cellular warriors at the battle of the bulge. *Science. 299,* 846-9. Reprinted with permission from AAAS.

identifies the known major messengers that work to control appetite process.

Leptin and Insulin

Fat cells were once thought to be passive storage depots for fat, but it is now known they play an active role in metabolism by producing substances that influence the central nervous system's control of appetite and metabolism. These substances include tumor necrosis factor alpha, resistin, leptin, adiponectin, and adipocyte complement-related protein of 30 kDa. Tumor necrosis factor alpha, resisten, and adiponectin all contribute to insulin

resistance. Insulin acts to inhibit production of appetite stimulating neuropeptide Y in the arcuate nucleus; however, decreased insulin sensitivity appears to blunt this effect. Much is still unknown about the mechanisms involved, and it is not yet clear how much of a role it plays in weight regulation (Marx, 2003).

Leptin, found in 1994, has received much attention as the first appetite hormone to be identified. Produced by adipocytes, it stimulates satiety and increases energy expenditure. At first it was thought by researchers to be the key for which they had been searching, and perhaps leptin deficiency was indeed the culprit in obesity. This theory proved to be true only in a handful of cases. Conversely, obese humans were found to have higher than normal blood levels of leptin, yet they were resistant to its effects.

Scientists now believe that leptin's main role may be in protecting against weight loss in times of reduced food supply, rather than against weight gain in times of plenty (Marx, 2003). But leptin may have yet an even more significant role in the treatment of obesity because it has been linked to the chronic inflammatory state found to be present in this disease and is believed to contribute to many of the comorbid disease problems of obesity (Harle & Straub, 2006). Chronic inflammation appears to also influence leptin's influence on the arcuate nucleus and may mute the body's response to its signal.

GENETIC EFFECTS

One of the least understood areas affecting obesity is that the contribution of genetics. There is evidence that hundreds of DNA sequences are associated with obesity, and obesity genetics is a rapidly growing field. Identifying specific genes that affect energy balance is compounded by environmental influences, which also have a cause and effect relationship to obesity.

The current view in relation to obesity genetics is that these gene components predominantly result in a susceptibility of the individual to develop obesity in the "right" environmental conditions, rather than cause obesity. Studies done with twins, adoptions, and families have shown estimates that between 50% and 70% of individuals have a hereditary component to their obesity (Cope, Fernandez, & Allison, 2004). This finding does not mean that their obese state is caused by genetics, only that it may contribute to development of this condition. Genetic obesity, directly caused by an invalidated gene regulating energy balance, is much less common. At present it could represent 5% of obesity cases and potentially a larger percentage of severely obese cases (Bouchard & Rankinen, 2005). A known example of this phenomenon is leptin deficiency, a rare cause of childhood obesity. When found, it is treatable with leptin injections, but actual cases have been few (Marx, 2003).

Genetic predisposition likely exists on a continuum, from directly linked genetic-caused obesity, to a genetic resistance to obesity. Figure 3-2 demonstrates the interaction between genetic predisposition, the obesity prone environment, and body mass index. Combinations of susceptibility alleles on several loci rather than a single gene defect likely cause the range of disposition towards obesity. Individuals with a strong disposition in an environment that does not favor obesity would likely only be overweight. In an environment that is strongly obesogenic, they likely would become obese or even severely obese (Bouchard & Rankinen, 2005).

Genetic relationships to energy intake and energy expenditure have been found. Research on genetics that regulate food intake focuses in the areas of taste preference, palatability of food, and genes affecting the arcuate nuclear regulation system. Some evidence also exists for genes influencing energy expenditure, particularly in muscle types that may predispose an individual to be active

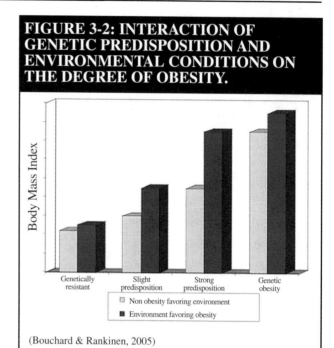

FIGURE 3-2: INTERACTION OF GENETIC PREDISPOSITION AND ENVIRONMENTAL CONDITIONS ON THE DEGREE OF OBESITY.

(Bouchard & Rankinen, 2005)

or inactive. REE may also be affected by genetics as well (Cope, Fernandez, & Allison, 2004).

The ultimate result of genetic research is to identify ways to prevent obesity, and to treat it more successfully. The study of genetics may help predict individuals and populations at risk in order to intervene prior to the onset of obesity. Treatments addressing components of genetic susceptibility may be developed, which may be beneficial in cases resistant to traditional methods. It must always be remembered, however, that the environment has an overreaching effect far beyond the individual genetic makeup and must be the focus of attention.

SUMMARY

Obesity is a complex phenotype, resulting from environmental influences, biological regulation, and genetic makeup. Research will continue to add to the knowledge base and allow more diverse treatment methodologies to develop. Public policy changes will be needed to address environmental components of this multifactorial problem.

This situation may be compared to treatment of another complex disease, diabetes. For many years, the cause of diabetes was unknown, and the standard treatment was to starve the patient to prevent the elevation of glucose. Patients were thought to have caused the diabetes by "eating too much sugar." In 1921, Frederick Banting and his assistant Charles Best discovered insulin and revolutionized the care of diabetic patients worldwide.

Obesity stands on the same threshold. Obese individuals today are told overtly and in more subtle messages that they are overweight because they "eat too much" and "exercise too little." What knowledge with the potential to revolutionize prevention and treatment of this epidemic awaits discovery?

EXAM QUESTIONS

CHAPTER 3
Questions 8-12

Note: Choose the one option that BEST answers each question.

8. A strong contributor to the obesity epidemic in the United States is the two- to fivefold increase in

    a. serving size.
    b. portion size.
    c. food availability.
    d. food cost.

9. The amount of food eaten at one sitting is

    a. measured in grams.
    b. variable by individual.
    c. equal to the serving size.
    d. universally measured on the Food Pyramid.

10. The component of energy expenditure that contributes the most to the total 24-hour energy expenditure is the

    a. thermic effect of food.
    b. exercise energy expenditure.
    c. adipose tissue energy expenditure.
    d. resting energy expenditure.

11. The arcuate nucleus, known as the satiety center, is located in the

    a. hypothalamus.
    b. gastrointestinal tract.
    c. adipocyte tissue.
    d. peripheral nervous system.

12. The percentage of obesity cases that are directly caused by a genetics is

    a. 0%.
    b. 5%.
    c. 50%.
    d. 75%.

REFERENCES

Bouchard, C. & Rankinen, T. (2005). Genetics and obesity: What does it mean to the clinician? *Obesity Management, 1*(3),100-4.

Committee on Food Marketing and the Diets of Children and Youth. (2006). *Food marketing to children and youth: Threat or opportunity?* Washington, DC: The National Academic Press.

Cope, M.B., Fernandez, J.R., & Allison, D.B. (2004). Genetic and biological risk factors. In J.K. Thompson (Ed.), *Handbook of eating disorders and obesity* (pp. 323-338). Hoboken, NJ: John Wiley & Sons, Inc.

Cummings, D.E., Weigle, D.S., Frayo, R.S., Breen, P.A., Ma, M.K., Dellinger, E.P., and Purnell, J.Q. (2002). Plasma ghrelin levels after diet induced weight loss or gastric bypass surgery. *New England Journal of Medicine, 346,* 1623-30.

Drewnowski, A. (2004). Obesity and the food environment: Dietary energy density and diet costs. *American Journal of Preventive Medicine, 27*(3S), 154-162.

Forman, J.N., Miller, W.C., Szymanski, L.M., & Fernhall, B. (1998). Differences in resting metabolic rates of inactive obese African-American and Caucasian women. *International Journal of Obesity, 22,* 215-221.

Fields, S. (2004). The fat of the land. *Environmental Health Perspectives, 112,* A821-A823.

Harle, P. & Straub, R.H. (2006). Leptin is a link between adipose tissue and inflammation. *Annals of the New York Academy of Sciences, 1069,* 454-62.

Ikramuddin, S., Leslie, D., Whitson, B.A., & Kellogg, T.A. (2007). Energy metabolism and biochemistry of obesity. *Bariatric Times, 4*(5).

Klein, S. & Romijn, J.A. (2008). Obesity. In H.M. Kronenberg, S. Melmen, K.S. Polonsky, & P.R. Larsen (Eds.), *Williams textbook of endocrinology,* (11th ed., pp. 1563-87). Philadelphia: Saunders.

Marx, J. (2003). Cellular warriors at the battle of the bulge. *Science, 299,* 846-9.

National Institutes of Health; National Heart, Lung and Blood Institute. (n.d.). *Portion distortion.* Retrieved September 5, 2008, from http://hp2010.nhlbihin.net/portion

Rolls, B.J., Morris, E.L., & Roe, L.S. (2002). Portion size of food affects energy intake in normal-weight and overweight men and women. *American Journal of Clinical Nutrition, 76,* 1207-1213.

Sharp, T.A., Bell, M.L., Grunwald, G.K., Schmitz, K.H., Sidney, S., Lewis, C.E., et al. (2002). Differences in resting metabolic rate between White and African-American young adults. *Obesity Research, 10,* 726-732.

United States Department of Agriculture. Economic Research Service: The Economics of Food, Farming, Natural Resources & Rural America. (n.d.). Retrieved September 5, 2008, from www.ers.usda.gov/data/foodconsumption/foodavailindex.htm

U.S. Department of Health and Human Services. (2001). *The Surgeon General's call to action to prevent and decrease overweight and obesity.* Rockville, MD: Office of the Surgeon General, U.S. Department of Health and Human Services, Public Health Service.

U.S. Department of Health and Human Services (1996). *The Surgeon General's report on activity and health.* Rockville, MD: Office of the Surgeon General, U.S. Department of Health and Human Services, Public Health Service.

Wansink, B. & Kim, J. (2005). Bad popcorn in big buckets: Portion size can influence intake as much as taste. *Journal of Nutrition Education and Behavior, 37,* 242-245.

Young, L.R. & Nestle, M. (2003). Expanding portion sizes in the U.S. marketplace: Implications for nutrition counseling. *Journal of the American Dietetic Association, 103,* 231-234.

CHAPTER 4

ASSESSING DIET AND ENERGY INTAKE

CHAPTER OBJECTIVE

After completing this chapter the learner will be able to describe how to analyze dietary intake and diet composition.

LEARNING OBJECTIVES

After completing this chapter, the learner will be able to

1. analyze the dietary intake of a patient.

2. describe ways to assist patients in learning to measure portion size.

3. describe how diet composition impacts weight loss efforts.

INTRODUCTION

The basis of analysis of obesity must include an assessment of energy intake and diet. Establishing and analyzing a patient's baseline history will form the foundation for therapeutic modifications for the individual patient. Most individuals have a completely erroneous assessment of their food intake and eating patterns. A written record is a useful tool in helping to quantify and qualify what the dietary needs and challenges may be.

MEASURING FOOD INTAKE

There are several basic methods that are used to assess dietary intake. All methods focus on quantitative assessment of the amount of food intake. However, efforts should also be made to obtain information on the quality of food choices by obtaining food preparation and source information.

Diet History

The diet history is an important part of the dietary assessment. It typically includes some form of food recall, further described below. In addition, food preferences and associated behaviors are evaluated, such as

- previous dieting history and results,

- food cravings or "favorite foods,"

- food allergies or aversions,

- dietary or nutritional supplements used, and

- eating behavior, such as binge eating or nighttime eating.

Diet interventions should incorporate the elements noted in the history so the patient can build on successful behavior and avoid previous problem areas.

Food Records

Food diaries are frequently used in the analysis of dietary intake. The 3-day dietary record is the most common time frame used for analyzing a person's diet, although a 7-day record more accurately represents the individual's intake (St. Jeor, 2002). Specific procedures vary, depending upon the nature of the recall, but the basic process is the same. The individual is instructed to record and describe everything eaten for 3 days on the food diary form provided. At least one weekend day (Saturday or Sunday) and one weekday should be included. All foods and beverages (including water) taken at each meal and between meals should be listed. Items such as gravy, jam, jelly, butter, margarine, salt, sauces, salad dressings, nuts, or sugar and milk added to cereal or beverages should be included. Also included are chewing gum and mints and it should be specified whether they are sugarless or not. Vitamin or mineral supplements should also be listed. It is important to be as specific as possible and include

- the brand name of the food if possible;

- whether the food was raw or cooked;

- how the food was prepared (fried chicken, baked chicken, etc.);

- the percentage of fat in milk and dairy products (1% milk, 2% cottage cheese);

- whether food (e.g., orange juice) was frozen, fresh, or canned; and

- any other specific information of this kind.

The diary should be completed after each meal or snack; failure to do so leads to underestimation of intake and an inaccurate record. If possible, foods should be weighed or measured using household measurements, such as cup, slice, tablespoon, teaspoon, pat (pat of butter), package, etc. For example, a ham sandwich may be listed as 2 slices of bread, 3 ounces of ham, 1 pat butter, 1 teaspoon of mustard, 1 leaf iceberg lettuce, 1 slice tomato.

Because the purpose of this diary is to estimate the adequacy of the individual's normal diet, it is important to conduct the survey before changes are made in the diet. Patients should be cautioned not to fast or to restrict their diet because it is more

helpful to get a picture of their common eating patterns. The days selected should be the most representative of normal dietary intake.

24-Hour Dietary Recall

This method is widely used, although it provides a narrower picture of dietary intake than food diaries. Multiple recalls from random, nonconsecutive days can provide a more representative assessment (St. Jeor, 2002). The 24-hour recall is a useful tool to monitor behavior during the intervention phase of therapy.

DIET ANALYSIS

Once the dietary history is completed, it must be analyzed. The U.S. Department of Agriculture (USDA) publications remain the most comprehensive and up-to-date information in the United States. Jean Penington's *Food Values of Portions Commonly Used* is a classic work that is still commonly used for quick analysis of foods as well (St. Jeor, 2002).

Many software programs exist that make this once tedious task much easier. Two examples are Food Processor: Nutritional Analysis and Fitness Software (ESHA Research, Inc, Salem, OR; 800-659-3742; www.esha.com) and Nutritional Care Management (Computrition, Inc., Chadsworth, CA; 800-222-4488; www.computrition.com (St. Jeor, 2002).

The USDA's National Nutrient Databank System provides a repository of over 6,200 foods. Its online search program is available at: http://www.nal.usda.gov/fnic/foodcomp/search/

Below is a list of several Web sites where diet records can be analyzed:

- Provides a free nutritional analysis tool: www.nat.uiuc.edu/mainnat.html

- A commercial site that allows you to analyze your diet online for free: www.dietsure.com

- Web site provided by the USDA for assistance with diet analysis and diet planning: www.mypyramidtracker.gov

These sites can also be used by individual patients to assist in ongoing dietary monitoring. (See Case Study 4-1.)

Case Study 4-1: Dietary Analysis

You are a dietitian working at a family practice clinic. The nurse practitioner at the same clinic has referred a patient to you for a diet assessment. The 55-year-old patient is George. George is 5'10" tall and weighs 264 lb. His body mass index is 38, and his predicted resting metabolic rate (RMR) is 2,234 kcal per day. George's RMR was measured a few days ago at a rate of 1,800 kcal per day. His predicted RMR is 25% above his measured RMR, but the discrepancy could be due to the fact that George is very obese, and fat tissue has a much lower metabolic rate than lean tissue. Your job is to assess George's diet intake to determine whether there is an energy imbalance.

Intervention/Solution

Upon completion of George's 3-day food diary, you will need to analyze the results. If you have access to a diet analysis software program, use that program to analyze George's diet. Online resources that may also be used include:

www.nat.uiuc.edu/mainnat.html
www.dietsure.com
www.mypyramidtracker.gov/

Units of Measure

1 cup =	8 oz	2 cups =	1 pint
1 coffee cup =	6 oz	4 cups =	1 quart
3 teaspoons =	1 tablespoon	3 oz meat =	size of a deck of cards
16 tablespoons =	1 cup		

Food Diary Day 1

Name: George Jabrinski   **Age:** 55   **Sex:** Male
Date: March 1, 20__   **Day of week:** Tuesday

Software code (if necessary)	Food or Beverage Consumed	Amount/Size	Kcal
	Breakfast		
	Fried eggs	2	
	Bagel (plain egg)	6 inch	
	Cream cheese (strawberry)	2 tablespoons	
	Cranberry juice cocktail	1 cup	
	Coffee (brewed)	1 cup	
	Creamer	1 teaspoon	
	Lunch		
	Hot ham and swiss sandwich (fast food)	1 large	
	Lettuce	1 leaf	
	Tomato	1 slice	
	V-8 juice (canned)	12 ounces	
	Potato salad	1 cup	

continued on next page

	Dinner		
	Spaghetti and meatballs	2 cups	
	French bread	2 slices	
	Light beer	12 ounces	
	Water	12 ounces	
	Margarine	2 teaspoons	
	Vanilla ice cream	1 cup	
		Total kcal per day: _____	

Food Diary Day 2

Name: George Jabrinski   **Age:** 55   **Sex:** Male
Date: March 3, 20__   **Day of week:** Thursday

Software code (if necessary)	Food or Beverage Consumed	Amount/Size	Kcal
	Breakfast		
	Cold cereal (Frosted Mini Wheats)	2 cups	
	2% milk	.25 cup	
	Toast (cracked wheat)	2 slices	
	Margarine	2 teaspoons	
	Honey	2 teaspoons	
	Grape juice (frozen concentrate)	1 cup	
	Coffee	1 cup	
	Creamer	1 teaspoon	
	Lunch		
	Cheeseburger (fast food)	1	
	French fries (fast food)	Large size	
	Chocolate milk shake (fast food)	Medium	
	Dinner		
	Coke (regular)	12 ounces	
	Roast beef	12 ounces	
	Mashed potatoes	1 cup	
	Gravy	.5 cup	
	Cooked carrots	.5 cup	
	Dinner roll	2	
	Margarine	2 teaspoons	
	Chocolate cake with frosting	1 slice	
		Total kcal per day: _____	

continued on next page

Food Diary Day 3

Name: George Jabrinski   **Age:** 55   **Sex:** Male
Date: March 5, 20__   **Day of week:** Saturday

Software code (if necessary)	Food or Beverage Consumed	Amount/Size	Kcal
	Breakfast		
	Pancakes	2.6 inch	
	Bacon	3 slices	
	Margarine	2 teaspoons	
	Syrup	6 tablespoons	
	Coffee	1 cup	
	Lunch		
	Burrito supreme (Taco Bell)	1	
	Lemonade	20 ounces	
	Dinner		
	Apple juice	12 ounces	
	Baked ham	10 ounces	
	Baked potato	1	
	Sour cream (low fat)	1 tablespoon	
	Peas (frozen)	.5 cup	
	French bread	2 slices	
	Margarine	2 teaspoons	
	Snack		
	Coke (regular)	12 ounces	

Total kcal per day: _____

Resolution

George was not too far off in his statement that he was eating healthy. His diet consists of approximately 2,900 kcal per day, of which 13% is protein, 29% fat, and 58% carbohydrates. The composition of George's diet is within the recommended healthy range, but his energy intake puts his body in the state of fat storage. His energy intake should be reduced and/or his energy expenditure increased for him to lose weight.

Resolution Process

Your analysis of George's diet revealed that he was consuming approximately 2,900 kcal per day. His RMR was measured at 1,800 kcal per day and his daily energy expenditure from exercise is about 150 to 200 kcal a day. (George walks for 30 minutes a day and estimates that he covers about 1.5 to 2.0 miles. Average energy expenditure for most people is roughly 100 kcal per mile.) Therefore, George's total energy expenditure is approximately 2,000 kcal per day. Even if his RMR were closer to his predicted RMR (2,232 kcal per day), George would still be eating more kcal than he expends.

As you look more closely at George's food intake, you can see that small changes in some of his food choices will reduce energy intake significantly. You also can see that his portion sizes are often higher than they could be. Therefore, it would not be hard to reduce George's energy intake without severely restricting his current diet. He could reduce some portion sizes and change a few of his energy-dense food choices.

PORTION SIZE AND SERVING SIZE

As discussed in Chapter 3, the portion size that an individual may be used to eating may equal two to three standard serving sizes. Because labels designate serving size and outline macronutrient proportions accordingly, it is necessary to learn to read labels and recognize standard serving sizes as a method of monitoring energy intake. The process of completing the dietary log is an opportunity to introduce this concept to the patient.

Ask the patient to check the package label to see how many "servings per container" are listed. Have the patient measure the serving size from the label onto a plate so that they can get a visual idea of the actual serving size. This step will help the patient to see how their "normal" portion size compares to the measured serving.

It is also helpful to compare serving sizes to everyday objects. Figure 4-1 shows some common objects and comparable serving sizes.

DIET COMPOSITON

Energy-dense diets (higher calories per unit weight or volume) are most often implicated with the rising prevalence of obesity in children and adults. The implication is that these diets contain a concentrated amount of energy (kcal) per unit weight, and this concentrated energy tips the body's energy balance toward energy storage. The contrasting implication is that foods low in energy density will cause satiation sooner than energy-dense foods and the energy intake will be one that favors weight maintenance or even weight loss. A simple way to look at it is that if a person gets full after eating 2 cups of food, 2 cups of ice cream will bring in more calories than 2 cups of lettuce. Preferences for energy-dense foods can also impact adherence to diet modifications, so analysis of food quality as well as quantity is important.

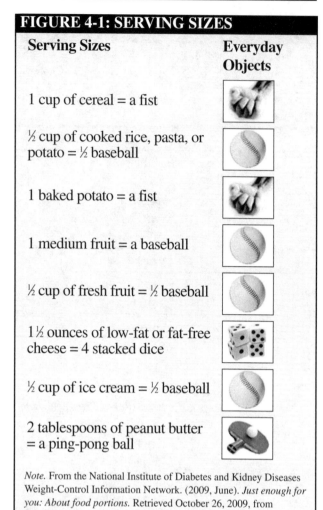

FIGURE 4-1: SERVING SIZES

Serving Sizes	Everyday Objects
1 cup of cereal = a fist	
½ cup of cooked rice, pasta, or potato = ½ baseball	
1 baked potato = a fist	
1 medium fruit = a baseball	
½ cup of fresh fruit = ½ baseball	
1½ ounces of low-fat or fat-free cheese = 4 stacked dice	
½ cup of ice cream = ½ baseball	
2 tablespoons of peanut butter = a ping-pong ball	

Note. From the National Institute of Diabetes and Kidney Diseases Weight-Control Information Network. (2009, June). *Just enough for you: About food portions.* Retrieved October 26, 2009, from http://www.win.niddk.nih.gov/publications/just_enough.htm

2002 Dietary Reference Intakes For Macronutrients

The National Academy of Science's Institute of Medicine Food and Nutrition Board has established revised guidelines for dietary intake to minimize chronic disease risk. The recommended daily proportions are that adults should obtain 45% to 65% of daily intake from carbohydrates, 10% to 35% from protein, and 20% to 35% from fat (Hellerstein & Parks, 2004).

Dietary Fat

Dietary fat was recognized as a main culprit in promoting obesity during the 1980s and 1990s. Hundreds of fat-free food products came onto the market. Fat-free and low-fat were highlighted on hundreds of food labels, and fat-free desserts became widely popular.

In order to maintain palatability of these low-fat and fat-free foods, refined sugar was often added. Many people who adopted a diet of low-fat and fat-free foods did not know that they were still consuming energy-dense foods. After a decade or more, the phobia of fat in our food diminished. It may be that Americans became tired of bland-tasting fat-free and low-fat foods, or maybe they saw it pointless to restrict fat in their diet when they were not losing weight. Nonetheless, fat has crept back into our foods and diets.

We know today that dietary fat can promote obesity, whether or not there is overeating. As discussed previously, high-fat foods are energy-dense foods, and can induce body fat storage by contributing large amounts of kilocalories for the volume of food consumed. We also know that dietary fat is digested, processed, and stored on the body more efficiently than dietary carbohydrate, or protein. This means that the thermic effect of food is less for dietary fat than carbohydrates and protein, and that a lower percentage of the total caloric value of fat is needed to store excess dietary fat as body fat than the percentage of total energy needed to store excess carbohydrates and protein as body fat.

New research is indicating that the type of fat may be more important than the quantity. Monosaturated fats have proven beneficial in lowering low-density lipoprotein (LDL) cholesterol levels, whereas saturated fats and trans-fatty acids are to be avoided. In addition, higher fat percentage in a calorie-restrictive diet can provide more satisfaction, and therefore contribute to dietary compliance and weight loss efforts (Hellerstein & Parks, 2004).

Dietary Fiber

Dietary fiber is defined as indigestible carbohydrate. Because all carbohydrates are sugars, dietary fiber is really carbohydrate that is not digestible. Dietary fibers are found most abundantly in fruits, vegetables, and whole grain products. The rule of thumb is that the less refined or less processed the carbohydrate, the more the dietary fiber. Dietary fiber has certain health benefits. The most familiar health benefits of dietary fiber are preventing cardiovascular disease and facilitating digestion. However, dietary fiber can also help with weight loss or reduced weight maintenance.

Dietary fiber may assist with weight control in several ways. First of all, some dietary fibers from fruits and vegetables reduce the overall absorption of fat and protein, which means that fewer kilocalories from a mixed diet that is high in fiber will be absorbed than for a mixed diet with low fiber. Dietary fiber can also decrease feelings of hunger or increase fullness. The majority of dietary fiber studies conclude that dietary fiber does reduce hunger (Howarth, Saltzman, & Roberts, 2001). Reduced hunger, induced by dietary fiber, also reduces actual energy intake. The combination of all of these effects of dietary fiber food intake and absorption does affect body weight. Several early studies on dietary fiber and weight control show that augmenting dietary fiber accelerates weight loss, whether the fiber comes in supplement form or real food.

Dietary Carbohydrates

A minimum intake of at least 130 grams of carbohydrates ensures adequate glucose for brain metabolism. No more than 25% of total calories should be from "added sugars"; those incorporated during processing. Diets high in processed carbohydrates lead to more rapid return of hunger as opposed to diets high in complex carbohydrates, which also provide greater satiety. In addition, lower fat, higher carbohydrate diets have been associated with elevations in serum triglycerides, and lower high-density lipoprotein (HDL) cholesterol, which is felt to contribute to heart disease development (Hellerstein & Parks, 2004).

Glycemic Index and Glycemic Load

Most nutritionists agree that the problem with refined sugar is its stimulating effect on blood glucose and insulin levels. Large fluctuations in blood glucose and insulin levels stress the metabolic system, and this glycemic stress can present a health risk. The glycemic index is a relative comparison of how a food item raises blood glucose levels relative to a standard bolus of ingested glucose. The magnitude of rise in blood glucose over a 2-hour period resultant from the ingestion of 50 grams of glucose is set as the standard of 100. Fifty grams of the comparison food is then consumed and the rise in blood glucose is plotted over the 2-hour period. For example, if the comparison food causes a rise in blood glucose that is 70% that of the standard glucose bolus, the glycemic index for the comparison food is 70.

Many nutritionists contend that the glycemic load is a better indicator of glycemic stress on the system than the glycemic index. The glycemic load is calculated by dividing the glycemic index by 100 and then multiplying it by the grams of carbohydrate per serving. Thus, the glycemic load takes into account the glycemic index, but also accounts for the total amount of carbohydrate consumed. For example, two foods could both have a glycemic index of 70, but the serving size for one food contains 20 grams of carbohydrate and the serving size for the second contains 10 grams carbohydrate. The glycemic load for the first food would be 14 and the second 7. Thus, eating one serving of food item number 1 would have a greater effect on blood glucose levels than eating a serving size of food number 2. Most refined carbohydrates tend to have a higher glycemic index and load, whereas most complex carbohydrates have a lower glycemic index, and load.

Consuming foods with a low glycemic index and/or load may help the obese person control weight by ensuring a slow steady flow of glucose into the bloodstream after eating, which can extend feelings of fullness. The risk of insulin resistance and diabetes can also be reduced in the obese person by consuming more foods with a low glycemic index and/or low glycemic load.

Dietary Protein

Higher proportion protein diets – those that consist of more than 25% of total energy intake – can also be problematic. The low proportion of dietary fiber and water content can lead to constipation, and may lead to increased filtration load on the kidneys. Other effects may include an increase in urinary calcium loss and contribution to osteoporosis. High-protein foods may also be high in saturated fat. They likely result in increased satiety, however, leading to decreased food intake and increased weight loss.

SUMMARY

Analysis of dietary intake is an important component of the baseline assessment. Food records should be evaluated for quantity as well as type and quality of food choices. Overconsumption of carbohydrates, fats, or proteins can lead to increased body weight. Diets that focus on only one macronutrient have limited effectiveness. Recent dietary guidelines provide a framework that recognizes that different diet strategies are necessary for different people, and therefore consist of more flexible ranges of macronutrients.

CHAPTER 4
Questions 13-15

Note: Choose the one option that BEST answers each question.

13. When completing a dietary recall log, a patient should be instructed to

    a. only include solid foods in the records list.

    b. record the food as soon as the meal or snack is over.

    c. reduce the amount of food to the designated serving size.

    d. include only weekend days in the log because food consumption is higher on those days.

14. When discussing portion size with an obese patient, the nurse should be aware that

    a. serving size and portion size are synonymous terms.

    b. the patient may be used to portion sizes that are considerably larger than serving sizes.

    c. food serving size on labels is consistent with the food pyramid serving size.

    d. government agencies regulate the standardization of serving sizes.

15. A diet associated with the rising prevalence of obesity is one that

    a. is high in protein.

    b. is low in carbohydrate.

    c. is high in energy dense foods.

    d. has a low glycemic load.

REFERENCES

Hellerstein, M.K. & Parks, E.J. (2004). Obesity & overweight. In F.S. Greenspan & D.G. Gardner (Eds.), *Basic and clinical endocrinology* (pp. 805-806). New York: McGraw Hill Companies.

Howarth, N.C., Saltzman, E., & Roberts, S.B. (2001). Dietary fiber and weight regulation. *Nutr. Rev, 59,* 129-139.

National Institute of Diabetes and Digestive and Kidney Diseases. Weight-Control Information Network. (2009, June). *Just enough for you: About food portions.* Retrieved October 26, 2009, from http://win.niddk.nih.gov/publications/just_enough.htm

St. Jeor, S.T. (2002). Measurement of food intake. In C.G. Fairburn & K.D. Brownell (Eds.), *Eating disorders and obesity* (2nd ed., pp. 126-129). New York: The Guilford Press.

CHAPTER 5

ASSESSING ENERGY OUTPUT AND PHYSICAL ACTIVITY

CHAPTER OBJECTIVE

After completing this chapter the learner will be able to describe techniques used to measure resting metabolic rate (RMR), physical activity, and fitness.

LEARNING OBJECTIVES

After completing this chapter, the learner will be able to

1. describe how different tools are used to measure and monitor energy expenditure and physical activity.

2. describe the relevance of RMR measurements in the treatment of patients.

3. determine appropriate physical activity monitoring tools for individual patients.

4. list components of a fitness assessment tool.

INTRODUCTION

One half of the energy balance equation is energy expenditure. Therefore, it is important that the health care professional be able to measure or estimate energy expenditure for the patient who is conscious about body weight. Monitoring energy expenditure from physical activity is also essential when helping patients with weight control because most weight management regimes include exercise programming. Tools used for measuring and monitoring energy expenditure range from expensive and sophisticated machines that are only found in medical centers to inexpensive gadgets and diaries that can be found in any setting.

MEASURING RESTING METABOLIC RATE

Calorimetry

The total energy expenditure of the body is the sum of the energy derived from the breakdown of dietary fat, protein, and carbohydrate; or in the case of weight loss, the breakdown of stored energy in the body. Heat is released in the process of metabolism, and the heat production of the body is directly related to the body's metabolism. The process of quantifying the body's energy expenditure through the measurement of metabolic heat production is called calorimetry. Direct calorimetry is the measurement of heat emission from a person enclosed in a temperature-controlled chamber. This method of quantifying energy expenditure is very expensive, cumbersome, and limiting. Therefore, direct calorimetry is not used in most clinical practices. Most health professionals use either indirect metabolic measures or prediction equations to quantify energy expenditure. See Table 5-1.

Heat liberated from the body, as a result of metabolism, is also directly related to respiration.

TABLE 5-1: COMMON PREDICTION EQUATIONS FOR RESTING METABOLIC RATE

Kleiber equation for predicting resting metabolic rate (RMR) according to body size:

$$RMR = 73.3 \times BM^{0.74}$$

Harris and Benedict equations for predicting RMR according to body size, height, age, and sex

$$RMR = 13.75 \times BM + 500.3 \times H - 6.78 \times age + 66.5 \text{ (men)}$$

$$RMR = 9.56 \times BM + 185.0 \times H - 4.68 \times age + 655.1 \text{ (women)}$$

RMR = kcal·d⁻¹ BM = body mass in kg. H = height in meters.

Thus, by measuring oxygen consumption and carbon dioxide production, one can also quantify energy expenditure. The respiratory gas exchange measurements are easily converted into calorie equivalents. This method of metabolic measurement is called indirect calorimetry, because heat released from the body's metabolism is measured indirectly, rather than directly.

There are several methods used to quantify energy expenditure through indirect calorimetry. The most familiar is some brand of metabolic cart that is connected to a treadmill or exercise cycle to measure exercise energy expenditure. A small hand-held device to measure human resting metabolism was introduced commercially in 2000. The unit, called the Body Gem, consists of a face mask or mouthpiece in which the individual breathes for 5 to 10 minutes. Sensors measure oxygen consumption, ventilation, temperature, humidity, and barometric pressure and provide a digital readout of RMR in kcals/day (Nieman, Trone, & Austin, 2003).

Although such measurements may not be routinely used in the clinical practice setting, referral of the individual patient to an exercise physiologist or other source of metabolic testing may provide information helpful in developing the treatment plan, as discussed in Case Study 5-1.

Case Study 5-1: Measuring Resting Metabolic Rate

You are a nurse practitioner at a family practice clinic. George is a 55-year-old patient who has developed hypertension. He is 5' 10" tall and weighs 264 lb. George states that he is eating a healthy diet and walking 30 minutes every day. He is convinced that his weight is caused by a metabolic problem. However, his blood workup, performed a week ago, is normal. You are suspicious of George's reported health behaviors, but without documentation cannot really deny that he is eating healthy and exercising. What should you do to discover the true root of the problem while not offending your patient? (*Note:* This chapter deals only with resting metabolic rate (RMR) and energy expenditure, so please ignore food intake for the time being.)

Intervention/Solution

George has a calculated body mass index of 38, which places him in the obese class II category. You have a RMR evaluation ordered for George. George's RMR is measured through indirect calorimetry at the local hospital endocrinology lab. The RMR report shows that George's resting oxygen consumption level is 0.250 L/min, which is equivalent to an RMR of 1,800 kcal/day. You explain to George that his metabolism is within the range of a normal person, but you admit the RMR may be on the low side of the normal range for somebody his size. Because George is in the obese class II category, you suspect that his weight problem is not all due to a slightly lower than normal RMR. You also want to have the dietitian perform a dietary intake for George.

Resolution Process

There are several hints or keys that guide you in what to do. Many obese individuals hope or are convinced that their weight problem is metabolic. This perception often stems from their frustration in controlling

continued on next page

weight when they believe they are doing what is necessary to control weight. George may be one of these people. George's blood profile did not show any hormonal imbalance or other abnormality that suggests a metabolic disorder. Thus, hypothyroidism is clearly not the issue. However, he still may have a slow metabolic rate that is not caused by a hormonal imbalance. You, therefore, request the RMR test at the local hospital endocrinology lab.

While waiting for the RMR lab tests, you calculate George's predicted RMR by using the Harris and Benedict equation for men (Table 5-1). His predicted RMR is 2,234 kcal/day. The RMR lab test comes back and the results show an oxygen consumption level of 0.250 liters per minute, which translates into 1,800 kcal/day. Average resting metabolic rate for the normal adult male is approximately 0.263 liters oxygen consumed per minute (One Metabolic Equivalent of Task (MET) = 3.5 ml kg^{-1} min;^{1} equal to 0.263L/min for a 75-kg man). George's metabolic rate is 95% of what is expected. Although this rate is comparatively low (5% below normal), much of George's extra weight is fat tissue, which has a very low metabolic rate. So, his metabolic rate is most likely normal, or slightly above normal relative to his lean body mass.

George's predicted RMR is about 400 kcal/day above his actual measured RMR. This predicted metabolic rate is almost 25% higher than measured. If George is following a diet based on energy predictions, he may be overconsuming without even knowing it. You therefore request a dietary intake assessment.

ASSESSING PHYSICAL ACTIVITY

Activity Monitors

The most plausible field methods for measuring either total energy expenditure or physical activity energy expenditure are pedometers, accelerometers, and heart rate monitors. Pedometers are more suited for monitoring physical activity than overall daily energy expenditure, whereas accelerometers and heart rate monitors are well-suited for both.

Pedometers have been around for several decades (see Figure 5-1). The pedometer itself is designed to measure steps taken during the day. However, only the total distance traveled is recorded on the pedometer, and there is no indication of intensity of physical activity. Therefore, pedometers are useful in gaining insight into overall energy expenditure, but do not provide any reference to exercise intensity or activity patterns throughout the day. An advantage of pedometers is that they are relatively inexpensive (some are given away free as promotions), and even children can learn how to use them.

Accelerometers are fairly new to the field and work on a principle different than pedometers.

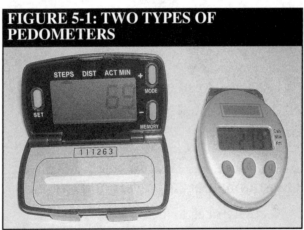

FIGURE 5-1: TWO TYPES OF PEDOMETERS

Accelerometers are really tiny force transducers that measure continuously the intensity, frequency, and duration of movement for extended periods. Accelerometers are valid and reliable for adults and children. However, there is no consensus about the accelerometer count thresholds for mild, moderate, and high exercise intensities in children. Correlations between accelerometer measures and calorimetry measures range from about 0.60 to 0.85, which are fairly high correlations. The advantage of accelerometers is that they can measure the intensity of energy expenditure throughout the day, and this information can be downloaded to a computer. The computer then generates the data and pinpoints the fluctuations in energy expenditure at any time of day. The computer also uses regression equations to calculate actual kilocalorie expenditure from activity counts. Accelerometers are probably one of the best tools for monitoring daily energy expenditure.

Heart rate is strongly related to respiratory rate and energy expenditure across a wide range of values. Heart rate monitors can accumulate data from short or long bouts of activity throughout the day (see Figure 5-2). Heart rate data can also be downloaded to a computer and the magnitude of fluctuations in heart rate during the day can be pinpointed. Regression equations are used to convert heart rate measures to kilocalorie expenditure.

FIGURE 5-2: THE HEART RATE MONITOR

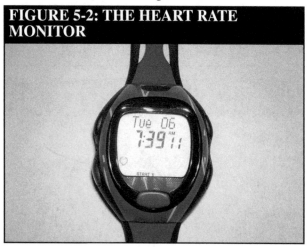

Questionnaires, Surveys, and Diaries

Activity questionnaires generally require a recall or observational report of the person's activity. Their accuracy is quite variable, from being a rather poor indicator of actual physical activity to being a relatively good measure of physical activity. Activity questionnaires for children tend to be less accurate than those intended for adults. The inaccuracy of activity questionnaires for children is due primarily to two issues:

- the younger the child the less capable the child is at reading, understanding, and completing the questionnaire; and

- many children cannot complete questionnaires, so the questionnaire has to be completed by an observing adult.

Physical activity diaries are commonly used to assess physical activity in children and adults because these diaries are inexpensive, unobtrusive, and easily administered. An adult physical activity questionnaire that is used internationally is the International Physical Activity Questionnaire (IPAQ; Craig et al., 2003). The IPAQ comes in a long and short version. Both versions ask the respondent to record his/her health-related physical activity for the past 7 days. Either version can be administered by a professional, either face-to-face or via phone interview, or they can be self-administered. The long version consists of 27 questions that focus on job-related physical activity, transportation-related physical activity, housework, recreation and sport activity, and sedentary or sitting time. The short version of the form asks only seven questions about time spent in vigorous physical activity, moderate intensity activity, walking, and sitting. The questionnaire can be obtained in several different languages. Figure 5-3 outlines the Self Administered short version and Figure 5-4 describes the scoring of the questionnaire.

One of the most popular questionnaires for older children and adolescents is the Previous Day Physical Activity Recall (PDPAR). The PDPAR was designed to provide accurate data on mode, frequency, intensity, and duration of physical activities; which is then used to estimate physical activity energy expenditure (Weston, Petosa, & Pate, 1997).

The PDPAR is an activity diary that is segmented into seventeen 30-minute intervals. The youth completing the questionnaire is provided with a list of 35 different activities in which youth normally engage. The youth then records the number of the activity in which he/she participated for any given 30-minute interval of the previous day. For the selected activity, he/she also records the appropriate intensity using the following descriptors: very light (slow breathing and little or no movement), light (normal breathing and movement), medium (increased breathing and moderate movement), and hard (hard breathing and quick movement). From the recorded data, an estimated

FIGURE 5-3: INTERNATIONAL PHYSICAL ACTIVITY QUESTIONNAIRE, SHORT FORM SELF-ADMINISTERED VERSION

In answering the following questions,

♦ **vigorous** physical activities refer to activities that take hard physical effort and make you breathe much harder that normal.

♦ **moderate** activities refer to activities that take moderate physical effort and make you breathe somewhat harder that normal.

1a.   During the last 7 days, on how many days did you do **vigorous** physical activities like heavy lifting, digging, aerobics, or fast bicycling,?

Think about *only* those physical activities that you did for at least 10 minutes at a time.

_____ **days per week** ⇨

or

☐ **none**

1b.   How much time in total did you usually spend on one of those days doing vigorous physical activities?

_____ **hours** _____ **minutes**

2a.   Again, think *only* about those physical activities that you did for at least 10 minutes at a time. During the last 7 days, on how many days did you do **moderate** physical activities like carrying light loads, bicycling at a regular pace, or doubles tennis? Do not include walking.

_____ **days per week** ⇨

or

☐ **none**

2b.   How much time in total did you usually spend on one of those days doing moderate physical activities?

_____ **hours** _____ **minutes**

3a.   During the last 7 days, on how many days did you **walk** for at least 10 minutes at a time? This includes walking at work and at home, walking to travel from place to place, and any other walking that you did solely for recreation, sport, exercise or leisure.

_____ **days per week** ⇨

or

☐ **none**

3b.   How much time in total did you usually spend walking on one of those days?

_____ **hours** _____ **minutes**

The last question is about the time you spent _sitting_ on weekdays while at work, at home, while doing course work and during leisure time. This includes time spent sitting at a desk, visiting friends, reading traveling on a bus or sitting or lying down to watch television.

4.   During the last 7 days, how much time in total did you usually spend *sitting* on a **week day?**

_____ **hours** _____ **minutes**

This is the end of questionnaire, thank you for participating.

This is the final SHORT LAST 7 DAYS SELF-ADMINISTERED version of IPAQ from the 2000/01 Reliability and Validity Study. Completed May 2001.

FIGURE 5-4: INTERNATIONAL PHYSICAL ACTIVITY QUESTIONNAIRE, SCORING

At A Glance
IPAQ Scoring Protocol (Short Forms)

Continuous Score

Expressed as MET-min per week: MET level x minutes of activity/day x days per week

Sample Calculation

MET levels   **MET-minutes/week for 30 min/day, 5 days**
Walking = 3.3 METs $3.3*30*5 =$ 495 MET-minutes/week
Moderate Intensity = 4.0 METs $4.0*30*5 =$ 600 MET-minutes/week
Vigorous Intensity = 8.0 METs $8.0*30*5 =$ 1,200 MET-minutes/week
                                         _____
                                         TOTAL   =   2,295 MET-minutes/week

Total MET-minutes/week = Walk (METs*min*days) + Mod (METs*min*days) + Vig (METs*min*days)

Categorical Score- three levels of physical activity are proposed

1. **Low**

   - No activity is reported **OR**
   - Some activity is reported but not enough to meet Categories 2 or 3.

2. **Moderate**

   Either of the following 3 criteria
   - 3 or more days of vigorous activity of at least 20 minutes per day **OR**
   - 5 or more days of moderate-intensity activity and/or walking of at least 30 minutes per day **OR**
   - 5 or more days of any combination of walking, moderate-intensity or vigorous-intensity activities achieving a minimum of at least 600 MET-minutes/week.

3. **High**

   Any one of the following 2 criteria
   - Vigorous-intensity activity on at least 3 days and accumulating at least 1500 MET-minutes/week **OR**
   - 7 or more days of any combination of walking, moderate- or vigorous-intensity activities accumulating at least 3000 MET-minutes/week

Please review the full document "Guidelines for the data processing and analysis of the International Physical Activity Questionnaire" for more detailed description of IPAQ analysis and recommendations for data cleaning and processing [www.ipaq.ki.se].

Revised November 2005

energy expenditure value is derived for each activity within the given time frame.

Many additional physical activity questionnaires and surveys have been designed for adults. Some of these have been intended for specific populations, such as cardiac patients. The reliability and validity of these questionnaires is variable, but all are acceptable.

Case Study 5-2 demonstrates how these tools may be used to monitor physical activity.

FITNESS TESTING

An important component of assessing an individual's current physical activity involves establishing a baseline fitness level. A simple fitness test can guide priorities in the treatment plan. Components of a fitness assessment include aerobic capacity, muscle strength and endurance, and flexibility. Aerobic fitness can be measured with a timed walk or step test over a short timed interval and accompanying heart rate change. Muscle strength can be measured by the number of push-ups or sit-ups done over a short time period. Flexibility can be measured by sit and reach exercises, with documentation of how close to the toes an individual can reach. These components are found in many fitness assessments, including the YMCA Fitness Assessment, the American College of Sports Medicine Fitness Assessment, and the President's Challenge Adult Fitness Test. An online version of the latter is available at www.adultfitnesstest.org.

Case Study 5-2: Monitoring Physical Activity (1 of 2)

You are a physical therapist at a large clinic. Ginger is a 50-year-old patient who has developed chronic back and knee problems. Ginger has a body fat content of 43%. It is decided that she should lose weight in order to alleviate some of the weight stress on her joints. As part of Ginger's weight loss program, she is prescribed an exercise protocol. The protocol calls for Ginger to exercise twice per day, 5 to 6 days per week, and expend 100 kcal per exercise session (200 kcal per exercise day). In order not to overstress her musculoskeletal system, Ginger is restricted to exercising at a low intensity. Your clinic has heart rate monitors, accelerometers, and pedometers. You are also familiar with the International Physical Activity Questionnaire (IPAQ). You are afraid that Ginger might overdo it because she is ambitious and was an athlete in college. Which tool will you use to monitor Ginger's exercise program on a day-to-day and week-to-week basis?

Intervention/Solution

Ginger is clearly obese at 43% body fat. You decide to monitor her exercise program by using an accelerometer. Ginger is to wear the accelerometer around her waist during the hours she is awake. After the first week, the accelerometer data illustrate that Ginger is adhering to her exercise program and that she is maintaining the appropriate intensity.

Resolution Process

The biggest key to this case study is that you will need to monitor Ginger's exercise sessions closely, without being present. You want to be sure of three things:

- Ginger exercises 5 to 6 days per week (and doesn't try to expend all of her exercise kilocalories in one day),

- Ginger exercises twice per day, so she can have a rest period between exercise bouts and avoids one prolonged exercise bout, and

- Ginger expends 200 kcal in exercise each day she exercises.

These three criteria will ensure that Ginger gets the appropriate exercise stimulus without overtaxing her musculoskeletal system.

continued on next page

You quickly rule out the IPAQ because it as a subjective measure that gives overall activity levels without regard for time or day. Next, you rule out the pedometer, as it will not give you intensity of exercise or timing of the exercise sessions. Your remaining choices are the accelerometer and heart rate monitor. Both devices record exercise intensity (the accelerometer directly and heart rate monitor indirectly), and both have time and day clocks (allowing you to know when Ginger exercises). Both devices calculate energy expenditure.

The accelerometer data reveal that Ginger exercised Monday through Saturday. Her exercise sessions occurred twice daily, in the morning and evening, and were spaced out enough to give Ginger time to recover between sessions. Each exercise session was estimated to be in the low-intensity range (data taken from the accelerometer algorithms). However, there were a few times when Ginger was exercising on the boarder of moderate intensity. She explained that she walked much faster at these times because she was pressed for time.

The accelerometer estimates for energy expenditure during each exercise session are listed in the table below. Ginger was on target for her energy expenditures each day.

Sunday	Monday	Tuesday	Wednesday	Thursday	Friday	Saturday
Off	105 kcal	140 kcal	90 kcal	135 kcal	80 kcal	95 kcal
Off	115 kcal	100 kcal	110 kcal	120 kcal	95 kcal	102 kcal

SUMMARY

Several methods for measuring and estimating energy expenditure have been utilized in clinical practice. Indirect calorimetry is the most common clinical method used to measure energy expenditure. Activity monitors, such as accelerometers, heart rate monitors, and pedometers, are relatively inexpensive devices used to monitor physical activity throughout the day. Questionnaires, such as the IPAQ, are used to gather physical activity information on children and adults. Fitness testing is also an important aspect of determining individual strength's and challenges and establishes a baseline for future measurements.

EXAM QUESTIONS

CHAPTER 5
Questions 16-19

Note: Choose the option that BEST answers each question.

16. A characteristic of the pedometer used to monitor physical activity is that it measures

    a. intensity of physical activity.

    b. only the total distance traveled.

    c. heart rate and respiratory patterns.

    d. specific patterns of physical activity.

17. Measurement of a patient's resting metabolic rate (RMR) is helpful in treatment, because the results

    a. can help with the treatment plan and may rule out a metabolic abnormality.

    b. are usually fascinating to the patient and encourage compliance with any diet regimen.

    c. will reveal whether the patient is exercising or not.

    d. will reveal whether the patient is at risk for a co-morbidity.

18. An advantage of using physical activity questionnaires or physical activity diaries to measure physical activity energy expenditure is that these tools

    a. are more reliable than accelerometers.

    b. are highly accurate for recording physical activity in children.

    c. are inexpensive and easily administered.

    d. record exercise heart rate.

19. Aerobic fitness is measured as one component of establishing a baseline fitness level. A method of assessing aerobic fitness is

    a. the length of time to do 50 push-ups.

    b. a timed walk and accompanying heart rate change.

    c. a resting blood pressure measurement.

    d. self-reported daily activity.

REFERENCES

Adult Fitness Test. (n.d.). Retrieved February 25, 2009, from www.adultfitnesstest.org

American College of Sports Medicine. (1997). Collection of questionnaires for health-related research. *Medicine and Science in Sports and Exercise, 29,* S1-S208.

Craig, C.L., Marshall, A.L., Sjostrom, M., Bauman, A.E., Booth, M.L., Ainsworth, B., et al. (2003). International Physical Activity Questionnaire: 12-country reliability and validity. *Medicine and Science in Sports and Exercise, 35,* 1381-1395.

International Physical Activity Questionnaire. (2002, November). Retrieved February 15, 2009, from http://www.ipaq.ki.se/questionnaires/IQLoTEL rev111402.pdf

Nieman, D., Trone, G., & Austin, M. (2003). A new handheld device for measuring resting metabolic rate and oxygen consumption. *Journal of the American Dietetic Association, 103,* 588-593.

Weston, A.T., Petosa, R., & Pate, R.R. (1997). Validation of an instrument for measurement of physical activity in youth. *Medicine and Science in Sports and Exercise, 29*: 138-143.

CHAPTER 6

EMOTIONAL LINKS TO OBESITY

CHAPTER OBJECTIVE

After completing this chapter the learner will be able to discuss skills needed to help patients recognize and overcome emotional eating.

LEARNING OBJECTIVES

After completing this chapter, the learner will be able to

1. explain the connection between habits and emotional needs.

2. state how a person uses food as an emotional coping mechanism.

3. describe how to help patients identify their emotional links to food and express their feelings about eating and exercise behaviors.

4. identify barriers to healthy eating for individual patients.

5. list behavioral tools to help patients overcome unhealthy emotional links to food.

INTRODUCTION

Many individuals with eating and/or weight problems have a difficult time distinguishing among hunger, thirst, emotions, and habitual eating behaviors. They eat as an emotional outlet or as a form of emotional expression. People also eat in accordance to established eating patterns, regardless of hunger. Once individuals learn how to separate their emotions from what they think is a need to eat, they can begin to establish healthier eating patterns.

HABITS AND EMOTIONAL NEEDS

Regardless of how medically sound a weight control program is, new behaviors will not become habits until they are well established patterns of repetitive behavior. Conversely, one's old unhealthy habits will not disappear until they are removed from the person's established behavior patterns. The best place to begin learning about habit change is by describing habits in general and then examining what it takes to change a habit. After these concepts are understood, one can learn how to help individuals change a personal habit permanently.

A research questionnaire administered to obese men and women revealed that more than 80% of them reported that their failures at weight control were attributed to the fact that they reverted back to old eating patterns and stopped exercising (Miller & Eggert, 1992). In other words, these people were unsuccessful in weight control because they were not able to sustain their newly learned eating and exercise habits. More recent research supports the same notion – people who are successful at weight loss maintenance permanently change their eating and exercise habits (Befort et al., 2008; Jakicic,

Wing, & Winters-Hart, 2002; Wing & Hill, 2001). This suggests that habits play a crucial role in behavior management. However, many people do not understand how their habits are established or what controls their habits. They usually can identify the habits that contribute to their unhealthy state of being when they critically evaluate the consequences of specific behaviors, but have a difficult time discerning how to break old habits and establish new ones.

If one were to ask the question, "what is a habit?," one's response might be that a habit is an enduring pattern of behavior that is fixed, automatic, repeated, unconscious, involuntary, and resistant to change. If our definition of a habit is correct, then one can easily see that the longer we engage in a habit, the stronger it becomes, and the stronger a habit becomes, the more difficult it is to change.

So, what does a person have to do to change a habit? Well, if a habit is a fixed, automatic, repeated, unconscious, involuntary behavior that is resistant to change, then to change a habit one must focus his or her attention on the habit so that he or she can make a conscious and deliberate behavior change. In other words, habits don't just change themselves. Many people with weight control issues have not been able to change their habits because this most important ingredient of the whole behavior change process was missing every time they tried to change. A person's undesired habits are destined to return unless replaced with other newly created habits that meet the previous needs served by the habits removed! (Miller, 1998)

Attempts at habit change fall short because people do not meet their needs that were served by the habits they were trying to change. The individual can refocus efforts, work diligently, and strive tenaciously to change habits; but if needs are not met in another acceptable way, ultimately the old habit will return. Why? The answer is because the drive to meet one's needs is stronger than the drive to change one's behaviors. This imbalance results in an internal struggle over healthier habits that do not seem to meet the individual's needs versus unhealthy habits that feel like they do meet the person's needs. One way to describe it is that during every unsuccessful attempt to change a habit, the intellectual being is fighting the emotional being. Intellectually, the person is convinced that the unhealthy habit should be changed, and that if he or she were determined enough and worked hard at it, he or she could change the old habit behavior. However, during the behavior change attempt, the emotional being wages a war to meet some type of emotional need, and because the emotional being only knows one way to meet this need (through the already established unhealthy habit) the person easily returns to the unhealthy habit. In order to change a habit permanently, the person needs to learn how to meet his or her needs in healthy ways so that newly developed behavior patterns can become habits.

It is part of the health professional's job to help the patient identify unhealthy habits, ascertain what needs are being met by the habits, and then design new healthier ways to meet the needs previously served by the habits (Adami, Campostano, Ravera, Leggieri, & Scopinaro, 2001; Larsen, van Strien, Esinga, & Engles, 2006; Miller, 1998). There are different approaches the health professional can use to help a patient through the habit change process. Regardless of approach, the health professional will be more effective if at the forefront of his or her mind is the fact that all habits meet needs. Case Studies 6-1 and 6-2 give two different approaches to helping the patient begin the process of habit change.

COMPULSIVE BEHAVIORS

Habits can also be compulsive behaviors. The thought of habits being compulsive behaviors does not dissociate habits from being need-fulfilling behaviors. Compulsive behaviors must also fulfill needs. However, we look at compulsive behaviors a little differently than habits. Most people generally

text continues on page 74

Case Study 6-1: Identifying Emotional Links To Behavior

You are a nurse who works at a cardiac rehabilitation clinic. Ed is a patient who has been in the program for 6 months and has problems maintaining a healthy diet. Ed is overweight, with a body mass index of 34.8. He would like to lose weight, but more importantly, he would like to establish healthier behaviors so he can reduce his cardiovascular risk. How can you help him identify some of his emotional links to unhealthy eating behaviors?

Intervention/Solution

Nurse: Hi Ed. How are you doing today?

Ed: Well, not too bad, but I still am struggling with my eating.

Nurse: Can you explain?

Ed: You know I missed the last two sessions, so I really haven't seen you in over a week.

Nurse: Yes, I know, but tell me about your eating.

Ed: I just cannot seem to give up the ice cream. In the last week, I must have eaten ice cream every day except once.

Nurse: Sounds like you are a little discouraged. Tell me about your week and your ice cream eating.

Ed: Last Monday I had a good session here at the clinic. So, I thought I was off to a good week. However, after I left the clinic, the day went sour. I got to work later than expected and worked like a dog on this project that was due at the end of the week. I was all stressed out when I got home, so I made a frozen dinner. Then afterward, I ate a huge bowl of ice cream before going to bed. Tuesday was not much better, and I found myself working late and eating ice cream again before bed. I vowed that I would not have ice cream again on Wednesday because I know it is not healthy, but after being chewed out by my boss for getting behind schedule on this project, I just gave in to the ice cream. Thursday, my work partner was sick so I had to handle many of her assignments to keep the project moving. I think I ate ice cream Thursday night as a reward for working so hard. I finished the project on Friday and turned it in. Then Friday night I tried to relax and watch some TV, but I couldn't sit in front of the TV without ice cream. Saturday I was out with my girlfriend, and was able to tell her about my horrible work week, but guess where we talked? We were at the ice cream parlor. This trying to eat healthy is wearing me out.

Nurse: Can you see any patterns in your ice cream eating?

Ed: Not that I can see. Maybe I am just weak.

Nurse: I don't think you are weak, Ed. I think you were just trying to take care of yourself.

Ed: How can you say I am taking care of myself when I am eating ice cream every night?

Nurse: Let me explain by asking you a few questions. How did you feel Monday night?

Ed: Stressed out.

Nurse: How did you feel Tuesday night?

Ed: More stressed and tired.

Nurse: And how about the rest of the week?

Ed: Wednesday, angry at my boss and more stressed, because I knew I had to make good on this deadline. Thursday, mad and stressed, because my partner was sick. Friday, stressed in the morning, but then relieved that I finished the project that afternoon. Saturday, relieved, but my girlfriend told me to calm down as I explained everything to her.

Nurse: Can you identify any strong emotions that surfaced daily last week?

Ed: I guess stress and anger, but how does that explain my eating ice cream on Friday and Saturday. I finished the project on Friday, and Saturday I was out with my girlfriend.

Nurse: One thing at a time. Let's first recognize that you were probably eating ice cream in an attempt to reduce stress and deal with your anger. You were using ice cream as a comfort food, to make yourself feel better.

continued on next page

Ed: So why Friday and Saturday? The stress was gone Friday after I finished the assignment.

Nurse: The deadline was gone Friday, but the stress lingered. More importantly, the need to deal with the stress and anger of the whole week had not yet been met. So, you ate ice cream on Friday in a further attempt to deal with these emotions. Furthermore, as you related your work week to your girlfriend on Saturday, the same emotions resurfaced. Why didn't you eat ice cream on Sunday?

Ed: I don't know.

Nurse: I am guessing that your need to relieve stress and anger was finally met on Saturday, when you related your work week to your girlfriend. Is she a good listener?

Ed: Yes.

Nurse: I bet she is, and that the ice cream all week long did not meet your emotional needs, but talking with her, and being with her did. We now need to figure out healthy ways you can deal with the emotions of stress and anger.

Resolution

Ed is like many other people who eat in response to their emotions. However, he could not put two and two together. Your keen ear and knowledge of the habits-meet-needs relationship allowed you to analyze Ed's behavior. An excerpt from your discussion with Ed is shown below, with key hints highlighted.

Resolution Process

Ed: Last Monday I had a good session here at the clinic. So, I thought I was off to a good week. However, after I left the clinic, the **day went sour.** I got to work later than expected and **worked like a dog** on this project that was due at the end of the week. I was all **stressed out** when I got home, so I made a frozen dinner. Then afterward, I ate a huge bowl of **ice cream before going to bed.** Tuesday was not much better, and I found myself **working late** and eating ice cream again before bed. **I vowed that I would not have ice cream again on Wednesday** because I know it is not healthy, but after being **chewed out by my boss** for getting behind schedule on this project, I just **gave in to the ice cream.** Thursday, my work partner was sick so I had to **handle many of her assignments** to keep the project moving. I think I ate ice cream Thursday night as **a reward** for working so hard. I finished the project on Friday and turned it in. Then Friday night I **tried to relax** and watch some TV, but I **couldn't sit in front of the TV without ice cream.** Saturday I was out with my girlfriend, and **was able to tell her about my horrible work week,** but guess where we talked? We were at the ice cream parlor. This **trying to eat healthy is wearing me out.**

Your first clue that Ed needed to deal with negative emotions came when Ed said that the day went sour. The first clue that the emotion was stress appeared when Ed said that he worked like a dog. This clue was confirmed with his statement, "I was all stressed out when I got home." Working late the next day only compounded the problem. The intellectual being tried to take control of Ed's behaviors when Ed vowed that he would not have ice cream again on Wednesday because he knew it is not healthy. He thought he gave in to ice cream because he got chewed out by his boss for getting behind schedule on the project. However, he really gave in to ice cream because he still hadn't met his need to deal with the stress. He ate ice cream on Thursday because he was further stressed that his partner was sick, not as a reward. The reward ploy was an attempt of the intellectual being to rationalize his behavior when, in fact, his behavior was totally rational – he was using ice cream to meet his emotional needs. Friday night he tried to relax, but could only relax when he had ice cream, because that is his learned method of dealing with stress. Then on Saturday his emotions were riled up again as he explained his work week to his girlfriend. However, talking with her was the only good emotional expression he had all week, and hence his needs were met. Trying to eat healthy is not wearing him out. Nor is stress wearing him out. What is wearing him out is trying to meet the need to deal with stress and not doing it in a satisfactory way or in a way that agreed with his intellect.

Case Study 6-2: Behavioral Assignment To Meet Needs

You are a nurse practitioner who works at a bariatric center. Christy is an obese patient who has been in the program for 3 months and has problems maintaining her eating and exercise behaviors. Christy may be eating in response to her emotions or in an effort to meet emotional needs. The assignment given below is one way in which patients can identify their emotional needs and determine whether these needs are being met in a healthy manner. They can then begin to meet their needs in a healthier way.

Patient Assignment:

In the appropriate column of the chart that follows, make a list of all your emotional needs. Write down anything that comes to mind. Remember that the list should contain emotional needs, not physical needs. Also remember that it is "OK" to have needs. Everyone has many needs, but a person becomes needy, so to speak, when he or she overwhelms others with inappropriate attempts to fulfill their needs.

After your emotional needs list is complete, write a description of how you currently meet each need in the corresponding box next to the need listed in the chart. Do not get discouraged if you realize that you have many unhealthy behaviors that you use to meet your needs. The important thing is that you recognize your needs and identify better ways to meet those needs.

Finally, review all of your need-fulfilling behaviors. For those behaviors that are unhealthy, list at least one healthier way that you can meet that need. There are no right or wrong answers. You select a healthier behavior that will work for you. Do not let the intellect control your decision-making process. Make sure the emotional needs are being met with each new behavior you propose.

During this upcoming week, consciously select two or three needs each day and deliberately participate in a healthier behavior to meet the need. Even if you don't think that a need is eminent, practice the behavior anyway. If you find that a certain need becomes paramount during the day, obviously select that need and corresponding healthier behavior to focus upon.

An example of how to perform this assignment is shown below. Christy has filled in her assignment sheet for you to review.

Resolution

Emotional Need	Current Behavior	New Healthier Behavior
to feel loved	Bake treats (cookies, pies, cakes, etc.) for family members and friends	Express my feelings to my spouse, do something special for my business partner
to feel secure	Eat foods I enjoy (usually snack foods that are high in fat and sugar)	Snuggle with my spouse, go visit a friend, go out with a group of friends
to feel important or needed	Work hard at my career or at volunteer service in community organizations	No change needed
to feel in control	Make demands, dominate conversations, dominate relationships, eat whatever I want	Prioritize my daily activities, schedule activities and events, exercise
to feel happy and fulfilled	Entertain friends, socialize, set and achieve goals, give to others	No change needed
to reduce stress or feel relaxed	Eat junk food when I am stressed out	Practice stress-relief techniques, exercise, express my feelings, have a massage
to feel physical pleasure	Eat foods that taste good (regardless of nutritional value)	Be sexual with my spouse, take a bath, take a walk on the beach

continued on next page

Resolution Process

Christy did a good job at identifying her emotional links to food. It is important for you, as the health professional, to make sure that the new healthier behaviors really meet Christy's needs. For example, Christy listed "exercise" as a stress relief. Exercise is a stress-relief technique but not for all people. In fact, the contrary may be true. Exercise may be a stress inducer for some people, particularly obese people. The thought of going to the gym, working with awkward equipment, wearing workout clothes that reveal the body, getting sweaty, and exercising with people who are physically fit can easily stress a person who is unfamiliar and unaccustomed to exercise. Exploring responses given in discussion will help Christy to form realistic goals and expectations of the results of her healthy behaviors.

turn back to page 70

---

view a compulsive behavior as something negative, whereas habits can be viewed as being either positive or negative. Compulsive behaviors, however, can also be positive actions. Let's say that you and a friend cross paths in the grocery store. Your friend smiles and says "Good morning, how are you today?" You automatically return the smile and respond "I am doing very well, thank you." Your smile and polite response came automatically, without thought – compulsively. In this case, the compulsive positive behavior did fulfill a need – the need to reciprocate in an encounter or the need to avoid discomfort that would arise if you said nothing. Fulfilling the need in this manner was totally appropriate and healthy.

We generally define unhealthy or negative compulsive behaviors in three ways (American Psychiatric Association, 2005; Miller, 1998). First...

A compulsive behavior is an overt act performed against one's better judgment.

Our next definition of compulsive behavior takes on a little stronger connotation.

A compulsive behavior is an irresistible, repeated, irrational behavior.

In this context, it seems like the person has lost control. The behavior (or some need) is controlling the person, not the person controlling the behavior. It is at this time in behavior that a person usually recognizes that he or she is compulsive because they feel out of control. The last definition of a compulsive behavior is the most intriguing. This

definition encompasses the other two definitions we have examined and applies to positive as well as negative compulsive behaviors.

A compulsive behavior is a repetitive act performed to relieve fear.

This third definition of compulsive behavior easily fits all compulsive acts. Take our previous example at the grocery store. We said that your automatic smile and polite response to your friend's greeting fulfilled a need; the need to reciprocate in the encounter and/or the need to avoid discomfort. In either case, fear was involved. Your automatic response (compulsive behavior) relieved you from any number of fears – the fear of not knowing what to say, the fear of an awkward conversation, the fear of having to communicate in depth, the fear of silence, the fear of embarrassment, etc. You see, the last definition of a compulsive behavior does fit. We participate in compulsive behaviors in order to relieve fear. Similar to habits, we can make valiant attempts to change our compulsive behaviors, but if these attempts do not deal with the underlying fear, we will ultimately return to our undesired behaviors. Why? It is because the emotional person does not like being afraid. So, the way to permanently change our unhealthy habits or compulsive behaviors is to identify the needs and fears associated with the undesired behaviors and learn how to fulfill these needs and relieve the fear in a healthier way.

There are various ways the health professional can help a patient identify and overcome fears related to eating and exercise behaviors. The easiest way is to just ask. For example, if a patient is consuming too much chocolate, a simple question may reveal some fears and emotional needs linked to chocolate. The health professional might ask, "Brittney, what would happen if you were not allowed to have chocolate anymore? Describe the worst case scenario." Brittney may respond, "Oh, I would probably get depressed. I would probably feel alone."

The words depressed and alone, suggest that Brittney is using chocolate to meet her need to deal with depression or discouragement. She may also be using chocolate to deal with fears of abandonment. The health professional can easily pick up on emotional links to eating behaviors such as these without being a psychologist. Another way to uncover fears related to eating and exercise behaviors is to have the patient perform an assignment to help gain insight into his or her emotions. An example of such an assignment is presented in Case Study 6-3.

Case Study 6-3: Compulsive Behaviors Used To Relieve Fear

You are a nurse practitioner who works at a women's health clinic. Sharon is an obese patient who has been in the program for 2 months and has problems maintaining her eating and exercise behaviors. Sharon may be eating in response to her emotions or in an effort to meet emotional needs. Have her perform the following assignment to identify and overcome her emotional fears related to eating and exercise.

Patient Assignment

In the left-hand column of the table below list your fears. These fears should be emotional or psychological, not physical. After you have listed your fears in the left column, identify some healthy ways that you can deal with or overcome your fears. Write these in the right-hand column under the heading "Overcoming My Fear."

During the coming week, select one fear that you want to focus upon each day. Practice the healthy behavior associated with the respective fear you have selected for the day. Some of your fears may seem irrational or not make sense to the intellectual mind, but to the emotional being they are real, nonetheless.

My fear	Overcoming my fear
Being thin	Talk to (by phone or in person) someone close (friend, relative, sibling, parent) who accepts me the way that I am; talk to the intellectual me about how society's image of body size is distorted; visualize being thin, what would really happen?
Being abandoned	Spend some time with a friend; write or call a loved one; extend a helping hand to someone in need; volunteer to take part in something at work or in the neighborhood that includes getting involved with people
Being a failure	Tell myself that success is not measured only in pounds lost, nor is success an all-or-nothing phenomena; assess other aspects of my life where I have achieved success; prioritize my immediate responsibilities into "must do," "should do," and "would like to do" categories and act accordingly; talk to myself about how success is not always determined by tangible accomplishments

Resolution

Sharon has a fear of becoming thin. This may seem silly, especially coming from someone who has been overweight for her whole life and has tried every diet and weight loss program you can think of in attempting to become thin. However, as Sharon examines her fear more closely, she realizes that her fear of becoming thin is really based in some of the cultural myths perpetuated by society with regard to performance expectations of thin people. As Sharon grew up, she learned from our ailing society that *thin people*

continued on next page

are happy, thin people are sexy, thin people are smart, thin people are high achievers, thin people get pro-motions, thin people have many friends, etc. So, in Sharon's emotional being, if she were to become thin, then she would have to be happy, have to perform better sexually, to demonstrate intelligence, achieve more, perform better on the job, and have many wonderful relationships. No wonder Sharon is scared to death of becoming thin even though she has wanted that more than anything her whole life. Anyone would rather cling onto unhealthy compulsive behaviors than have to live up to Sharon's perception of society's expectations for a *thin* person.

Sharon has identified some fears that affect her self-efficacy about being successful at controlling her weight. If she can practice steps to remove these fears, she will more likely be successful in her weight loss program. It took great insight for Sharon to discover what fears were affecting her weight control behaviors. The health professional may need to assist patients in identifying fears if fears are not immediately forthcoming. Some possible probing questions are: "What would it be like to reach the weight you think is ideal for you?" "What is the scariest thing about being thin?" "Can you describe a living environment that scares you the most?" "How would you never want anybody to describe you?"

EATING DISORDERS ASSOCIATED WITH OBESITY

Binge eating disorder and night eating syndrome are two emotional disorders that are associated with obesity. They warrant discussion related to emotional links to obesity because evidence of these types of behaviors may emerge during any stage of treatment. Failure to recognize their existence can set the patient up for failure related to behavioral change.

Binge eating is characterized by consuming large amounts of food in a short period of time, accompanied by a perceived loss of control during the episode. The overeating is not followed by behaviors such as vomiting or laxative abuse, but it is often accompanied by feelings of guilt. Approximately 20% to 30% of individuals seeking weight loss report binge eating behavior (Phelan & Wadden, 2004). Three treatment methods have been found to be effective: psychotherapy, pharmacotherapy, and behavioral weight loss programs (Allison & Lundgren, 2006).

Psychotherapy using cognitive behavioral therapy or interpersonal psychotherapy reduced the number of binge episodes, with reductions from 48% to 96%. This result was not accompanied by weight loss. Selective serotonin reuptake inhibitors were found to also be effective and produced decreases in weight. Other drugs have also been found to reduce binge episodes, notably the appetite suppressant sibutramine (Meridia) and the anticonvulsant topiramate (Topamax) (Allison & Lundgren, 2006).

Traditional behavioral weight loss programs have also proven beneficial in reducing binge episodes and in weight reduction. It is important to monitor eating behavior during weight loss efforts because persistent binge eating behavior may need additional methods of treatment such as those noted above.

Night eating syndrome is manifested by evening hyperphagia – consuming 25% or more of total daily calories after the evening meal and/or frequent nocturnal awakenings with ingestion of food. Nocturnal eating may serve to reduce anxiety, act as a sleep aid, placate cravings, or battle fears related to insomnia. Night eating syndrome occurs more frequently with obesity and psychiatric comorbidity, with rates of 9% to 14% found in patients studied at obesity treatment clinics (Allison & Lundgren, 2006). Treatment with selective serotonin reuptake inhibitors has reduced the occurrence of night eating syndrome and weight. Psychotherapy has also been used. Attention to sleep hygiene is also important, as well as a structured diet to consume the daily calorie load several hours prior to the designated hour of sleep.

COPING MECHANISMS

Patterns of behavior often relate to coping with various issues in the individual's lifestyle. How individuals think about themselves, relate to others, and cope with life's stress is important to understand. Kushner (2007) developed a tool that analyzes lifestyle patterns of eating, exercise, and coping. He identified seven patterns in each domain, and found that obese patients typically utilized all seven coping patterns. Patterns identified were emotional eating, self scrutinizing behavior, persistent procrastination, people-pleasing behavior, fast-paced lifestyle behaviors, self-doubt behavior, and overreaching achievement behavior. He then identified strategies to address each of these categories in order to help the individual achieve weight loss goals and, more importantly, lifestyle change. Much of this work relies on the individual's ability to recognize and understand their own emotional needs. The following section describes this process.

EMOTIONAL EXPRESSION

Many obese people have difficulty distinguishing between emotional needs, physical needs, hunger, and appetite. When people learn how to separate their emotions from what they think is a need to eat, they can begin to establish healthier eating patterns. The first step in this separation process is to be able to identify and feel emotions. Although this step may seem easy, it is one of the biggest and most difficult steps on the pathway to healthy weight management. The reason this step is so difficult is because we are taught from childhood just the opposite – not to feel our emotions. We are taught by our families, friends, and society that our emotions are not important and that we should not be feeling (Miller, 1998). Case Study 6-4 illustrates this point.

What is the natural reaction for someone if every time they tried to express themselves they were ignored, told to shut up, sent away, or hidden in a closet? They would try to find some way to strike back; or, if an outright attack seemed hopeless, they would find some way to pacify themselves until they were in a better position to strike back. Food is a primary emotional pacifier in

---

Case Study 6-4: Examples Of Repressing Feelings

The following vignettes illustrate how we are taught to ignore our feelings.

Example #1:

It is late at night on a warm summer evening. Clouds have rolled in, and a thunderstorm develops. A few minutes later there is a knock on the bedroom door. A 4-year-old girl, Jackie, pops her head through the doorway.

"Mommy, can I come sleep with you? I'm scared."

"No! Go back to bed."

"But it's thundering and lightening, and I'm scared."

"No you're not. You are a big girl now and you don't need to be afraid every time it starts raining. We have talked about this before, and decided that there is nothing to be afraid of; so go back to bed."

Jackie closes the door and returns to her room.

The parents think that they have successfully taught their daughter how to handle her fear of thunderstorms, but they have actually taught her that her emotions are unimportant or not valid, and that the way to deal with unpleasant feelings is to ignore them or suppress them.

continued on next page

Example #2:

Here's another example of how we are taught not to feel.

Six-year-old Tommy comes in the house crying because his older siblings will not let him join them in a game they are playing.

"Daddy, they won't let me play with them."

Father opens the kitchen window and yells at the other kids, "You let your brother play with you. If you can't learn to play together, you will all have to come in the house."

He turns to his son and says, "Now stop crying Tommy. Big boys don't cry."

So, Tommy goes outside to play. He is feeling better now because he gets to play with his siblings.

Dad thinks he has dealt with the problem. However, Tommy was also taught to ignore his feelings; and moreover, he may not even know what he was feeling at the time he came in the house because no emotion was recognized or mentioned in the discussion with his father.

Example #3:

A third example can be used to illustrate how ignoring or repressing our feelings is perpetuated into adulthood.

You get into an argument with your boss at work, with a spouse, friend, partner, or whomever. You leave the encounter upset and unsettled. As you begin to relate the incident to a friend, your friend says, "Oh, just forget about it. You are making a big deal about this. Let it go, and in a few days it will be as if nothing happened."

So, what transpired? Your feelings once again have gone unrecognized and been invalidated. You repress your feelings or ignore them, thinking that if you do not acknowledge them, they do not exist. Nonetheless, they do exist; and you have a need to recognize them for what they are and to deal with them.

today's society. That is exactly what happens when the feelings from the emotional being are suppressed. So, in order for people to stop using unhealthy eating behaviors as a counterattack or a pacifier for unexpressed emotions, people need to allow themselves to feel their emotions. Thus, the first rule for resolving emotional eating issues is to validate all emotions. To do this, one must recognize and acknowledge that…

All emotions are real.

By recognizing a feeling for what it is or validating the emotion, one acknowledges the emotional being inside. The next step is to allow that emotional being the opportunity to be expressed. This step is critical, because regardless of whether one acknowledges his or her emotions or not, emotions will be expressed in one way or another. In other words...

All emotions will emerge.

This fact can be illustrated through a couple of glaring examples. You may see on the news or read in the paper a story of a U.S. postal worker who shoots and kills some of his coworkers, or a story about a man who enters a fast-food restaurant and starts shooting at people with a semi-automatic rifle. When neighbors and relatives are interviewed, they describe the offender as being quiet, well-mannered, and introverted. These descriptions seem inconsistent with the violent behavior pattern exemplified by the offender. Obviously, the paradox is solved by understanding that the quiet, well-mannered, introverted behaviors were surface behaviors controlled by the intellectual being for the purpose of covering up some sort of rage, anger, or frustration residing inside the emotional being. Then in one uncontrollable surge all the pent up emotions emerged into a destructive behavior.

Take as another example an argument that occurs between you and your boss. You leave work with an unresolved conflict, and you go home with much repressed anger. When you arrive home, dinner is not on the table waiting, so you belittle your spouse. There is no conversation at dinner, but after dinner the kids are playing excitedly and your spouse yells at them to quiet down. The kids do not feel they can argue with their parent, so they kick the dog that is lying there doing nothing. The dog wakes up and chases the cat. You can see from this example that there is a lot of emotional release in this family, but that it is all emerging in unhealthy, inappropriate ways.

Many times we hang on to our inappropriate or unhealthy eating behaviors because they fulfill the need we have to soothe or disperse our emotions. Food tastes good. Food makes us feel good. Food gives us pleasure. Food is a comfort. As one former patient stated, "food is my friend."

It is not inappropriate to use food to manage our emotions once in a while, but to use food consistently for emotional release or to have eating be our only emotional expression is physically and emotionally unhealthy (Adami et al., 2001; Larsen et al., 2006; Miller, 1998). So, each obese patient needs to examine his or her own relationship with food. Have them seriously consider…

What is my emotional relationship with food?

This question is more thought provoking than it may seem. Many patients have buried their emotions so deep, that the only emotional expression they have is food. Many of them feel that if food were taken away from them, they would have nothing left. How does a person get to this state of being, to where they can no longer recognize their feelings? There are a multitude of reasons for each individual that are not easy to delineate, but the cumulative effect is the same. As a result of personal, family, social, and environmental experiences, the person commonly learns that emotional expression is painful and something that should be avoided. Emotions are continually repressed until the emotional being is imprisoned. Once impris-

oned, there is no risk, so to speak, of that emotional person communicating with someone on the outside. Hence, the possibility of experiencing emotional pain is eliminated (at least the individual thinks it was eliminated).

However, as discussed already, all emotions will emerge. So what happens? The emotions start to emerge in unhealthy or inappropriate ways. If the person has a strong moral character, the intellectual being will not allow the emotions to emerge in destructive behavior toward someone else (e.g., murder, rape, physical abuse). Oftentimes the intellectual being will not allow the emotions to emerge in outright self-destructive behaviors; such as alcoholism, drug abuse, or sexual promiscuity, either. Eliminating these behaviors that are morally taboo limits the possibilities for emotional release to just a few, and frequently eating becomes the choice.

Hopefully, the health professional, can see how ignoring the emotional person inside can get people into trouble. The professional should also be aware that achieving healthy weight management requires the integration of multiple facets of behavior that are not as simple as just cutting back on food intake or getting on an exercise program. The fear of becoming emotional or expressing emotions appropriately is a big issue for many people. However, the health professional can help patients overcome emotional eating issues by facilitating expression of the patient's emotions.

FACILITATING EMOTIONAL EXPRESSION IN THE OBESE PATIENT

All health care professionals who deal with obese patients on a regular basis and who provide weight control intervention for patients must be attuned to how to help the patient deal with emotional issues. How much intervention is provided may depend on the knowledge and skill of the provider and the needs of the situation; but even if the patient is working with a clinical therapist, psychologist, or psychiatrist, a basic understanding of the impact of emotional issues is necessary for all health care providers involved.

Helping the obese patient identify and express emotional links related to eating and exercise behaviors is not as difficult as it may appear. It is generally a matter of asking the appropriate question or probing one step further in the interview. Case studies 6-5 and 6-6 illustrate how these approaches can be used by any level of health care provider.

EMOTIONAL EXPRESSION AND EATING

One of the best ways to help people discover how they use food to meet their emotional needs is to have them record their feelings and eating behaviors simultaneously. That way they can begin to see how certain feelings are linked to specific eating behaviors. The technique is to have the patient record their feelings several times during the day. At the same time they note their feelings, have them record if they have any strong desire to eat or

Case Study 6-5: Emotional Listening

It is common for a health professional to overlook emotional links to eating and exercise behaviors, especially when things seem to be going well. When the patient is compliant with his or her program, the health professional tends to overlook the possibility of underlying emotional links that may later sabotage the behavior. This case illustrates how a professional can uncover emotional links to eating behavior that otherwise would have gone unrecognized.

You work as a nurse at a weight loss clinic. Jack is a patient who has been with the clinic for a few weeks. He is struggling with healthy eating. He has successfully completed 2 weeks on his new diet. His goal was to cut out all "junk" food. He has come to you for a follow-up visit. Compare the following two versions of the same situation:

Scenario #1

Nurse: Good to see you again, Jack. Last time we met, you planned to remove the junk food from your kitchen in an attempt to reduce the amount of junk food you consumed. Were you able to do it?

Jack: Yes, all the junk food is gone, and I have not had any chips in 2 weeks.

Nurse: Great, so will you be able to do the same thing until we meet again in 2 weeks?

Jack: Yes, probably.

Nurse: I am sure you can do it. You were successful this week.

Scenario #2

Nurse: Good to see you again, Jack. Last time we met, you planned to remove the junk food from your kitchen in an attempt to reduce the amount of junk food you consumed. Were you able to do it?

Jack: Yes, all the junk food is gone, and I have not had any chips in 2 weeks.

Nurse: Wow! Removing all junk food from the kitchen and going without chips must have been difficult. How do you feel about it?

Jack: I miss the chips. I almost went out and bought some a couple of times.

Nurse: So, how did you resist?

Jack: Willpower.

Nurse: That's commendable, but how does not having junk food make you feel?

Jack: Well, to be honest, I feel deprived. I also feel guilty sometimes for still craving chips.

Nurse: Those feelings are natural. Maybe we should think of a strategy that will help you deal with these feelings. How does that sound?

Jack: What do you mean?

continued on next page

Nurse: Well, we could negotiate for you to have a small amount of junk food, but still keep to your diet. That might help you from feeling deprived, and then when you have the chips you might not feel guilty because it is a part of your contract. On the other hand, you may decide to give up chips all together. If this is the case, then we need to find a way for you to indulge yourself in something else, not necessarily food, so you don't feel deprived and guilty for wanting to indulge. I am sure there are other possibilities we can come up with if we put our heads together.

Resolution/Discussion Process

The nurse in scenario #1 complimented Jack on the achievement of his goal, and because there did not appear to be any behavioral issues the nurse had Jack commit to the same goal for the next 2 weeks. All seemed fine when Jack agreed, so the nurse ended what she thought was a successful discussion with a behavioral commitment from Jack. The nurse missed an opportunity to pick up on a clue that Jack was having an internal struggle when Jack's commitment response was, "Yes, probably."

The nurse in Scenario #2 took the opportunity to explore Jack's feelings by simply asking how Jack felt about giving up junk food. Jack expressed that he was feeling deprived and guilty. These emotions may have been present in Scenario #1, but were never expressed, validated, or dealt with. In Scenario #2, the nurse validated Jack's feelings – *"Those feelings are natural."* The nurse then began a dialogue as to how Jack might be able to deal with these feelings. Jack and the nurse can now work together to design a strategy to help with the feelings of deprivation and guilt. Jack's total abstention from junk food may be too restrictive at this time. He may want to reconsider his commitment to the behavior change step, or he may need to have junk food totally out of his environment. In this case, the strategy would have to find a way to meet the emotional needs of deprivation and guilt.

The key to the success with this patient is that Jack was able to express his feelings. If these feelings were not explored (Scenario #1), Jack may have kept the goal to refrain from junk food for the time being, but ultimately his emotional being would have forged a counterattack and Jack most likely would have binged on chips. The binge itself would have brought on more guilt. By discussing these feelings early, the chance for future relapse from the junk food restriction is greatly reduced and alternative options for emotional expression can be explored before Jack goes on a binge.

drink, and what they desire to eat or drink. Alternatively, each time the patient eats or drinks, have them record what they are feeling. Reviewing the diaries of patients' feelings and eating/drinking behaviors can help them unravel their emotional links to food.

Another way to help patients discover their emotional links to food is to have them use the feelings chart presented in Figure 6-1. The way this assignment works is to have patients record their feelings whenever they are inclined to participate in an eating behavior that is not part of the established eating plan. Have them record what they are experiencing emotionally in the appropriate box of the feelings chart when the temptation or inclination to eat inappropriately comes. Checkmarks can be

made alongside the S, M, T, W, Th, F, S letters, which represent the days of the week. If patients unconsciously succumb to the temptation to eat inappropriately, they can later record what they were feeling at the time. At the end of the week, patients can look to see if there were any feelings that were consistently associated with the desire to eat inappropriately. After this discovery is made, strategies to meet the emotional need more appropriately can be instituted, such as in Case Study 6-7.

Case Study 6-6: 1 To 10 Scaling Of Emotions

It is common for a health professional to overlook emotional links to eating and exercise behaviors. The most frequent situation in which these emotional links are overlooked occurs when things seem to be going well. In other words, when the patient is compliant with his or her program, the health professional tends to overlook the possibility of underlying emotional links that may later sabotage the behavior. This case illustrates how a 1-minute conversation can avoid a future behavior relapse.

You work as a nurse at a clinic that does not provide exercise on site. However, you do encourage exercise for all of your patients. Sue is a patient who just began an exercise program. This past week was her first week of exercise on her own. She has come to you for a follow-up visit. Compare the following two versions of the same scenario:

Scenario #1

Nurse: Glad to see you again, Sue. Last week we set a goal that you would exercise three times this week at the cardio conditioning class held in the basement of your apartment complex. Were you able to accomplish that?

Sue: Yes, I went to a session on Tuesday, Wednesday, and Saturday.

Nurse: That's great. Do you think you can do that again next week?

Sue: I guess so.

Scenario #2

Nurse: Glad to see you again, Sue. Last week we set a goal that you would exercise three times this week at the cardio conditioning class held in the basement of your apartment complex. Were you able to accomplish that?

Sue: Yes, I went to a session on Tuesday, Wednesday, and Saturday

Nurse: That's great. So, on a scale of 1 to 10, with 10 being "I am so excited about exercise I want to go out and run a marathon," and 1 being "I hate exercise so much, I never want to do it again," where did your exercise attempts fall this week?

Sue: Oh, I would say about a 2.

Nurse: Can you describe why a rating of 2?

Sue: I have never felt so intimidated and humiliated in my life! I was twice the size of everybody in the cardio class, and I felt so embarrassed in my exercise clothes.

Nurse: I am sorry to hear that you were so intimidated, humiliated, and embarrassed. What do you think we can do to help you become more comfortable with exercise

Resolution Process

The nurse in scenario #1 complimented Sue on the achievement of her goal, and because there did not appear to be any behavioral issues; the nurse had Sue commit to the same goal for next week. All seemed fine, so the nurse ended what she thought was a successful discussion that included a behavioral commitment from Sue.

The nurse in Scenario #2 was able to use a simple 1 to 10 scaling technique to get Sue to express her feelings about the exercise sessions. When Sue did this, negative emotions of intimidation, humiliation, and embarrassment were expressed. As in Case Study 6-5, these emotions may have been present in Scenario #1, but were never expressed, validated, or dealt with.

As in Case Study 6-5, expression of feelings enables the patient and nurse to discuss ways to achieve the goal successfully and/or modify the behavioral commitment. The scaling technique is a simple tool to help the patient safely identify discomfort and be able to express feelings. It may well allow the individual who is reluctant to acknowledge or voice feelings to more easily recognize them.

turn back to page 80

FIGURE 6-1: THE FEELINGS CHART

S M T W Th F S **ANGRY**	S M T W Th F S **ANXIOUS**	S M T W Th F S **ARROGANT**	S M T W Th F S **BASHFUL - SHY**
S M T W Th F S **BORED**	S M T W Th F S **DEPRESSED**	S M T W Th F S **DETERMINED**	S M T W Th F S **DISAPPOINTED**
S M T W Th F S **ENVIOUS**	S M T W Th F S **EXHAUSTED**	S M T W Th F S **FRIGHTENED**	S M T W Th F S **FRUSTRATED**
S M T W Th F S **GRIEF**	S M T W Th F S **GUILTY**	S M T W Th F S **HAPPY**	S M T W Th F S **HURT**
S M T W Th F S **LONELY**	S M T W Th F S **MEDITATIVE**	S M T W Th F S **MISCHIEVOUS**	S M T W Th F S **OPTIMISTIC**
S M T W Th F S **PLAYFUL**	S M T W Th F S **PUZZLED**	S M T W Th F S **REGRETFUL**	S M T W Th F S **RELIEVED**
S M T W Th F S **SAD**	S M T W Th F S **SEXY**	S M T W Th F S **SURPRISED**	S M T W Th F S **SUSPICIOUS**
S M T W Th F S **SYMPATHETIC**	S M T W Th F S **WITHDRAWN**	S M T W Th F S **OTHER**	S M T W Th F S **? I DON'T KNOW**

Case Study 6-7: Emotional Links To Food

You are a nurse practitioner at a large hospital. One of your responsibilities is patient education. You are currently running a small support group for weight control. One of the group members is having difficulty maintaining a healthy diet. Two weeks ago you asked him to begin keeping track of his feelings when he had impulses to eat inappropriately. He has returned to the group this week to receive guidance.

Scenario

Fred has struggled to lose 30 lb and continues to struggle with his eating behaviors. He insists that he is not an emotional eater. The past 2 weeks he has been recording his feelings when he has impulses to eat unhealthy. Can you discover any of Fred's emotional links to unhealthy eating by reviewing his recorded feelings?

Resolution

Fred placed several markings for the negative feelings of angry, anxious, depressed, disappointed, exhausted, frustrated, and puzzled. Fred also marked the feelings of determined and withdrawn several times, which may or may not be seen as negative emotions. Fred also indicated that he had impulses to eat unhealthy when he was feeling happy and optimistic. Your initial review of Fred's feelings chart suggests that he desires to eat unhealthy when he experiences mostly negative emotions. However, his frequent association of unhealthy eating with neutral emotions and positive emotions does not seem to fit the pattern you initially found. Only through further questioning about Fred's feelings and their causes can you accurately conclude that your first impression was correct.

As you talk with Fred about the root of his recorded feelings, you discover that Fred is a professor at a junior college in the city where you live. His department has undergone some attrition of faculty over the past 2 years. What was a faculty of 10 professors is now a faculty of 6. Consequently, Fred and his colleagues have needed to take on additional workloads to keep the department running effectively. This added workload, in addition to the realization that the situation would not be remedied for another couple of years, has placed an emotional burden upon Fred.

Initially, Fred was in denial about his emotional eating. However, as he reviews his feelings chart (shown right), he realizes that his unhealthy eating is linked to emotions. He can now admit that the negative emotions associated with work have driven him to eat inappropriately. However, he is puzzled with the idea that he has possible eating links to positive emotions. A more careful look at the feelings chart unveils the answer.

Fred marked optimistic several times on Sunday and Monday – the beginning of the week. It is at the beginning of the week when he feels optimistic about overcoming the struggles at work. So, his positive feeling of optimism is also associated with the emotional distress at work. Fred marked happy several times on the weekend. The weekend is when Fred catches up on his sleep and spends time with friends and family. Weekends are his rejuvenation time. He thinks that because he had a long hard work week he deserves relief. Subconsciously, however, Fred gets some of this relief by "relieving" himself from what his emotional being sees as a restrictive diet.

Fred's problem eating revolves around his inability to deal with the stressors of his job. Fred seems to be using food as a coping mechanism to deal with the emotional distress associated with work. His unhealthy eating is rooted in his attempts to deal with the emotional distress of his job. He is on a roller coaster of emotions – going from happiness and optimism at the beginning of the week through determination and several negative emotions during the week, to emotional release on the weekend. Your next step is to help Fred find healthier ways to meet his emotional needs.

continued on next page

Note the boxes that Fred checked off in his feelings chart.

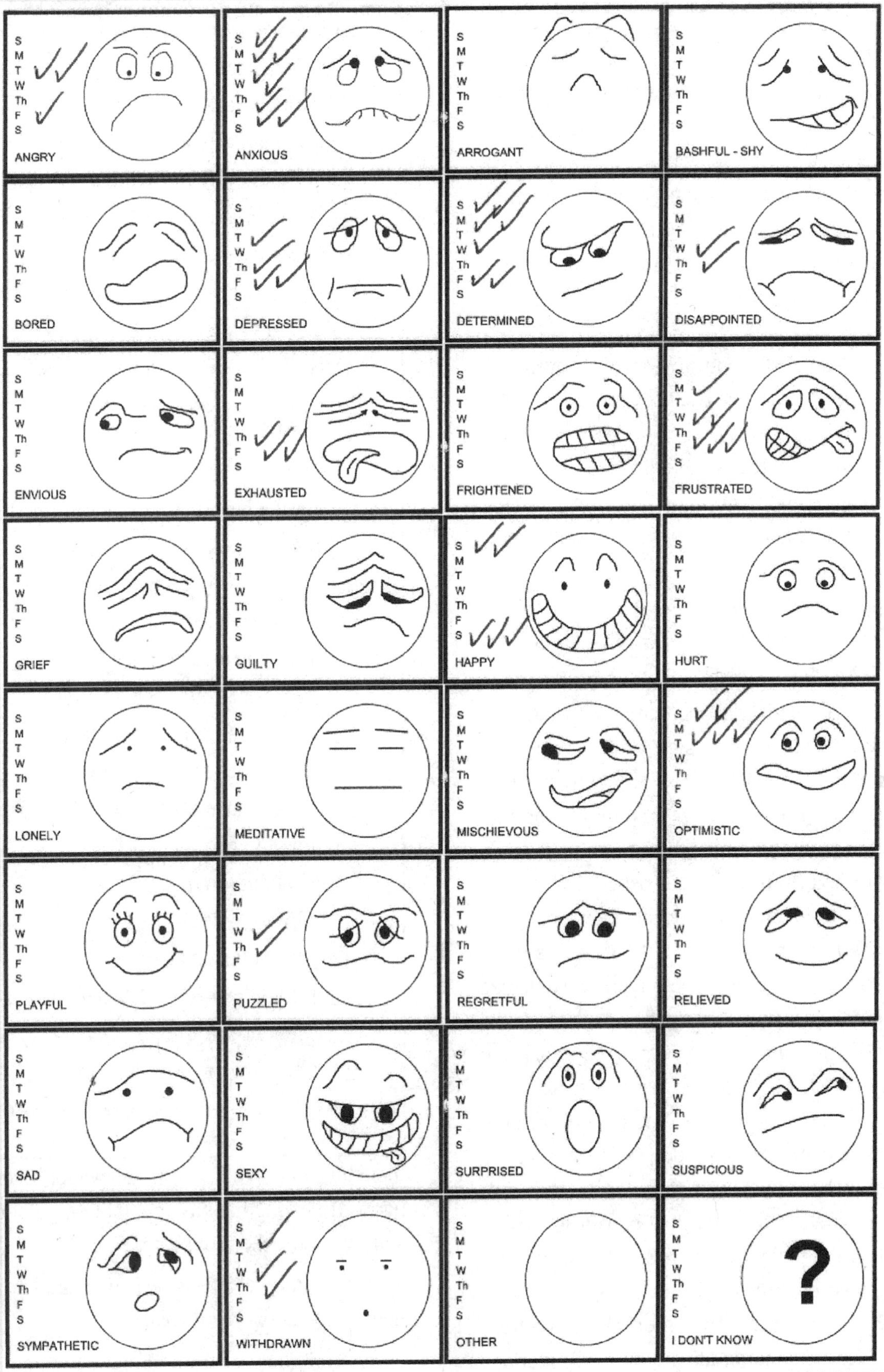

IDENTIFYING AND OVERCOMING BARRIERS TO HEALTHY EATING

The first step in removing individual barriers to healthy eating is to identify those barriers. Once a person's barriers to healthful eating are identified, a realistic strategy to remove or at least minimize those barriers can be designed. Most people can identify some of their barriers to eating healthy, but they often have trouble identifying all barriers. More importantly, people have a difficult time developing lasting strategies to help them overcome barriers to healthy eating. The checklist in Table 6-1 can be used as a starting point to help the obese patient identify barriers to healthy eating. This checklist can be used during the initial intake interview and periodically as the patient becomes more self-aware. It also can be used as a tool to measure progress as barriers are overcome one at a time. Notice how several of the barriers listed in the table have an emotional component.

Once barriers to eating healthy have been identified, the next step is to design strategies to overcome or minimize each one of the barriers. This step can be done in several ways. It may be helpful to have the patient identify things that worked in the past to help him or her eat better. The patient may be able to identify specific situations that minimize a barrier or maximize a barrier. A simple method that can be used to help patients strategize is for them to identify a barrier they want to tackle, and then decide on a strategic plan to attack the barrier head on. For example, a patient may state that he or she does not have time to cook healthy food. Possible strategies to address this barrier are to discover healthy meals that can be made in under 10 minutes, to use a slow cooker to cook a meal when the patient is at work all day, or learn how to make healthy food selections at a restaurant. The main thing to remember is to help patients find personal strategies that will work in

their lifestyle. What helps one person overcome a barrier to eating healthy may not help another person overcome the same barrier.

Case Study 6-8 provides an example of how to help a patient overcome barriers.

TABLE 6-1: IDENTIFYING INDIVIDUAL BARRIERS TO HEALTHY EATING

Please check all those that apply:

_____ I skip meals.

_____ I often binge.

_____ I often overeat or stuff myself.

_____ I eat too much fried food.

_____ I eat too much fast food.

_____ I eat too much refined sugar.

_____ I consume too much butter or oil.

_____ I don't eat enough fruit.

_____ I don't eat enough vegetables.

_____ I don't have any family support to eat healthy.

_____ I eat when anxious.*

_____ I eat when depressed.*

_____ I eat when lonely.*

_____ I eat to avoid relationships.*

_____ I eat when frustrated.*

_____ I eat when I am angry.*

_____ I eat because I am not assertive.*

_____ I eat because I am a perfectionist.*

_____ I don't have time to eat healthy.

_____ I don't have time to cook.

_____ I snack too much.

_____ I eat out too much.

_____ I love sweets.

_____ I love chocolate.

_____ I don't have any motivation to eat healthy.

_____ I don't drink enough water.

_____ Other reason not listed above.

*The patient may not be able to identify these emotional links to eating.

Case Study 6-8: Overcoming Barriers To Healthy Eating

You are a nurse who has a Master's degree in Exercise and Nutrition. You own your own business, where you do personal training, private consulting, and rehabilitation/health promotion. Your private client, Becky, has been working with you for 2 months. Becky is overweight, but not obese. She would like to lose a little weight, but more importantly she wants to prevent future weight gain. Today you go to her home for a personal consultation session. She reports that she is having difficulty maintaining her healthy eating patterns.

Scenario

Your session today with Becky includes personal training. You have the option of talking about Becky's eating during the personal training session, afterwards, or both. How will you approach the discussion about her eating behaviors? In other words, what type of information will help you guide her to maintaining healthier eating patterns?

Resolution

The first objective is helping Becky to identify her personal barriers to healthy eating. In order to accomplish this objective, you need to discuss Becky's current eating behaviors and what she sees as the problem. Becky immediately tells you she overeats quite often, even to the point of stuffing herself. As you discuss her overeating episodes, you realize that Becky is not binging. Becky is truly hungry when she eats. So, binging is not a barrier. You gather some of this overeating information by having Becky describe her typical eating day. You contrast this typical eating day to what Becky describes as a great eating day, and then to what she describes as a terrible eating day.

A pattern of behaviors seems to emerge. It appears that Becky eats better on the weekends than weekdays. It also becomes evident that Becky eats too much fast food during the week. Becky did not originally identify this as a barrier to healthy eating, but when she described her terrible eating days, fast food is always consumed; sometimes twice in the same day. Her good eating days are predominantly on weekends, when she has a lot of free time. Her bad days are generally weekdays when she is pressured, rushed, and does not have time to plan meals or cook. Therefore, she often skips eating breakfast, sometimes skips lunch or has fast food for lunch, and then overeats at dinner. You also learn that her food choices for fast food are not healthy, and are void of fruits and vegetables.

Although Becky only identified one barrier to eating healthy (overeating), you help identify four barriers:

- overeating,
- skipping meals,
- eating too much fast food, and
- not eating enough fruits and vegetables.

All four of these barriers are interrelated. Becky skips meals because she is rushed. She grabs fast food because she is pressured for time. When she arrives home after work, she is so famished she overeats. On the weekends, Becky has more time to plan meals and cook. She also consumes more fruits and vegetables on weekends because she eats at home.

Now that you have identified Becky's barriers to eating healthy, you begin to strategize with her. Becky lives two blocks away from a farmer's market. So she decides to shop for fresh fruits and vegetables at the farmer's market on the weekend. On the weekdays, when Becky is stressed, she has decided to grab some fruit and vegetables to eat on the way to work. (Becky rides the city Metrorail to work). This strategy integrates more fruits and vegetables into her diet and stops her from skipping breakfast. Becky decides to prepare a lunch for work 3 days a week and allows herself to eat fast food twice a week. On Sunday, Becky will prepare a fresh lunch for Monday, and two other days during the week she will eat leftovers from dinner.

continued on next page

One of the fast food days, Becky will go to the store across the street from her work and buy something from the salad/food bar. The other fast food day is open for her choice.

You have thus far decreased Becky's tendency to skip meals, decreased her fast food intake, and increased her fruit and vegetable intake – all without a great time commitment. Next, you want to strategize around her dinner meals, so if she is hungry after work, she will have something healthy to eat. Becky has a slow cooker she got for Christmas years ago. She rarely uses it. Her strategy is to cook one slow cooker meal a week. Her preparation can be the night before, or in the morning. In either case, the food can cook all day and be there for her when she returns home from work. A second strategy is for Becky to prepare two dinner meals on the weekend and have them ready or frozen for later during the week. Her last strategy is to eat one commercially prepared meal for dinner during the week (e.g., Lean Cuisine, Weight Watchers).

All of these strategies are realistic to Becky and still allow her some flexibility without a lot of restraint. The last thing you two prepare is a monitoring tool. The tool you decide upon is a simple behavior record. Becky has made a chart where she counts how many times she overeats during the week, how many times she eats unhealthy fast food, and how many times she skips meals. You will assess her behaviors when you again meet with her in 2 weeks.

Your discussion with Becky focused on helping her discover her personal barriers to eating healthy. With your help, Becky identified her barriers as: skipping meals, eating too much fast food, not eating enough fruit and vegetables, and overeating. She was then able to design some strategies to overcome these barriers to healthy eating and to utilize a monitoring system.

SUMMARY

The key to successful weight loss is sustaining healthy eating behaviors. Most people who are unsuccessful at maintaining healthy eating behaviors have not identified personal barriers to eating healthy and have no strategies in place to help them overcome their personal barriers to healthy eating. Once patients identify their barriers to healthy eating, design strategies to overcome these barriers, and instill an eating monitoring system; the chance for successful weight maintenance increases dramatically. One of the most common barriers to eating healthy is the inappropriate use of food to meet emotional needs. Helping the patient understand the emotional links to food is an essential component of any effort to achieve weight loss.

EXAM QUESTIONS

CHAPTER 6
Questions 20-24

Note: Choose the one option that BEST answers each question.

20. In order for a person to be successful at changing an unhealthy behavioral habit, the person needs to replace the existing habit with a

    a. new habit that is healthier.

    b. habit that is socially acceptable.

    c. new habit that meets the needs served by the existing habit.

    d. commitment to increase exercise.

21. Individuals participate in compulsive eating behaviors in order to cope with certain

    a. uncertainties.

    b. stress.

    c. fears.

    d. inconsistencies.

22. One of the best ways to help patients identify their emotional links to eating is to have them

    a. eat something they dislike and then state how this made them feel.

    b. go without eating a meal purposely and describe their feelings.

    c. eat an unlimited quantity of any food for 24 hours and then record the resulting feelings.

    d. record their feelings and eating behaviors simultaneously.

23. One of the most common barriers to healthy eating is

    a. not having enough money to buy healthy food.

    b. not knowing how to read food labels.

    c. eating in response to one's emotions.

    d. that healthy food tastes bad.

24. A way to help patients design strategies to overcome their barriers to healthy eating is to

    a. assist them in identifying barriers to healthy eating.

    b. give them a list of healthy foods.

    c. search the Internet for healthy eating strategies.

    d. check the tabloids for strategies famous people have used successfully.

REFERENCES

Adami, G.F., Campostano, A., Ravera, G., Leggieri, M., & Scopinaro, N. (2001). Alexithymia and body weight in obese patients. *Behavorial Medicine, 27,* 212-215.

Allison, K.C. & Lundgren, J.D. (2006). Eating disorders in obese individuals. *Obesity Management, 2*(6), 110-3.

American Psychiatric Association. (2005). *Diagnostic and statistical manual of mental disorders* (4th ed., *Text Revision).* Arlington, VA: Author.

Befort, C.A., Stewart, E.E., Smith, B.K., Gibson, C.A., Sullivan, D.K., & Donnelly, J. E. (2008). Weight maintenance, behaviors and barriers among previous participants of a university-based weight control program. *International Journal of Obesity 32,* 519-526.

Jakicic, J.M., Wing, R.R., & Winters-Hart, C. (2002). Relationship of physical activity to eating behaviors and weight loss in women. *Medicine and Science in Sports and Exercise, 34,* 1653-1659.

Kushner, R.D. (2007). Lifestyle patterns approach for obesity management. *Obesity Management, 3*(6), 121-4.

Larson, J., van Strien, T., Esinga, R., & Engles, R. (2006). Association between alexithymia and emotional eating in obese individuals. *Journal of Psychosomatic Research, 60,* 237-246.

Miller, W.C. (1998). *Negotiated peace: How to end the war over weight.* Needham Heights, MA: Allyn & Bacon.

Miller, W.C. & Eggert, K.E. (1992). Weight loss perceptions, characteristics, and expectations of an overweight male and female population. *Medical, Exercise, Nutrition and Health, 1,* 42-46.

Phelan, S. & Wadden,T.A. (2004). Behavioral assessment of obesity. In J.K. Thompson (Ed.), *Handbook of eating disorders and obesity* (pp. 393-420). Hoboken, NJ: John Wiley & Sons, Inc.

Wing, R.R. & Hill, J.O. (2001). Successful weight loss maintenance. *Annual Review of Nutrition, 21,* 323-341.

CHAPTER 7

BEHAVIOR MODELS

CHAPTER OBJECTIVE

After completing this chapter the learner will be able to describe the most common theories of behavior.

LEARNING OBJECTIVES

After completing this chapter, the learner will be able to

1. describe the components of each of the common models of behavior.

2. identify the components of the social cognitive theory of behavior in the context of a patient interview.

3. identify the components of the theory of planned behavior in the context of a patient interview.

4. identify the stages of change for patients.

INTRODUCTION

The previous chapter devoted much time to the emotional links among eating and exercise behaviors. These emotional links, along with other influences, are what control an individual's behavior on a moment-to-moment basis. They control the decision process that dictates whether or not a person is going to participate in a specific behavior. The purpose of this chapter is to help the profes-

sional gain an appreciation for the nature of the behavior change process. Several behavior models are presented in the context of helping the professional understand some of the behaviors directly associated with obesity.

KNOWLEDGE-ATTITUDE-BEHAVIOR MODEL

The knowledge-attitude-behavior (KAB) model, sometimes called the knowledge-attitudes-skills Behavior model, is probably the oldest of the behavior models. This model is the assumed model that underlies most educational settings from ancient times to today. The primary resource in this model is the accumulation of knowledge. The KAB model proposes that as knowledge accumulates, attitudes change; and that these changes in attitude promote behavior change. A hidden assumption in the model that is generally not discussed is that increased knowledge also gives the person the skills to change behavior (Miller, 1998). In other words, there must be something self-empowering about knowledge that provides the individual with the skills or self-efficacy to change behavior.

If one were to apply the KAB model to obesity management, it would require a person to gain knowledge of the basic principles and benefits of healthy eating and exercise behaviors, to develop positive attitudes about the importance of healthy behavior management, and to acquire the necessary skills to overcome any barriers that may hinder adoption of a healthier lifestyle. This application can be illustrated in the following example.

Suppose John has an eating problem that is a direct result of only one behavior (which is highly unlikely, but it works for this example). The problem is that John has too much fat in his diet. The program he enlists to help him conquer this problem seems excellent. He learns from the program about the disease risks associated with a high-fat diet, about low-fat foods, about blood triglycerides and cholesterol, and about everything imaginable for dealing with dietary fat and health (KNOWLEDGE). All of this knowledge leads him to a real healthy attitude about low-fat diets and healthy dietary behaviors (ATTITUDES). This program is so good that it helps him develop skills relevant to cooking low-fat meals, making low-fat substitutions in recipes, reading food labels, making alternate food choices, etc. (SKILLS). The end result is that John now consumes a low-fat diet.

One can see, from the example, that there are assumptions and undefined constructs that must be in place to make the KAB model work. One assumption is that John's lack of knowledge of the deleterious effects of a high-fat diet, in and of itself, is what causes him to eat a high-fat diet. Thus, in the KAB model, it is assumed that John eats a high-fat diet simply because he doesn't know any better. In the KAB model, the "how-to" knowledge is difficult to distinguish from the constructs of skills and self-efficacy, which are important constructs in other behavior models. Therefore, knowledge may be incorporated into larger conceptual frameworks that provide some understanding of behavior change, but increasing knowledge itself does not seem to be very useful in promoting behavior change.

HEALTH BELIEF MODEL

The Health Belief (HB) model is similar or possibly an extension of the KAB model for behavior change (Baranowski, Cullen, Nicklas, Thompson, & Baranowski, 2003). The constructs of the HB model are much different from the KAB model, but the underlying foundation is the same – knowledge and attitudes. The primary constructs of the HB model are:

- perceived susceptibility or risk of becoming or staying obese,

- perceived severity of being obese,

- perceived benefits of changing health behaviors,

- perceived barriers to changing health behaviors,

- cues to action that trigger perceptions about susceptibility or risk, and

- self-efficacy about performing a specific health behavior.

One can see from the list of HB model constructs, that knowledge underlies most of them – knowledge about susceptibility and risk, knowledge about disease severity, knowledge about behavior benefits, and knowledge about changing behavior. Furthermore, attitudes are tightly linked to knowledge, in the HB model. Perceptions about obesity are the same as attitudes about obesity, which are rooted in knowledge. Knowledge and attitudes, then, are the primary motivators for change within the HB model. Self-efficacy, in the HB model is what allows the person to make a successful behavior change. The HB model can be applied to obesity through the following example:

Bev is obese and begins to receive cues regarding the risks of being obese. She watches a program about the rising prevalence of obesity in the United States, learns of an obese friend who just suffered a heart attack, recalls that her family has a history of heart disease, etc. Then, at some critical point, the accumulation of cues reaches a threshold that stimulates Bev to take action to reduce her body weight.

The actions she takes are in direct relation to the perceived benefits of those actions, and her own self-efficacy about those actions. Bev's experience suggests that individuals behave, or choose between opposing behaviors, in accordance to their perceived health threat. Although the HB model seems appealing, its validity has not been confirmed.

SOCIAL COGNITIVE THEORY

The social cognitive theory (SCT) is probably the most commonly used and most familiar behavior model for the prevention and reduction of obesity. The SCT proposes that behavior is a function of the interaction between the person and the environment. Personal concepts that affect behavior are:

- skills to perform the behavior,

- self-efficacy that one can perform the behavior under different circumstances, and

- outcome expectancies that will occur as a result of performing the behavior.

The environmental concepts of the SCT are:

- modeling the behavior after another person's example, and

- availability of whatever is needed to perform the behavior (e.g., exercise equipment) (Baranowski et al., 2003).

The personal and environmental concepts of the SCT model lead to motivation and self-control. Outcome expectancies are what motivate the person to change behavior, but self-control is what allows the person to behave. In other words, an obese person with hypertension learns that a physical activity can cause weight loss and a reduction in blood pressure. These outcome expectancies motivate the person to exercise. The person achieves self-control over exercise by goal setting, monitoring progress, rewarding one's self for behaving, and problem solving when goals are not achieved. Note how outcome expectancies are closely related to attitudes in other behavioral models.

The SCT is the behavioral model most health professionals use, even though they may not know it. An example of how it is implemented is shown in Case Study 7-1.

Case Study 7-1: Exercise and The Social Cognitive Theory

The Social Cognitive Theory (SCT) proposes that behavior is a function of the interaction between the person and the environment. The person has certain outcome expectancies that are influenced by his skills and self-efficacy. Skills and self-efficacy are modified by behavior modeling and available resources. This case study illustrates how the SCT can be applied to an obese patient who is contemplating an exercise program. The dialogue occurs between an exercise physiologist (EP) and the patient (Bill). See if you can identify the components of the SCT in the dialogue.

Scenario:

EP: I understand that you are here to design an exercise program to help with your weight control. Is that right, Bill?

Bill: Yes, I need help. I don't know much about exercise programs.

EP: Well, it is not hard to figure out when you understand some of the basics. What are your weight loss expectations with regard to exercise?

Bill: I would ultimately like to lose 40 pounds, but I know that won't all happen with exercise. I am also on a 500 kcal restricted diet.

EP: That information will help us as we design your program. Have you ever used exercise as a form of weight control?

Bill: No, not to lose weight, but I have exercised in the past.

EP: Tell me more.

continued on next page

Bill: I used to be quite the athlete in high school. I got a varsity letter in cross country, basketball, and tennis. However, I really have not exercised much since I got out of college 12 years ago.

EP: So, it sounds like you like sports. It also looks like you were a runner. Are you considering getting back into sports or running for your exercise program?

Bill: I would like to. I think it's like riding a bike. Once I get back into it, I am sure it will all come back to me.

EP: I am sure it will. How would you like to start?

Bill: Probably just running. I think that after I lose a little weight through running I can get back into playing tennis or something.

EP: Sounds like a good plan to me. Let's think of some goals that you can reach for with your exercise program (discussion on goals ensues). Now let's figure out how you will reward yourself if you meet your goals (discussion on rewards ensues). The reward for your short-term goal will come up on 4 weeks. Why don't we sit down in 2 weeks and see how the program is going. We can modify things at that point if we need to.

Bill: Sounds good to me.

EP: Now, you did say that you are going to run on your lunch hour at work because they have an exercise facility. Is that correct?

Bill: Yes, you got it.

EP: Before we finish, I want to show you how to take your heart rate during exercise because that is how you will monitor your exercise intensity.

Resolution

EP: I understand that you are here to design an exercise program to help with your weight control. Is that right, Bill?

Bill: Yes, I need help. **I don't know much about exercise programs.** *(This statement indicates a lack of exercise programming skills, not exercise skills. It infers a possibility of self-efficacy problems.)*

EP: Well, it is not hard to figure out, when you understand some of the basics. What are your weight loss expectations with regard to exercise?

Bill: I would ultimately **like to lose 40 pounds,** *(one goal is stated, along with an expectation.)* but I know that won't all happen with exercise. I am also on a 500 kcal restricted diet. *(This statement shows a realistic expectation.)*

EP: That information will help us as we design your program. Have you ever used exercise as a form of weight control?

Bill: No, not to lose weight, but **I have exercised in the past.** *(This statement demonstrates some skills and alludes to a positive self-efficacy.)*

EP: Tell me more.

Bill: I used to be quite the athlete in high school. I got a varsity letter in cross country, basketball and tennis. However, I really have not exercised much since I got out of college 12 years ago. *(This statement shows much self-efficacy, with a little hesitation.)*

EP: So, it sounds like you like sports. It also looks like you were a runner. Are you considering getting back into sports or running for your exercise program?

Bill: I would like to. I think it's like riding a bike. Once I get back into it, I am sure it will all come back to me. *(This statement demonstrates more self-efficacy.)*

EP: I am sure it will. How would you like to start?

Bill: Probably just running. I think that after I lose a little weight through running I can get back into playing tennis or something. *(Shows realistic expectations.)*

EP: Sounds like a good plan to me. Let's think of some goals that you can reach for with your exercise program (discussion on ensues). Now let's figure out how you will reward yourself if you meet your goals (discussion on rewards ensues). The reward for your short-term goal will come up on 4 weeks. Why

continued on next page

don't we sit down in 2 weeks and see how the program is going. We can modify things at that point if we need to. *(All of this relates to goals, rewards, and monitoring. These are all part of the SCT model.)*

Bill: Sounds good to me.

EP: Now, you did say that you are going to run on your lunch hour at work because they have an exercise facility. Is that correct? *(Checking on availability.)*

Bill: Yes, you got it.

EP: Before we finish, I want to show you how to take your heart rate during exercise because that is how you will monitor your exercise intensity. *(Demonstrates modeling.)*

Resolution Process

All of the components of the SCT are present in the case study. The clues to the SCT are given in bold text, whereas the italicized text delineates the specific component of the model.

TRANSTHEORETICAL MODEL AND STAGES OF CHANGE

The transtheoretical model (T) for behavior change has become a very popular model to explain behaviors in various realms. The popularity of the T model stems from its mapping out specific stages of change that are supposed to occur in the behavior change process. Unfortunately, the bulk of the research does not show that the T model is valid for obesity (Baranowski et al., 2003). Some of the problems with the model are that its constructs are not standardized, staging people is not consistent across different behaviors and among different people, the length of each stage is not consistent or clearly defined, and how to manipulate a person through the stages is not delineated. Notwithstanding these problems, many obesity experts like using the T model for obesity intervention because the stages of change are appealing.

Different variations of the T model propose different stages, but the most common variation proposes five stages, which are:

1. *Precontemplation* – no thought of changing behavior or suppressing thoughts about changing behavior (indefinite). People in precontemplation tend to have low levels of confidence and are externally motivated (Blair, Dunn, Marcus, Carpenter, & Jaret, P., 2002).

2. *Contemplation* – thinking about changing behavior within the next 6 months, but taking no action to change. Patients acknowledge the benefits of behavior change but feel the barriers are overwhelming.

3. *Preparation* – anticipating a behavior change within the next 1 to 2 months, and defining how to change the behavior. They may have made attempts in the past, but they need a plan. While their self confidence is higher, they are still primarily externally motivated (Blair et al., 2002).

4. *Action* – in the process of changing behavior or have changed behavior within the past 6 months. This stage requires the greatest amount of energy and the patient is at the highest risk of relapse. Motivation at this stage is external and internal (Blair et al., 2002).

5. *Maintenance* – expending effort to retain the changes made during the action stage (6 months to 4 years). Self-confidence at this stage is high, with internal motivation predominant. The new behavior has become part of the individual's value system.

The T model proposes that behavior change is a process that initiates with changes in cognition that occur across the first three stages. These cognition changes are similar to the gaining of knowledge and formation of attitudes in the KAB model. New knowledge and attitudes formed lead one to a decisional balance, or weighing the pros and cons of performing a behavior. The self-efficacy factor comes into play during the preparation and action stage, where the person plans and participates in the new behavior. A self-control factor comes into play during the action and maintenance stage. Thus, the T model seems to map out the process that is contained within some of the other behavior models.

Change strategies can be used no matter where the individual is at in the process. These include both cognitive and behavioral strategies. Cognitive strategies include:

- increasing knowledge

- comprehending the benefits

- warning of risks

- caring about consequences to others

- increasing healthy opportunities.

Behavioral techniques include:

- making a commitment

- enlisting social support

- substituting alternatives

- rewarding yourself

- reminding yourself.

Case Study 7-2 further discusses how these strategies can be used to address the level at which the patient may be.

Case Study 7-2: Stages of Change for Exercise

You are a Diabetes Educator for a county hospital. Herman is a new patient who will be attending the upcoming diabetes education course. He is meeting with you today to register for the course and pick up any course materials he will need. Can you identify in which stage of change Herman currently resides?

Scenario

Diabetes Educator: Hello, Herman. I assume you are here to register for the diabetes education course coming up next week.

Herman: Yeah, the doc said I have to take it.

Diabetes Educator: You were recently diagnosed with diabetes, weren't you?

Herman: No, I have had diabetes for a while, but I never attended the course. The doc got pretty mad at me and insisted I get into this session of the course.

Diabetes Educator: So, if you were diagnosed with diabetes a while back, why didn't you attend the course sooner?

Herman: I don't know. I guess I didn't think it was that important.

Diabetes Educator: And if the doc didn't get after you today, you probably wouldn't have signed up for this session either?

Herman: Don't get me wrong. I'm sure you teach a fine course. I just thought my diabetes was doing fine without the course.

Diabetes Educator: Well, your diabetes may be doing just fine, but the course will help you understand more about diabetes and how to manage it.

Herman: I guess so. See you next week.

continued on next page

Resolution

Diabetes Educator: Hello, Herman. I assume you are here to **register for the diabetes education course coming up next week.**

Herman: Yeah, the **doc said I have to take it.** *(Herman is registering for the course because his doctor has recommended he do so. This is external motivation, which suggests that Herman is really in a stage lower than preparation or action.)*

Diabetes Educator: You were recently diagnosed with diabetes, weren't you?

Herman: No, **I have had diabetes for a while, but I never attended the course.** The **doc got pretty mad at me and insisted I get into this session** of the course. *(These comments reinforce the fact that Herman is not in the preparation or action stages. Having been diagnosed for a while suggests that Herman is not even in the contemplation stage; he is in the precontemplation stage.)*

Diabetes Educator: So, if you were diagnosed with diabetes a while back, why didn't you attend the course sooner?

Herman: I don't know. I guess I didn't think it was that important. *(This comment further suggests that Herman is in precontemplation stage.)*

Diabetes Educator: And if the doc didn't get after you today, you probably wouldn't have signed up for this session either?

Herman: Don't get me wrong. I'm sure you teach a fine course. **I just thought my diabetes was doing fine without the course.** *(This comment confirms that Herman is in precontemplation. However, he may have moved to contemplation following his doctor's insistence he take the course.)*

Diabetes Educator: Well, your diabetes may be doing just fine, but the course will help you understand more about diabetes and how to manage it.

Herman: I guess so. See you next week. *(This comment hints that Herman may have changed his attitude. He may have just moved along to contemplation or preparation.)*

Resolution Process

The transtheoretical model's stages of change for Herman are present in the case study. The clues to identifying Herman's stage of change are given in bold text. How the clues are interpreted is shown in italics. If Herman had come to register for the diabetes education course voluntarily, he would have been categorized as being in either the preparation or action stage. Herman can still benefit from the cognitive strategies in the diabetic course. Increased knowledge can help him begin to see what effects his diabetes will have on his life. Warning of risk will help him to see the down side of not changing any of his unhealthy behaviors. Increasing exposure to healthy opportunities will help him to see ways he may not have thought of to improve his health. Even though the locus of motivation is external, this information can help move Herman through the stages of change.

For discussion's sake, suppose Herman was already in the contemplation or even the action stage. The same information presented related to increasing his knowledge about his disease and awareness of risks and health opportunities can help to motivate him and help form a plan for needed changes. It can also reinforce information that the individual may already have assimilated. The class setting can be used to manage and meet the needs of individuals at various stages of the change process. Hopefully, Herman will soon move from the precontemplation stage in the care of his diabetes; however, each individual will move through the process at his or her own pace. Small changes can be built upon because readiness to change can be viewed as a continuum, rather than an all-or-nothing state.

THEORY OF PLANNED BEHAVIOR

The theory of planned behavior (TPB) contends that human action is guided by

- one's attitude toward the behavior in question,

- the perceived social pressure to perform the behavior (subjective norm), and

- the ease or difficulty with which one can actually perform the behavior (perceived control).

A modified version of the TPB adds the construct of self-efficacy. The combination of attitude, subjective norm, perceived control, and self-efficacy leads to the formation of an intention to perform or not to perform a given behavior. Generally, favorable attitudes and positive subjective norms, in combination with a high level of perceived control and self-efficacy, lead to a greater likelihood of actually performing the behavior (Baranowski, et al., 2003).

Specific salient beliefs underlie each of these cognitive constructs: behavioral beliefs (underlying attitude), normative beliefs (underlying subjective norms), control beliefs (underlying perceived behavioral control), and capability beliefs (underlying self-efficacy). The constructs for an individual are appraised by weighing the strength of the respective belief by a valuation of that belief. Thus, in order to understand why a person maintains a certain construct (attitude, subjective norm, perceived behavioral control, or self-efficacy) toward a specific behavior, it is necessary to assess the construct's beliefs as well as its respective valuations.

The constructs of attitude and self-efficacy, in the TPB are similar to what they are in other behavior models. The constructs of subjective norm and perceived control are unique to the TPB. Subjective norm is a function of the strength of a person's belief about whether certain people want the person to do the behavior and the strength of the person's desire to comply with those desires.

Similarly, perceived control is a function of the strength of the person's belief about whether there are factors that facilitate or inhibit performing a behavior and the strength of the power of these factors.

Many researchers have studied the correlates of physical activity and diet within the paradigm of the TPB. Their research has generally shown that the TPB is an efficacious model for explaining health behaviors for different populations. Most recently, the TPB has been shown to be a valid model to explain the correlates of physical activity in overweight adults (Boudreau & Godin, 2007). However, procedures for changing the components of the TPB in obesity interventions are not defined.

Case Study 7-3 uses TPB.

SUMMARY

The correlates and determinants of behavior are not well understood. Several behavioral models have been proposed to explain the determinants of behavior as well as the process of behavior change. The most common of these behavior models are the knowledge-attitude-behavior model (KAB), the health belief model (HB), the social cognitive theory (SCT), the transtheoretical model (T), and the theory of planned behavior (TPB). Each of these models proposes specific constructs that command a person's behavior. Knowledge, beliefs, attitudes, control, and self-efficacy are constructs that in one way or another are common to all the major behavior models. The health professional can better help the obese patient change health behaviors if the professional understands the patient's behavioral constructs.

Case Study 7-3: Theory of Planned Behavior and Obesity Treatment

You are a nurse at a family practice clinic. Skip is a 45-year-old man who has been a patient of the clinic for years. He does not visit the doctor regularly because he just doesn't like going to the doctor. Skip may also avoid the doctor because Skip is obese and could be in denial about how obesity is affecting his health. Skip is 5' 6" tall and weighs 243 lb. His body mass index is 39.3. Skip has come to the doctor for a physical checkup. See if you can determine Skip's attitude, strength of subjective norm, perceived control, and self-efficacy about losing weight through diet and exercise.

Scenario

Nurse: Hi Skip. I see you are here for a basic physical today. I haven't seen you in a few years. Everything OK?

Skip: Yeah, everything is OK. I just don't like going to the doctor, and I know you are going to tell me I need to lose weight.

Nurse: I am not going to harass you, Skip. I am just concerned about your health and what problems you may be facing in the future.

Skip: I know. My wife says the same thing.

Nurse: So your wife is worried about your weight? Who else?

Skip: Yes, she is. My parents also talked to me about it. Some of my friends have said something, either to me or behind my back to my wife. They all think I should lose some weight.

Nurse: Is it important for you to do what these people want you to do?

Skip: My wife definitely. My folks too. Some of my friends, yes. Others not so much.

> *Interjected comment: This first part of the dialogue evaluates Skip's subjective norm. Skip feels a lot of social pressure to lose weight. He also wants to comply with what important people in his life desire. Thus, Skip's subjective norm for trying to lose weight is high.*

Nurse: If you were to make a serious attempt at losing weight, what would that mean to you?

Skip: It means I would have to exercise and watch my eating.

Nurse: Is exercise and watching what you eat a good thing or a bad thing?

Skip: Not so good. I would have to fit exercise into my schedule. I would get all sweaty. I would have to buy exercise clothes. I would surely have to eat out less. I would need to do more grocery shopping.

Nurse: These things appear to be an inconvenience to you, but how bad are they?

Skip: Well, I really do have time for exercise. Plus, my wife goes to our gym 4 days a week. I could go with her. Obviously, I have a place to shower. I am embarrassed about my weight, so getting exercise clothes would be uncomfortable. Eating out less may be difficult because I do like the variety of restaurants here in the city, and don't really like to cook. Grocery shopping wouldn't be that bad, if I did it during the week and not on the weekend when the stores are crowded.

> *Interjected comment: This part of the dialogue evaluates Skip's attitudes about trying to lose weight. First, his attitudes about what losing weight entails is not so good. The nurse then has Skip describe how bad it would be, and he reveals the strength of his attitudes.*

Nurse: Sounds like you already have figured out a way to get around some of the inconveniences of trying to lose weight. If we came up with a reasonable diet and exercise plan, how sure are you that you could follow it?

Skip: 90% sure.

continued on next page

Nurse: Really? So, you could exercise even though there are demands at work? You will sacrifice eating out sometimes, even though your friends do it all the time? You will be able to cook a healthy meal, even if you get home late from work? You will be able to exercise, even on the weekends?

Skip: Like I said, my wife exercises at the gym all the time. I can go with her, even when work is crazy. On the weekends, my wife is always wanting to walk downtown and see the sites, rather than drive. I don't mind cooking, I just have become lazy. I will probably fall victim to peer pressure to eat out once in a while. That's why I said 90%.

Interjected comment: This part of the dialogue evaluates Skip's perceived control. He perceives to have high control over the aspects of the weight loss plan.

Nurse: Sounds reassuring. So, you know how to cook. Are you able to make healthy choices at the grocery store? And do you know how to use the equipment at the gym, or do you need somebody to teach you?

Skip: Yes to all of those. I guess the reason I have not done anything about my weight is that I got depressed because I gained it all. I never thought I would become fat.

Interjected comment: This last part of the dialogue evaluates Skip's self-efficacy. Notice how the nurse questions specific behaviors.

Resolution

Skip's attitude about trying to lose weight is mediocre. He has some fairly strong attitudes about the inconveniences of eating healthy and exercising. Skip has a high subjective norm. His closest relationships want him to lose weight, and he wants to do what they want. His perceived control is high and self-efficacy is also high. Skip's prognosis for successful weight loss is good.

Resolution Process

The comments injected into the dialogue between you and Skip reveal how the constructs of the theory of planned behavior can be used to evaluate a person's potential for successfully changing a behavior.

EXAM QUESTIONS

CHAPTER 7
Questions 25-28

Note: Choose the one option that BEST answers each question.

25. The knowledge-attitude-behavior model assumes that

    a. increased knowledge about an issue will promote an attitude change, which will lead to a change in behavior.

    b. knowledge and attitudes are ingrained, and therefore, behavior is difficult to change.

    c. as one continues to behave in a certain way, one's knowledge and attitudes about that behavior increase.

    d. knowledge will invariably lead to sustained behavior change.

26. The behavioral model that is most often used in the treatment of obesity is the

    a. transtheoretical model.

    b. theory of planned behavior.

    c. health belief model.

    d. social cognitive theory.

27. The transtheoretical model for behavior change contains which five stages of change that a person must pass through in order to establish a permanent pattern of behavior?

    a. Recognition, Awareness, Guilt, Attitude Change, Behavior Modeling

    b. Pre-contemplation, Contemplation, Preparation, Action, Maintenance

    c. Recognition, Attitude Change, Skill Development, Action, Maintenance

    d. Resistance to Change, Recognition, Awareness, Skill Development, Behavior Modeling

28. An obese, 50-year-old women tells you that she is confident she can maintain an exercise program of dance because she used to dance on a performance team in college, her husband and neighbor are pressuring her to dance again, there is a new dance club being formed at the community recreation center, and the club meets when she is available. This scenario fits best which behavior model?

    a. Knowledge-attitude-behavior model

    b. Transtheoretical model

    c. Health belief model

    d. Theory of planned behavior

103

REFERENCES

Baranowski, T., Cullen, K.W., Nicklas, T., Thompson, D., & Baranowski, J. (2003). Are current health behavioral change models helpful in guiding prevention of weight gain efforts? *Obesity Research, 11*, 23S-43S.

Blair, S.N., Dunn, A.L., Marcus, B.H., Carpenter, R.A., & Jaret, P. (2002). *Active living every day facilitator guide,* (pp. 8-18). Champaign, IL: Human Kinetics.

Boudreau, F. & Godin, G. (2007). Using the theory of planned behavior to predict exercise intention in obese adults. *Canadian Journal of Nursing Research, 39*, 112-125.

Miller, W.C. (1998). *Negotiated peace: How to end the war over weight.* Boston: Allyn & Bacon.

CHAPTER 8

COMMUNICATION SKILLS FOR WORKING WITH THE OBESE PATIENT

CHAPTER OBJECTIVE

After completing this chapter the learner will be able to describe communication strategies that foster a therapeutic relationship with the obese patient.

LEARNING OBJECTIVES

After completing this chapter, the learner will be able to

1. identify caregiver behaviors needed to gain information relevant to patient behavior.

2. facilitate patient behavior change by asking the right questions and probing for the right information.

3. describe principles of approaching the topic of obesity with a patient.

4. use the technique of motivational interviewing to structure a patient encounter.

INTRODUCTION

The health care professional, who plans on working with the obese patient, will develop a unique relationship with the patient. As illustrated in many chapters of this book, the etiology and management of obesity are multifaceted. In order to help the obese patient make the necessary behavior changes to overcome obesity, the health care profes-sional needs to understand how the internal and external environments of the patient affect the patient's behaviors. This understanding can only be gained through effective communication, and effective communication can only occur if the health care professional knows what to look for and how to interpret messages sent by the patient. The purpose of this chapter is to review standard communication techniques in the context of caring for the obese individual and to introduce concepts related to effective communication and intervention with this population.

LISTENING SKILLS

Listening skills are the most important skills a professional can develop to help guide effective problem-solving and behavior-changing strategies for the obese patient. Without listening skills, the professional is incapable of demonstrating other counseling skills, such as empathy, understanding, and support. Practicing true listening skills will help the professional become more aware of the subtle aspects of communication. Earlier chapters in this book have presented how emotions, perceptions, and attitudes affect the patient's behavior. The effec-tive listener will be able to detect these subtle aspects of communication by understanding how they are expressed through things like tone of voice, pitch of voice, speed of talking, and body language. True listening is not just hearing words, it is receiving and understanding the message. Often the root of the message is not embedded in words, but in emotions, perceptions, and attitudes.

Openness

The first listening skill the professional needs to develop is that of openness. Openness is the willingness to receive communication and to allow others to influence your perception (Knapp, 2007). It means being receptive to outside stimuli that can change your perception of reality. Openness requires the ability to receive messages that may conflict with your pre-established attitudes and beliefs. Openness does not require you to accept the attitudes or beliefs contained in another person's message; openness only requires that you do not distort the message of others before you receive it. That way you allow the possibility of that message changing your perception. In other words, you are "open" to something new.

Openness of the professional is portrayed to the patient through verbal and nonverbal communication. Body position communicates, in a physical way, how open you are to the patient's message. A tense body position tells the patient that you are not receptive. The nonverbal message of a tense body position is, "I have too many other things disturbing me to give full attention to your message." A closed body position also sends a message of not being open. Sitting in the chair with your legs crossed, arms folded across your chest, and upper body slumped over says to the patient, "I am withdrawing or retreating from you and, hence, your message is not welcome." On the other hand, sitting in the chair with both of your feet on the floor, arms at your side or on the chair armrests, and your body erect with a slight tilt toward the patient sends the message, "I am giving you all of my attention and am eager to hear what you have to say" (Givens, 2008).

Messages of openness or reticence are also communicated verbally. The verbal message of openness is not direct, but indirect. No health care professional would ever say to a patient, "I really do not want to hear what you have to say." However, the professional may indirectly be portraying the same closed message to the patient when making suggestions, giving advice, planning a strategy, asking questions, etc.

VERBAL COMMUNICATION

The professional who knows how to communicate well with the patient sends verbal messages back to the patient that tell the patient how the patient's message is being received and understood. Effective listening responses can be classified into several general categories. Each of these types of verbal responses communicates to the patient exactly what the professional perceives as the true message coming from the patient and how the professional interprets this message.

Affirmation

The patient's success at lifestyle change depends upon his or her intrinsic value and ability to problem solve and cope. The affirmation of patients is the basis for maintaining rapport between the professional and patient, and the basis for improving the patient's self-efficacy (Gable, 2007; Knapp, 2007). Messages of affirmation, from the professional, need to continually confirm the patient's worth and ability. The first affirmation message that should be sent to a patient is that of respect. Always address a patient by title or last name until some mutually agreed-upon salutation has been determined. Next in importance is to verify the patient's right to feel and to validate his or her emotions (see Chapter 6). When patients feel that you are receptive to and respective of their feelings, they develop trust in you (Knapp, 2007). Trust is the basis of interpersonal rapport and also the foundation of the patient's self-efficacy.

If you are not sure about the message a patient is communicating, ask for clarification in a manner that is not judgmental and in a manner that places the burden of communication upon you, not the patient. For example, the statement "I understand what you are saying to mean…" sounds much better than "so, you mean to say…" Avoid using the word "why" as much as possible. The question, "why did you do that" can much better be phrased as "how did you come about doing that" or "what brought you to the decision to do that." Another word to avoid as much as possible is "but." Replace the word "but" with the word "and" when referring to a patient's behavior. Remember that the word "but" in a sentence tends to negate everything preceding it. If you say to the patient, "I see you did well on reducing your fat intake this week and well at reducing your sweets, but you did not exercise like you committed," the patient will remember your judgment most, not exercising. It is better to say, "I see you did well on reducing your fat intake this week and well at reducing your sweets, and you did not exercise like you committed." Using the conjunction "and" rather than "but" helps the patient not to isolate and focus only on the negative.

Confrontation

Often the patient is not aware of or in denial about some behaviors, thoughts, and feelings. One method of approaching this problem is to confront the patient. Confrontation in this sense is used to identify opposition to change and is not adversarial. This process helps the patient recognize faulty thinking, inaccurate beliefs, and feelings that have become a barrier to lifestyle change. There are three areas of confrontation that are common in obesity therapy (Curry & Jaffe, 1998). The most common is the demonstration of discrepancies between what a patient says he or she is feeling and a more commonly expected response to the same situation. The second area of discrepancy is when a patient's words and behaviors are incongruent. The

third area for confrontation in obesity therapy is when the patient's behaviors do not match his or her beliefs. Confrontation must be done with sensitivity because it can create an environment of defensiveness and lead to poor therapeutic outcomes (Resnicow & Blackburn, 2005).

Reiteration

It is common for a patient to make statements that need clarification or statements that demonstrate distorted thinking patterns of the patient that need to be confronted. In these situations, the professional reiterates what a patient has said so the patient can clarify or reflect on the message he or she sent. If the professional is uncertain about how to interpret a message sent by the patient, the professional can reiterate exactly what a patient has said in order to elicit more detailed information from the patient about what was just said. For example, the professional may say, "Can you explain what you meant when you said, 'I hate to exercise?'" Reiteration can also be used as a method of confrontation to help the patient reflect upon what he or she has just said. For example, the professional may state, "You just said, 'I hate to exercise,' am I right?" "However, earlier today you said, 'exercise makes me feel good,' correct?"

Paraphrasing

The professional can paraphrase the main ideas that a patient has expressed in order to summarize the message(s) sent by the client. Paraphrasing can also be used to summarize or verbalize the emotions and nonverbal messages sent by the patient. Using the patient's words when paraphrasing will diminish the likelihood of misinterpretation or starting an argument over semantics. After each paraphrase, the professional should receive the patient's feedback about the paraphrase. The patient can agree with the professional's summary, clarify the summary, or deny the summary.

Interpreting

This technique is an extension of reiteration and paraphrasing. With this technique the professional offers an interpretation of the patient's message in order to help the patient either come to his or her own interpretation of the message sent, or to understand how the message the patient sent is being received. Interpretations carry the risk that they may not be accurate. Interpretations should always be offered as tentative so that the patient can affirm, clarify, or deny their meaning. The professional may say, "When you say that exercise makes you feel good, but that you also hate exercise, it tells me that there must be some type of internal conflict around your exercise participation. Maybe it would be helpful for us to talk about what you like about exercise versus what you don't like about it."

Probing

Formulating statements and questions for the purpose of getting additional information is called probing. There are two key skills the professional must develop in order to gain valuable information while probing:

- phrase all questions and probing statements so that the patient senses that any answers will be accepted without being judged,
- ask open-ended questions or make statements that elicit an open-ended response

(Knapp, 2007).

The question, "Did you eat all of the chocolate?" seems judgmental, whereas the question, "How much of the chocolate did you eat?" does not. The statement, "Please tell me why you did not exercise this week," seems judgmental, whereas the statement "Please tell me what stopped you from exercising this week" does not. The question, "Did you stay on your diet plan this week?" is close-ended because it can be answered with a "Yes" or "No" response and no more. The question, "Can you tell me about how your diet plan went this week?" is open-ended, because it requires the patient to elaborate.

NONVERBAL COMMUNICATION

Nonverbal communication, more often than not, conveys the true message in communication. Words can be manipulated and strategically spoken, but body language is almost impossible to censor. The professional, who is a skilled communicator, has the awareness necessary to understand nonverbal messages received in communication and the self-awareness necessary to send messages nonverbally. Consequently, listening to nonverbal communication can help you better understand the patient and your straightforward nonverbal responses to patient messages will increase your effectiveness in communicating with patients. The most common functions of nonverbal communication are to

- augment the meaning of words,
- negate the meaning of words, and
- express emotion

(Curry & Jaffe, 1998).

A patient who stomps his foot on the ground at the same time he says, "I am going to beat this thing one step at a time." is augmenting his words through his foot action. In contrast, a patient who is clenching her fist while she says, "I am not angry." is negating her words by the message she sends with her clenched fist. A patient whose eyes well up with tears as she relates how she regained all the weight she lost last year is expressing emotion through nonverbal communication.

Most of the time during obesity treatment, these functions of nonverbal communication occur spontaneously or subconsciously, which makes it easier for the professional to pick up on the true meaning of the communication. The professional can also reinforce messages sent to the patient by carefully paralleling the nonverbal communication with the spoken word.

Learning how to receive and send nonverbal messages requires practice. The best practice technique the professional can use to develop nonverbal communication skills is the test of congruence. Ask yourself, "Is the patient's verbal message congruent with the nonverbal message?" "Is what I am saying congruent with what I am portraying nonverbally?"

INITIATING A DISCUSSION WITH PATIENTS

Health care providers often feel uncomfortable approaching the patient to discuss weight issues. The communication techniques described previously are useful in all patient encounters; however, specific guidelines have been developed to use when talking with patients about obesity. The approach involves starting the discussion in the context of overall health. Words such as "obesity" or "fatness" are perceived by patients to be prejudicial, so use "excess weight" or "overweight" instead (Wadden & Tsai, 2005). The discussion should lead to clarification of the patient's goals, which may include the decision not to undertake weight loss. Respecting the right of the patient to choose this action helps establish a rapport and increases the provider's approachability for future discussion. Discussion can focus on healthy behavior changes to promote health and prevent further weight gain as well.

MOTIVATIONAL INTERVIEWING

Motivational interviewing, a counseling technique that was originally developed to treat addictions, is being increasingly used to modify behavior in chronic disease, particularly related to diet and physical activity. This technique helps individuals work through ambivalence about behavior changes and set goals that meet their own core values. The goal in motivational interviewing is to help patients think about and express their own reasons for and against change and form their own solutions in a "negotiated" fashion with the provider. A core

principle for motivational interviewing is that the individual is more likely to act upon that which they voice (Resnicow & Blackburn, 2005).

The first step in using motivational interviewing is to involve the patient in setting the agenda for the session. The patient can decide what behaviors to talk about during the session or what goals to focus on. Obtaining permission at key transitional points makes sure the patient is still engaged. For example, the provider may ask permission to discuss the next step or to make suggestions.

Throughout the session, reflective listening using the communication techniques previously described ensures the exchange remains patient-driven. Hearing their own words back often helps identify patients' beliefs, values, and motivations (Resnicow & Blackburn, 2005).

In the traditional communication method, information flows from the provider to the patient. In motivational interviewing, the focus is on the patient's feelings about the information. The provider might say, "You may have heard that exercise is a key component to weight loss, and several of my patients have found that it enhanced their efforts to lose weight. What is important to me is what you think about including it in your plan."

Change is commonly met with resistance, as a result of ambivalent feelings that accompany most life modifications. Bessesen and Stuht (2005) identified two components of meaningful change behavior: a compelling need to change and a high level of confidence in doing so. When ambivalence is detected, the patient is asked to rate the target behavior on a scale of 0 to 10, with 0 being no problem, and 10 being a very serious problem. For example, "On a scale of 0 to 10 (with 10 the highest) how important is it for you to…?" If the patient rates the behavior as a 7 or greater, they likely see a compelling need for change. To follow up, ask "On a scale from 0 to 10 (with 10 the highest), assuming you wanted to change, how confident are you that you could…?" If a lower number is chosen, a discussion can be initiated about why the patient feels this way and what may be the perceived barriers to behavior change. The provider can then prompt the patient to offer his or her own solutions to these barriers. One way to do this is to ask "What would it take you to get to a 9 or a 10 from where you are now?"

The motivational interviewing approach to the situations described as confrontational is to attempt to "unstick" the entrenched patient by using a "negative reverse" statement and repeating the patient's statement back to him or her, in a neutral way. In doing so, the patient may hear the incongruity of his or her own statement and start to gain insight and understanding into behavior and possible solutions. This approach also diverts the defense that the patient may be prepared to deliver related to an expected confrontation. In any case, the approach can build a better clinician/patient rapport, and ultimately facilitate the patient's readiness and willingness to change.

Case studies 8-1 and 8-2 incorporate many of the techniques described in this Chapter.

Case Study 8-1: Communicating Effectively

You are a nurse who works for a university hospital that provides a number of bariatric services. Today you will be meeting with Maggie Montgomery, who lost more than 50 pounds 2 years ago, but has regained the lost weight. The purpose of your meeting is to interview Maggie about coming back into the weight loss program. Because the hospital provides various weight loss services, you will need to determine which approach is most appropriate for Maggie. Can you identify the listening skills and communication techniques the nurse used during the interview?

Scenario

Nurse: Hello, Mrs. Montgomery. I am glad you came in today.

Maggie: Oh, you can just call me Maggie. No need to be so formal.

Nurse: OK, Maggie. Have a seat. I can see by looking at your file that you participated in our group therapy program a couple of years ago. Can you explain how it went?

Maggie: It went very well. I lost over 50 pounds. I also learned a lot about exercise and nutrition. I really liked the psychologist who ran the group. She was so inspiring. (Maggie relaxes, smiles, and points to herself when she says, "I lost over 50 pounds.")

Nurse: Wow! That's commendable! Fifty pounds is a lot of weight. You must be proud of yourself.

Maggie: Yeah, but I gained it all back again. That's why I've returned. I am nothing but a failure. I am never going to lose this weight and keep it off. It's hopeless.

Nurse: Maggie, I know you may feel discouraged, but you are not a failure. You lost 50 pounds and you learned a lot about being healthy. Plus, you returned to the clinic, which means there must be some hope inside that you can overcome your weight problem.

Maggie: I guess I am not a total failure, but it sure is discouraging.

Nurse: I am sure it is. Let's talk in more detail about your experiences last time. What do you think went well for you in the group therapy?

Maggie: Well, I liked the monitoring chart I used for recording my exercise. Recording the minutes and distance I walked helped me measure my progress toward my goal. I also liked the fact that I made my goal of walking 500 miles. Oh, and I definitely liked the reward I got for reaching my goal.

Nurse: So, you liked the process of monitoring your exercise in a way that could document your progress toward a goal, and rewarding yourself for reaching that goal. Is that correct? (Maggie nods her head yes.) What else went well?

continued on next page

Maggie: Like I said. I really loved Tina, the psychologist. She just had a way of getting me excited about becoming healthy. Each week she taught us something new, and we were always learning about what's going on inside ourselves. And the behavior assignments she gave us each week seemed to be exactly what I needed.

Nurse: Sounds like you liked Tina because she connected with you in a way that motivated you to find solutions to your individual behavioral issues. Is that right? (Maggie nods her head yes.) What else can you identify that went well in your last weight loss attempt?

Maggie: Nothing really.

Nurse: OK, then can you tell me about what did not go well last time?

Maggie: Well, I almost don't want to tell you, because you will think I am being critical. (Maggie crosses her legs and folds her arms across her chest.)

Nurse: Maggie, I will stop you if I feel your criticism is destructive, but I really want to know how you feel. Only you can tell me that.

Maggie: OK, the problem was some of the group members. A couple of them were real jerks. This one lady just would not stop talking. She dominated the whole group. Then there was this other chick, who really didn't participate at all. She never spoke and did not do the behavioral assignments we had each week.

Nurse: So, the problem was some of the group members. A couple of them were real jerks.

Maggie: Well, I guess they were not really jerks. It's just that I would have enjoyed it more if the whole group were cohesive.

Nurse: Tell me what else did not go well last time.

Maggie: I wish I could have had more time myself. I really wanted to open up more and get Tina's perspective on my own problems. She helped me a lot, and several times I just wanted to block the other group members out so Tina and I could continue with my issue until I felt satisfied. I guess that's it. The bad thing about the group was that I had problems with some of the other members and that I did not get enough time for myself.

Nurse: Sounds like there is a common thread here, with respect to the negative aspects of the group. Can you describe a way to get around the group therapy problems of annoying group members and not enough time to focus on your own issues?

Maggie: No.

Nurse: What about individual therapy? How do you think individual counseling with Tina would work for you?

Maggie: I never thought of it. Do you think she will do it? I would love to work with her.

Nurse: I am sure Tina would do it. I am also sure you will be more successful with Tina than with group therapy. You are very introspective and observant. Those are good qualities to have in therapy.

Resolution

The key to the success of this interview was effective communication. During the interview process, Maggie sent numerous messages. Some of these messages were verbal and some were nonverbal. Some of the messages Maggie sent conflicted with each other and with her beliefs or values. You also needed to gain more information than Maggie voluntarily offered. Note how the clues to the case study resolution through effective communication are highlighted in the bold text that lies in parentheses.

continued on next page

Resolution Process

Nurse: Hello, Mrs. Montgomery. (**Affirmation – by showing respect**) I am glad you came in today.

Maggie: Oh, you can just call me Maggie. No need to be so formal.

Nurse: OK, Maggie. Have a seat. I can see by looking at your file that you participated in our group therapy program a couple of years ago. Can you explain how it went? (**Open-ended question – better than asking something such as, "Did it go well?"**

Maggie: It went very well. I lost over 50 pounds. I also learned a lot about exercise and nutrition. I really liked the psychologist who ran the group. She was so inspiring. (**Maggie relaxes, smiles, and points to herself when she says, "I lost over 50 pounds." The nonverbal messages show pride.**)

Nurse: Wow! That's commendable! Fifty pounds is a lot of weight. You must be proud of yourself. (**Affirmation – reaffirming that Maggie has the right to feel proud, even though she has returned to the clinic because of relapse, and validating the emotion that was expressed nonverbally by Maggie**)

Maggie: Yeah, but I gained it all back again. That's why I've returned. I am nothing but a failure. I am never going to lose this weight and keep it off. It's hopeless.

Nurse: Maggie, I know you may feel discouraged, (**Affirmation**) but you are not a failure. You lost 50 pounds and you learned a lot about being healthy (**Gentle confrontation – Maggie's statements demonstrated all-or-nothing thinking, which is a thinking distortion.**) Plus, you returned to the clinic, which means there must be some hope inside that you can overcome your weight problem. (**Continued confrontation with some interpreting of the subconscious message of hope that was communicated by Maggie's return to the clinic**)

Maggie: I guess I am not a total failure, but it sure is discouraging.

Nurse: I am sure it is. (**Affirmation**) Let's talk in more detail about your experiences last time. What do you think went well for you in the group therapy? (**Probing – the goal is to gather information as to Maggie's perception of the positive aspects of her previous attempt. This perspective about what went well will help plan for the upcoming attempt.**)

Maggie: Well, I liked the monitoring chart I used for recording my exercise. Recording the minutes and distance I walked helped me measure my progress toward my goal. I also liked the fact that I made my goal of walking 500 miles. Oh, and I definitely liked the reward I got for reaching my goal.

Nurse: So, you liked the process of monitoring your exercise in a way that could document your progress toward a goal, and rewarding yourself for reaching that goal. Is that correct? (Maggie nods her head yes.) (**Paraphrasing – note how a closed-ended question was used here appropriately just to confirm that the nurse's paraphrasing was correct.**) What else went well? (**Open-ended question to probe for more information; better than asking, "Was there anything else that went well?"**)

Maggie: Like I said. I really loved Tina, the psychologist. She just had a way of getting me excited about becoming healthy. Each week she taught us something new, and we were always learning about what's going on inside ourselves. And the behavior assignments she gave us each week seemed to be exactly what I needed.

Nurse: Sounds like you liked Tina because she connected with you in a way that motivated you to find solutions to your individual behavioral issues. Is that right? (Maggie nods her head yes.) (**Paraphrasing and interpretation – Paraphrasing was used first, with a request for confirmation of the interpretation of Maggie's message.**) What else can you identify that went well in your last weight loss attempt? (**Open-ended question**)

continued on next page

Maggie: Nothing really.

Nurse: OK, then can you tell me about what did not go well last time? (**Open-ended question, probing**)

Maggie: Well, I almost don't want to tell you because you will think I am being critical. (**Maggie crosses her legs and folds her arms across her chest – a nonverbal sign that relays the message of withdrawal or distrust.**)

Nurse: Maggie, I will stop you if I feel your criticism is destructive, but I really want to know how you feel. Only you can tell me that. (**Openness demonstrated, with some affirmation**)

Maggie: OK, the problem was some of the group members. A couple of them were real jerks. This one lady just would not stop talking. She dominated the whole group. Then there was this other chick, who really didn't participate at all. She never spoke and did not do the behavioral assignments we had each week.

Nurse: So, the problem was some of the group members. A couple of them were real jerks. (**Reiteration – labeling group members as "jerks" is pretty harsh. Even though the behavior of other group members was not to Maggie's liking, using reiteration may help Maggie soften her critique and look further inside to see what else was negative about the group.**)

Maggie: Well, I guess they were not really jerks. It's just that I would have enjoyed it more if the whole group were cohesive.

Nurse: Tell me what else did not go well last time. (**Open-end question; better than asking, "Anything else?"**)

Maggie: I wish I could have had more time myself. I really wanted to open up more and get Tina's perspective on my own problems. She helped me a lot, and several times I just wanted to block the other group members out so Tina and I could continue with my issue until I felt satisfied. I guess that's it. The bad thing about the group was that I had problems with some of the other members, and that I did not get enough time for myself.

Nurse: Sounds like there is a common thread here, with respect to the negative aspects of the group. Can you describe a way to get around the group therapy problems of annoying group members and not enough time to focus on your own issues? (**Paraphrasing that is followed up with a probing question**)

Maggie: No. (**In this case the previous question ended up being closed-ended. If the answer was yes, then a description of the solution would be required. The "no" answer redirects the nurse.**)

Nurse: What about individual therapy? How do you think individual counseling with Tina would work for you? (**Open-ended question**)

Maggie: I never thought of it. Do you think she will do it? I would love to work with her.

Nurse: I am sure Tina would do it. I am also sure you will be more successful with Tina than with group therapy. You are very introspective and observant. Those are good qualities to have in therapy. (**Affirmation – builds self-efficacy and is sincere**)

Case Study 8-2: Using Motivational Interviewing

Now let's take the scenario we saw in Case Study 8-1, and apply the techniques of motivational interviewing.

You are a nurse who works for a university hospital that provides a number of bariatric services. Today you will be meeting with Maggie Montgomery, who lost more than 50 pounds 2 years ago, but has regained the lost weight. The purpose of your meeting is to interview Maggie about coming back into the weight loss program. Because the hospital provides various weight loss services, you will need to determine which will be most appropriate for Maggie. The explanation and discussion of motivational technique used is in parentheses

Scenario

Nurse: OK, Maggie. Have a seat. I can see by looking at your file that you participated in our group therapy program a couple of years ago and lost 50 pounds. That's really great! What would you like to talk about today? (**Agenda setting, ensuring that Maggie is engaged in the process**)

Maggie: Well, as you can see, I have gained the weight back. I'd really like to talk about how I did that. I feel like such a failure. I am never going to lose this weight and keep it off. It's hopeless.

Nurse: It sounds like you are feeling really discouraged about your weight gain (**Reflective listening**)

Maggie: Yes, I am. But I did lose more than 50 pounds. I also learned a lot about exercise and nutrition. And I really liked the psychologist who ran the group. She was so inspiring. I just don't think I can do it again. (**Maggie has ambivalence about trying to lose weight again. Despite her previous success she feels like she won't succeed.**)

Nurse: So you feel that there isn't any point in trying the program again? (**Negative reverse statement, repeating Maggie's words in a neutral manner**)

Maggie: Well, I guess if I really felt that way I wouldn't have come in today.

Nurse: Maggie on a scale of 0 to 10, with 10 being the highest, how important is it for you to lose the weight you have regained. (**Use of the 0 to 10 scale to elicit readiness to change**)

Maggie: Oh, it is absolutely a 10. I have started to have health issues again, and my joints are really bothering me. I felt so much better when I was at the lower weight.

Nurse: Alright, so can we discuss what you found most helpful with your successful experience? (**Asking permission to transition to the new topic, making sure that Maggie is still engaged in the discussion**)

Maggie: Sure, there were two things, really. I especially liked the monitoring chart I used for recording my exercise. Recording the minutes and distance I walked helped me measure my progress toward my goal. I also liked the fact that I made my goal of walking 500 miles. Oh, and I definitely liked the reward I got for reaching my goal.

Nurse: So, you liked the process of monitoring your exercise in a way that could document your progress toward a goal, and rewarding yourself for reaching that goal. (**Reflective listening**) What else went well?

Maggie: I really loved Tina, the psychologist. She just had a way of getting me excited about becoming healthy. Each week she taught us something new, and we were always learning about what's going on inside ourselves. And the behavior assignments she gave us each week seemed to be exactly what I needed.

Nurse: It sounds like you and Tina connected in a way that was very helpful (**Reflective listening**).

Maggie: Yes, it really was.

continued on next page

Nurse: Maggie, it's clear that you want to lose the weight, and you have identified two behaviors that helped you last time. Let's take the first one, monitoring your exercise and rewarding yourself for reaching your goal. On a scale of 0 to 10, with 10 being the highest, how confident are you that you could resume this activity? **(Use of the 0 to 10 scale to identify Maggie's confidence in her ability to change her behavior)**

Maggie: Hmm, well I'd say about a 9. I can do that easily.

Nurse: That's great. So how about discussing what type of exercise works best for you? **(Asking permission to move the agenda on to the specifics of the behavior change)**

Maggie: Sure, well I find I can get bored with the same thing all the time. And I don't really remember exactly what I should start with…what do you think?

Nurse: Well, you may have heard that the most recent research recommends 30 minutes a day of moderate activity, which includes brisk walking; however, many of my patients start out with a modified version of 15 minutes a day. They find it manageable to fit in the time, and it doesn't require a lot of preparation, but what's important to me is what you think might work for you. **(Allowing patient to interpret information, reject or accept it)**

Maggie: I can do that. I still have a treadmill in my basement. I will start with 15 minutes a day and add 5 minutes every week. How does that sound?

Nurse: It sounds like a plan. Now on a scale of 0 to 10, how confident are you that you will do your planned exercise? **(0 to 10 scale for confidence in change behavior)**

Maggie: 11! (Laughing)

Nurse: (Laughing with Maggie) OK, well we will check your progress on that at our next visit. You also mentioned Tina's support group activities. Can we talk about getting you back into it again? **(Asking permission to change to the second topic)**

Maggie: OK, I guess. **(This is a less than enthusiastic response, so the nurse decides to use the same tool to determine Maggie's readiness for change in this area is)**

Nurse: On a scale of 0 to 10, how important is it for you to attend the therapy group that Tina runs?

Maggie: I'd have to say a 5. I mean I liked what I learned in the group, and it was very helpful.

Nurse: That's interesting. You are not a 1, so it sounds like you found the group beneficial, but you're not a 10 on the scale. What would it take you to get to a 10? **(Exploring the response on a scale number helps to identify barriers to the behavior change as well as strengths.)**

Maggie: Yes, the information presented was beneficial, but the problem was some of the group members. A couple of them were real jerks. This one lady just would not stop talking. She dominated the whole group. Then there was this other chick, who really didn't participate at all. She never spoke and did not do the behavioral assignments we had each week.

Nurse: So, the problem was some of the group members. A couple of them were real jerks. **(Reflective listening)**

Maggie: Well, I guess they were not really jerks. It's just that I would have enjoyed it more if the whole group were cohesive.

Nurse: What else would make the experience a "10"? **(Use of 0 to 10 scale)**

Maggie: I wish I could have had more time myself. I really wanted to open up more and get Tina's perspective on my own problems. She helped me a lot, and several times I just wanted to block the other group members out so Tina and I could continue with my issue until I felt satisfied. I guess that's it. The bad thing about the group was that I had problems with some of the other members, and that I did not get enough time for myself.

continued on next page

Nurse: Sounds like there is a common thread here, with respect to the negative aspects of the group. In what ways might we get around the group therapy problems of annoying group members and not enough time to focus on your own issues? (**Rolling with resistance and patient-generated solutions**)

Maggie: I'm not sure.

Nurse: Some of my patients have found that individual therapy is helpful? How do you think individual counseling with Tina would work for you? (**Allowing patient to interpret information**)

Maggie: I never thought of it. Do you think she will do it? I would love to work with her.

Nurse: Tina does offer individual counseling as well as the groups. It sounds like this might be a good plan for you. Now on a scale of 0 to 10, how confident…?

Maggie: (Interrupting the nurse, laughing) I am on to this 0 to 10 thing. I am a number 8 if I can try counseling with Tina on an individual basis.

Nurse: (laughing) That's the spirit!

As you can see, there are parallels in this method, but also differences. The focus of both methods is on patient-centered communication, and practice of these techniques will make them easier and more comfortable to use in the clinical setting.

SUMMARY

The health professional can understand how patients' internal and external environments affect their behaviors only through effective communication. Effective communication occurs when the health professional knows how to interpret messages sent by the patient and how to respond effectively. True listening is not just hearing words, it is receiving and understanding the message, and the root of the message is often sent non-verbally. Openness is the most important listening skill because it shows a willingness to receive communication and to allow others to influence your perception. Methods for demonstrating listening when communicating include affirmation, confrontation, reiteration, paraphrasing, interpreting, and probing. The most common functions of non-verbal communication are to augment the meaning of words, to negate the meaning of words, and to express emotion. Communication strategies are simply tools that help enhance the personal relationship between the professional and patient. That relationship is the most important factor in successful obesity counseling.

EXAM QUESTIONS

CHAPTER 8
Questions 29-33

Note: Choose the one option that BEST answers each question.

29. The most important skill a health professional can develop in order to guide the obese patient in the behavior change process is the skill of

    a. empathy.

    b. compassion.

    c. emotional support.

    d. listening.

30. Openness in communication is described as

    a. the willingness to receive communication from others that will affect your perception.

    b. being honest and open about all issues on the table.

    c. opening up for discussion things that are difficult to talk about.

    d. talking until you have covered everything you need to say.

31. The best "probing" questions a professional can ask a patient are those that

    a. delve deep into the patient's psyche.

    b. require the patient to reveal intimate feelings.

    c. are nonjudgmental and are open-ended.

    d. put the patient on the spot, so he cannot deny the truth.

32. In approaching a patient to discuss weight issues, it is important to

    a. avoid words such as obesity or fatness in the discussion.

    b. use all methods to convince the patient of the need to lose weight.

    c. set goals for the patient to achieve.

    d. leave it up to the patient to raise the issue when ready.

33. A core principle for motivational interviewing is that

    a. it provides firm guidelines for patients to follow.

    b. the individual is more likely to act upon that which they voice.

    c. confrontation is a key element in establishing goals.

    d. as a professional, the provider sets the agenda for sessions.

REFERENCES

Bessesen, D. & Stuht, J. (2005). CORE tools and patient information. *Obesity Management, 1*(8), 168-70.

Curry K.R. & Jaffe, A. (1998). *Nutrition counseling and communication skills.* Philadelphia, PA: W. B. Saunders Company.

Gable, J. (2007). *Counseling skills for dietitians* (2nd ed.). Oxford, UK: Blackwell Publishing, Ltd.

Givens, D.B. (2008). *The nonverbal dictionary of gestures, signs and body language cues.* Spokane, WA: Center for Nonverbal Studies Press.

Knapp, H. (2007). *Therapeutic communication: Developing professional skills.* Los Angeles: Sage Publications.

Resnicow, K. & Blackburn, D. (2005). Motivational interviewing in medical settings. *Obesity Management, 1*(8), 155-9.

Wadden, T.A. & Tsai, A.G. (2005). Weight management in primary care: Can we talk? *Obesity Management, 1*(1), 9-14.

CHAPTER 9

DIETARY MODIFICATION

CHAPTER OBJECTIVE

After completing this chapter the learner will be able to identify sound approaches to dietary modification.

LEARNING OBJECTIVES

After completing this chapter, the learner will be able to

1. discuss common methods used to reduce daily caloric intake.

2. list the components and amounts of a balanced dietary diet modification program.

3. describe the contribution of commercially available diet programs.

4. identify specific health risks that need to be monitored more closely during dietary modification weight loss programs.

INTRODUCTION

The first goal of weight management is to decrease total calorie intake. This approach may be tailored to achieve weight maintenance, moderate weight loss, or aggressive weight loss. For most patients, a gradual weight loss is appropriate. According to the Expert Panel on the Identification, Evaluation, and Treatment of Overweight and Obesity in Adults (2002), the recommended rate of weight loss is 10% of body weight over a 6-month period, with a 1- to 2-lb loss per week. Setting realistic expectations helps reduce the risk of failure, but this technique is often difficult because many obesity sufferers are looking for the "quick fix." The diet modification should start with deciding on realistic mutual goals with the individual.

There have been numerous kinds of diets over the years in clinical practice and commercial settings. These diets can be categorized into two types: those that focus on reducing caloric intake and those that focus on changing diet composition. Diets that only restrict caloric intake try to disrupt the energy balance by reducing the total amount of calories consumed. Diets that change diet composition focus on restricting the intake of fat and/or carbohydrate as an indirect method of reducing total amount of calories consumed. The most success is achieved by addressing both of these components.

CALORIC RESTRICTION

Low-Calorie Diets

Most people attempting to lose weight have experimented with some form of LCD. The conventional LCD consists of a diet restricted to 1,200 kcal/day. This level of energy intake produces an unequal caloric deficit for each patient, depending upon individual daily consumption. Those with a relatively low baseline energy intake may sense only a slight level of dietary decrease with an LCD, whereas those with a high baseline intake may feel severely deprived. For example, a patient with a daily intake of 2,000 kcal/day will only reduce their intake by 40% if placed on a conventional LCD of 1,200 kcal/day, whereas a patient with a baseline intake of 3,000 kcal/day will have a 60% reduction. The predicted weight loss on a LCD will vary, depending on how much the restricted intake differs from the intake necessary for body energy balance.

More commonly, an approach to reducing the caloric intake by a set amount of 500 to 1,000 kcal/day is used, resulting in a total caloric intake of 800 to 1,500 kcal/day. The goal at this level is a 1- to 2-lb weight loss per week. A person with a baseline intake of 2,000 kcal/day will then consume 1,500 kcal/day on the LCD, whereas the person with a baseline intake of 3,000 kcal/day will consume 2,500 kcal/day. Under these conditions, the anticipated weight loss for each patient will be the same. In this case, 1 lb per week because 1 lb of fat is equivalent to 3,500 kcal.

LCD are probably the safest of all the energy restricted diets, because it is thought that all essential vitamins and minerals can still be obtained through a 1,200 kcal diet, though a supplement is typically recommended. Balance and variety of food intake can be maintained with a 1,200 kcal diet, and no serious side effects or health risks have been associated with LCD.

Very-low-calorie Diets

VLCDs were designed to produce a faster rate of weight loss than that seen with LCDs. The energy content of a VLCD is less than 800 kcal/day or less. One form of the VLCD that is popular is the protein-sparing-modified fast, or the liquid protein diet. The caloric content of this type of VLCD is about 450 kcal/day. The energy content of the diet is made up of protein, in hopes that a small amount of dietary protein will reduce body protein and potassium losses seen with total fasting.

Indiscriminate use of VLCD is not recommended because of health risks associated with this type of diet. In the 1970s, several deaths caused by abnormal heart rhythms were seen. The most common complication seen currently with the VLCD is cholelithiasis, induced by rapid weight loss (Plodkowski & St. Jeor, 2003). The VLCD should only be implemented under medical supervision, so that electrolyte abnormalities and other deficiencies such as anemia can be closely monitored. Because of the health risks, VLCDs are only to be prescribed for a short period of time, usually less than 16 weeks (Plodkowski & St. Jeor, 2003).

One of the biggest problems with a VLCD is compliance. A review of six randomized controlled trials for VLCD reported that dropout rates ranged from 15% to 40% (Tsai & Wadden, 2006). The liquid protein diet or protein-sparing modified fast is not very palatable, and patients never reach the point of fullness or satisfaction. Thus, after weeks of no real food, the temptation to eat or the desire to feel satisfied often overrides the motivation to continue dieting.

Portion Control

Several popular diets have been developed using portion-controlled caloric restrictions. Previous chapters have discussed the effects of increased portions on the rate of weight gain in this country. However, portion control awareness, along with balanced diet composition, have also been shown to be effective in reducing weight (Heber, 2002). This weight loss can be achieved with reduced portions of the individual's normal diets or with meal replacements. Meal replacements tend to provide more balanced diet composition than personal diet selection may provide. Additionally, meal replacements are often found to be more effective because self monitoring/modification of diet portions tends to significantly underestimate actual caloric intake. New technology has reduced this problem, because web-based programs that instantly calculate calorie intake and programs for personal handheld devices are readily available (Plodkowski & St. Jeor, 2002). Web programs that use this type of approach are now being widely marketed.

DIET COMPOSITION

The second goal of a dietary weight reduction addresses diet composition. There are many different approaches to this goal, and controversy continues about which macronutrient balance provides the best effects (Plodkowski & St. Jeor, 2002). Depending on the individual's health risks and comorbidities, the diet plan may require additional modification.

Low-fat Diets

The 1990s was the decade of dietary fat phobia. More than two decades of research and clinical trials surrounding dietary fat and cardiovascular disease led to the consensus that dietary fat was a health hazard. Obesity research from the late 1980s and early 1990s also discouraged people from eating fat. Studies in animals and humans suggested that a high-fat diet could produce obesity even without overeating. At the same time, exercise scientists contended that exercise endurance was best supported by a low-fat or high-carbohydrate diet. Thus, it seems like all factions of health and disease saw dietary fat as the cause of all our health problems. Hundreds of commercially available products that were either low-fat or nonfat hit the market in the 1990s advertised as weight-loss aids.

There is no fixed definition for a low-fat diet. However, the typical low-fat diet is in reality an LCD, consisting of 1,200 to 1,700 kcal. The fat content of a low-fat diet is generally 10% to 15% of the total energy value. This means for a 1,500 kcal diet, the fat content would be equivalent to 150 to 225 kcal, or 16 to 25 grams of fat per day (1

gram of fat is equivalent to approximately 9 kcal). A 15% diet may not appear that restrictive, especially if the caloric content is 1,500 kcal. Yet, a closer look reveals that a 15% fat diet can be quite restrictive for the average American.

The average American diet contains from 32% to 36% dietary fat. Let's assume that an overweight woman is consuming 2,000 kcal per day, of which 35% is dietary fat. This means that she is consuming 78 grams of fat each day (0.15 x 2,000 kcal = 700 kcal fat @ 9 kcal/gram, fat = 78 grams). If she were to consume a 1,500 kcal diet of 15% fat, her dietary fat intake would be 25 grams, and she would be reducing the amount of fat in her diet by 53 grams. This is a reduction in dietary fat of about two-thirds, even though her energy intake is only reduced by one fourth.

Another way to look at it is to examine how much fat is in some typical foods people eat. Table 9-1 shows how much fat is contained in some foods we eat daily. Accordingly, if the woman in the example were to eat two slices of toast for breakfast, with a pat of butter on each, she would already have reached her dietary fat allotment for the day. If she were to eat a peanut butter sandwich and cup of whole milk, she would reach her fat limit for the day. If the woman were to eat a quarter pound hamburger (without condiments), she would surpass her fat allotment for the day. Even if a person were to consume a healthy diet of fruits, vegetables, and grains; that person would be eating a significant amount of fat. Vegetables contain vegetable oils and breads and cereals contain a small amount of oil. So, one can see that maintaining a diet of 10% to 15% fat can be difficult.

One of the problems with low-fat diets is that they are not very palatable. Fat gives texture and flavor to our food. Taste tests show that people prefer foods that are high in fat and sugar over foods that are low in fat and sugar. When the bulk of the fat is removed from the diet, it loses a lot of flavor. Many food producers try to adjust for the loss in

TABLE 9-1: FAT CONTENT IN COMMON FOODS

Food	Serving Size	Fat per Serving (g)
Bread	Slice	1.0
Butter	1 pat (1 tablespoon)	11.5
Cheddar cheese	1 ounce	9.0
Corn oil	1 tablespoon	14.0
Cream cheese	1 ounce	0.0
Hamburger	Quarter pounder	28.5
Ice Cream	1 cup	12.0
Italian salad dressing	2 tablespoons	8.0
Milk (whole)	1 cup	8.0
Mayonnaise	1 tablespoon	9.0
Peanut butter	2 tablespoons	16.0
Potato chips	1 ounce	10.0

flavor of a low-fat food by increasing its sugar content. A word of caution should be shared with all those who seek low-fat foods – read the food label. Reduced fat, low-fat, or nonfat terms do not necessarily mean low calorie.

Comparing the calorie value of a serving of a low-fat food item to the regular variety of the same item will reveal whether or not the low-fat item is also low-calorie. Another comparison can be made by matching the amount of sugar in the low-fat version to the regular version of a food. If the low-fat version has a lot more sugar, you can assume that the food producer added sugar to the low-fat version to enhance its taste.

People who cannot adjust to a diet containing 10% to 15% fat can often maintain a diet consisting of 20% to 25% fat. If the woman in the example above were to maintain the 1,500 kcal diet, but at 25% fat rather than 15% fat, she would be allowed to consume 42 grams of fat a day instead of 25. Even small amounts of fat that are taken out of the diet will increase weight loss and improve health. Simple changes in behavior, such as drinking skim milk or low-fat milk rather than whole milk will help.

Low-fat diets do produce positive benefits. Reducing dietary fat content will decrease blood lipid levels and reduce the risk of cardiovascular disease in individuals who are obese, even in the absence of significant weight loss. Moreover, most low-fat diets have more dietary fiber than their high-fat counterparts. Increasing dietary fiber can prevent cardiovascular disease and cancer while assisting in weight loss. These health benefits of a low-fat diet completely overshadow any health risks. However, one must not completely eliminate fat from the diet. A minimal amount of dietary fat is necessary to sustain good health.

A healthy diet must contain essential fats. Essential fats are those fats that must be consumed because the body cannot make them. There are two types of essential fats, linoleic acids (omega-6 fatty acids) and linolenic acids (omega-3 fatty acids). These essential fats can be found in foods such as canola oil, sunflower seeds, walnuts, leafy vegetables, fish, shellfish, sesame seeds, avocados, and flaxseed or linseed oil. People on a low-fat diet must concern themselves with getting the essential fats. A good way to do this is to eat fish, nuts, and leafy green salads.

There is great controversy as to whether low-fat diets, in and of themselves, can produce substantial weight loss. Replacement of fat calories with the same number of carbohydrate and/or protein calories will reduce the amount of fat in the diet, but will probably not induce a significant amount of weight loss. People who are successful at weight loss on a low-fat diet are those people who initially consume a high-fat diet and then reduce their energy intake along with their dietary fat intake. The long-term effectiveness of low-fat diets on obesity has not been studied sufficiently to make any definite conclusions.

Low-carbohydrate/High-protein Diets

Low-carbohydrate/high-protein diets first became popular in the 1960s and 1970s. These diets eliminate or severely restrict the consumption of fruits, vegetables, beans, and grains, while consumption of meat, poultry, fish, nuts, seeds, and eggs is unrestricted. The high-protein content of the low-carbohydrate/high-protein diet is claimed to prevent muscle breakdown and the loss of lean body mass. The high-fat content of this type of diet is claimed to place a person in the ketogenic state, which suppresses appetite. Body weight loss is rapid during the first week or two on the low-carbohydrate/high-protein diet, because the carbohydrate restriction causes the body to lose a lot of water as body carbohydrate stores are depleted. However, much of this lost weight is regained when the person starts consuming carbohydrates again.

The most popular of the low-carbohydrate/high-fat diets is the Atkins diet. This diet was developed by Dr. Robert Atkins in the early 1970s following Dr. Atkins, own struggle with weight following his medical school training. Dr. Atkins popularized his diet in a series of books, starting with *Dr. Atkins' Diet Revolution,* published in 1972. His diet lost popularity during the 1980s and 1990s, but then became a national obsession after his revised book, *Dr. Atkins' New Diet Revolution,* was published in 2001. The Atkins diet became so popular that restaurant menus began offering entrees without carbohydrates. Cheeseburgers were offered without the bun, and restaurant menus highlighted certain menu items with icons stating "Atkins Friendly."

Several health risks are associated with low-carbohydrate/high-protein diets. A diet that is high in animal protein and low in fiber can raise cholesterol levels, putting the person at higher risk for cardiovascular disease. Cancer risk increases when fruits, vegetables, whole grains and beans are eliminated from the diet. Excess protein consumption can place a person at risk for developing kidney stones and osteoporosis. Although all of these health risks seem likely with a low-carbohydrate/high-protein diet, there are no long-term weight-loss studies to document that health is jeopardized on this type of diet. The American Heart Association has issued a statement that although high protein diets may not be harmful to most healthy people in the short term, they are not proven to be effective in the longer term, and can produce an overall unhealthy diet (St. Jeor et al., 2001).

Balanced Deficit Diet

In recent years, a more realistic approach to diet composition has evolved. After the caloric restriction recommendation has been decided, attention is turned to how to achieve the diet modification goal in a balanced manner. This approach more closely follows the average diet choices of adults in the United States. The National Cholesterol Education Program developed the Adult Treatment Panel III guidelines, which included a therapeutic lifestyle changes diet (2001). This approach recommends the following diet composition:

- Fat intake is 25% to 35% of total calories per day.
  - Saturated fat less than 7%
  - Polyunsaturated fat up to 10%
  - Monounsaturated fat up to 20%
- Carbohydrates are 50% to 60% of total calories.
- Protein is approximately 15% of total calories.
- Daily cholesterol intake is less than 200 mg/day.
- Have 20 to 30 grams of fiber per day.

A key component of the balanced diet is to ensure that any recommendations are in keeping with the comorbidities that the individual has. Diets low in saturated fats help reduce low-density lipoprotein cholesterol levels, thus this type of fat should be limited. Diets high in carbohydrate can raise serum triglycerides. The total amount of carbohydrates is the most important determinant of blood glucose levels, rather than the type of carbohydrate, as previously thought (Plodkowski & St. Jeor, 2003). The Diet and Lifestyle Guidelines from the American Heart Association (Lichtenstein et al., 2006) give specific recommendations in how to achieve these goals:

- Balance caloric intake and physical activity to achieve and maintain a healthy body weight.

- Consume a diet rich in vegetables and fruits.

- Choose whole-grain, high-fiber foods.

- Consume fish, especially oily fish, at least twice per week.

- Limit intake of saturated fat to 7% of energy, trans fat to 1% of energy, and cholesterol to less than 300 mg/day by

    - choosing lean meats and vegetable alternatives,

    - consuming fat-free (skim) or low-fat (1% fat) dairy products

    - minimizing intake of partially hydrogenated fats

- Minimize intake of beverages and foods with added sugars.

- Choose and prepare foods with little or no salt.

- If you consume alcohol, do so in moderation.

- When you eat food prepared outside of the home, follow these Diet and Lifestyle Recommendations.

The goal of the American Heart Association in developing the guidelines was not just to provide guidelines for individuals with heart health risks, but to provide guidelines for all individuals in order to prevent development of increased health risks. The guidelines are appropriate for children older than the age of 2 and all adults (Lichtenstein et al., 2006). Table 9-2 outlines practical tips on implementing the American Heart Association guidelines.

Many tools now exist to assist in monitoring dietary composition. The National Heart, Lung and Blood Institute's Obesity Education Web site provides resources to help patients and professionals. The Aim for A Healthy Weight project has an online menu planner, a body mass index calculator, and other tools. Printed materials geared toward assisting individuals to make lifestyle changes can be downloaded or purchased. The current Web site is: http://www.nhlbi.nih.gov/health/public/heart/obesity/lose_wt/index.htm

Commercial Weight Loss Programs

The weight loss industry is big business in the United States. It is estimated that Americans spend between $40 and $50 billion dollars each year on commercial weight loss products and programs. Advertising claims made by commercial weight loss programs are monitored by the Federal Trade Commission (FTC), but the industry is not required to submit any data on safety or efficacy of their programs. The FTC only steps in when it suspects that companies are making false or misleading claims. Several years ago, the FTC convened a panel of experts to make recommendations on how the public could become better informed about commercial weight loss programs and avoid deception in the commercial industry. The panel recommended that commercial weight loss programs and service providers disclose information about four aspects of their programs and services (Partnership for Healthy Weight Management, 2008). These four aspects are:

- a description of the key components of the program or service and what they entail,

- qualifications of the staff or provider,

- all costs associated with the program or service, including any hidden costs or continuing fees, and

- risks associated with the treatment.

TABLE 9-2: PRACTICAL TIPS TO IMPLEMENT THE 2006 AMERICAN HEART ASSOCIATION DIET AND LIFESTYLE RECOMMENDATIONS

Lifestyle
- Know your caloric needs to achieve and maintain a healthy weight.
- Know the calorie content of the foods and beverages you consume.
- Track your weight, physical activity, and calorie intake.
- Prepare and eat smaller portions.
- Track and, when possible, decrease screen time (e.g., watching television, surfing the Web, playing computer games).
- Incorporate physical movement into habitual activities.
- Do not smoke or use tobacco products.
- If you consume alcohol, do so in moderation (equivalent of no more than one drink in women or two drinks in men per day).

Food choices and preparation
- Use the nutrition facts panel and ingredients list when choosing foods to buy.
- Eat fresh, frozen, and canned vegetables and fruits without high-calorie sauces and added salt and sugars.
- Replace high-calorie foods with fruits and vegetables.
- Increase fiber intake by eating beans (legumes), whole-grain products, fruits, and vegetables.
- Use liquid vegetable oils in place of solid fats.
- Limit beverages and foods high in added sugars. Common forms of added sugars are sucrose, glucose, fructose, maltose, dextrose, corn syrups, concentrated fruit juice, and honey.
- Choose foods made with whole grains. Common forms of whole grains are whole wheat, oats/oatmeal, rye, barley, corn, popcorn, brown rice, wild rice, buckwheat, triticale, bulgur (cracked wheat), millet, quinoa, and sorghum.
- Cut back on pastries and high-calorie bakery products (e.g., muffins, doughnuts).
- Select milk and dairy products that are fat free or low fat.
- Reduce salt intake by
    - comparing the sodium content of similar products (e.g., different brands of tomato sauce) and choosing products with less salt;
    - choosing versions of processed foods, including cereals and baked goods, that are reduced in salt; and
    - limiting condiments (e.g., soy sauce, ketchup).
- Use lean cuts of meat and remove skin from poultry before eating.
- Limit processed meats that are high in saturated fat and sodium.
- Grill, bake, or broil fish, meat, and poultry.
- Incorporate vegetable-based meat substitutes into favorite recipes.
- Encourage the consumption of whole vegetables and fruits in place of juices.

Note. From "Diet and Lifestyle Recommendations Revision 2006: A Scientific Statement From the American Heart Association Nutrition Committee," by A.H. Lichtenstein et al.. Reprinted with permission of the American Heart Association. *Circulation, 2006;114*:82-96. ©2006 American Heart Association, Inc. Retrieved September 24, 2009, from http://circ.aha.journals.org/content/full/114/1/82#TBL3

The FTC hopes that the commercial weight loss industry will voluntarily subscribe to these guidelines so that future legislation concerning product and service disclosure will not be necessary.

In the early 1990s, the National Institutes of Health and the Food and Drug Administration requested data from the weight loss industry about the effectiveness of commercial programs for people with various degrees of obesity. Information was received from only two nonmedical programs and two medically-supervised programs. The data from the nonmedical programs were fraught with design problems, poor response rates to surveys, high dropout rates, and inadequate follow-up (Hyman, Sempos, Saltsman, & Glinsmann, 1993). The data were inadequate to draw any conclusions. Data from the medically-supervised programs showed that physician-directed VLCD programs reduced disease risk and assisted with weight loss, but further data were deemed necessary to draw substantial conclusions. Furthermore, the data provided were not always representative of the commercial services provided to the public (Hyman et al., 1993).

A review of the major commercial weight loss programs in the United States shows that not much has changed since the early 1990s (Tsai & Wadden, 2005). The review included any commercial program available in the United States for which there were published, objective, scientific efficacy data. Only 108 studies were found, but most of those were deleted from review because of incomplete data, inadequate follow-up, and insufficient reporting. Only 10 studies were ultimately reviewed.

Weight Watchers was the only nonmedical program in the United States that published data from a clinical trial. Weight Watchers conducted two clinical trials that showed clients losing about 5% of initial weight over 3 to 6 months (Tsai & Wadden, 2005). In one trial, 3% of initial weight loss was maintained after 2 years. Attrition rate on Weight Watchers is reported to be about 25%.

Optifast and Health Management Resources were the only medically-supervised programs to be reviewed (Tsai & Wadden, 2005). Studies showed that those persons who complete the comprehensive program can expect to lose 15% to 25% of initial weight in 3 to 6 months. However, these people gradually regain weight to where at 4 years after intervention, their net weight loss amounts to only 5% of their original body weight. However, these data represent the best case scenario, because they do not include the substantial percentage of persons who did not complete treatment or declined to participate in follow-up assessments (Tsai & Wadden, 2005).

In summary, although commercial program successes are highly advertised, there is little research to support many of their claims. They do often provide structure, and when used within the previously discussed parameters of diet modification, can be useful tools for some individuals. These benefits should be weighed against the costs to the individual and other resources that are available.

Case Study 9-1 provides an example of applying dietary modification guidelines.

MONITORING SPECIFIC HEALTH RISKS DURING DIETARY CHANGE AND WEIGHT LOSS

Whether or not the weight loss program is being medically managed, the risk profile of the

Case Study 9-1: Applying Dietary Modification Guidelines

You are a nurse who works for a family doctor in a small country town. In addition to your responsibilities as nurse, you are the business manager for the office and handle all patient consulting and education. Joan is an obese patient for whom the doctor has recommended weight loss. Joan has a body mass index of 33, and has been diagnosed with metabolic syndrome.

You are assigned to help her get started on a program that will help her lose weight. There are no commercial weight loss programs in town, but the town has a community recreation center. The recreation center employs two personal trainers. You met with Joan 2 weeks ago and she performed a 3-day dietary record of her eating. You analyzed her diet and are ready to meet with her about different diet options for losing weight. What type of diet can you suggest for Joan?

continued on next page

Intervention/Solution

A summary of Joan's diet analysis is listed below. There are several diet options that can be used to help Joan lose weight. Your explanation of the different options for Joan is also given below.

Daily caloric intake		2,500 kcal	
Dietary fat	34%	850 kcal	94.4 grams
Dietary protein	12%	300 kcal	75.0 grams
Dietary carbohydrate	54%	1350 kcal	338 grams

What clues from Joan's diet analysis would help you suggest some dieting approaches for her?

Diet Modification Options

Low-calorie Diet (LCD) – Joan's caloric intake is 2,500 kcal per day. If she were placed on an LCD that restricts her intake to 2,000 kcal per day, she should lose 1 lb per week. An alternative LCD would be for Joan to consume 1,500 kcal per day. This amount would be a restriction of 1,000 kcal per day, and should result in a weight loss of 2 lb per week. Joan could still use the food exchange lists and menu planners for this more restrictive LCD.

Very-low-calorie Diet (VLCD) – A more rapid weight loss could be achieved with a VLCD. This type of a diet requires medical supervision and would have to be supplied by a commercial program or a clinical supplier of VLCD food products. The VLCD food products would replace normal foods, and a vitamin/mineral supplement would be given. The diet would last 12 to 16 weeks. In Joan's case, she has metabolic syndrome, characterized by high triglycerides and low high-density lipoprotein levels, as well as increased abdominal circumference. According to the American Heart Association dietary guidelines, very low fat diets should not be used in this setting, and a VLCD is a very low fat diet.

Diet Composition Analysis – Joan's diet is higher in fat than the recommended diet of less than 30% fat. Therefore, Joan could easily transform her diet into a healthier diet while losing weight. Because her diet is now high fat, the fat restriction would not need to be drastic in order for Joan to lose weight. The rate of weight loss would be directly related to the number of calories removed from the diet when fat is removed from the diet. Joan's dietary record shows that, on average, she eats one-fourth pound of regular ground beef per day, 2 cups of whole milk per day, 2 ounces of cheese per day, and one tablespoon of mayonnaise per day (among other things). If Joan switched from eating ground beef that is 75% lean to 90% lean, her fat intake would be reduced by 17 grams and her caloric intake by 153 kcal. If she switched from whole milk to skim milk, she would reduce her fat intake by 16 grams and her caloric intake by 144 kcal. If her cheese intake and mayonnaise were changed to the low-fat variety, she would reduce her intake of fat another 13.5 grams and caloric intake by 122 kcal. These simple changes would amount to a reduction in fat intake of 46.5 grams and a caloric reduction of 419 kcal per day. At this level of consumption, Joan would lose weight at a rate of approximately 1 lb every 8 days. Her diet would contain 2,081 kcal per day, of which 21% would be fat.

Joan's diet is 54% carbohydrate and 12% protein. Her protein intake is on the low side; the recommended is 15% of calories. She could increase her protein intake by eating more vegetables, lean meats, poultry, beans, or fish.

Her carbohydrate intake is about what is recommended. A low-carbohydrate/high-protein diet would be a drastic change in Joan's normal eating patterns, and probably not sustainable. However, if Joan understood all of the possible risks of a low-carbohydrate/high-protein diet, she could be placed on this type of diet, but would need to be medically supervised. In this case, a reduction in her daily caloric intake can be achieved through modification of her dietary fat and portion control of other food choices. The following

continued on next page

Web site from the National Heart, Lung and Blood Institute's Aim for a Healthy Weight can help her plan menus that will meet her dietary needs: http://hp2010.nhlbihin.net/menuplanner/menu.cgi.

If Joan does not have Internet access, written materials are available for download online, or to purchase from the National Heart, Lung and Blood Institute's Health Information Center, 302-592-8573, or email: nhlbiinfo@nhlbi.nih.gov.

Resolution

After discussing the diet recommendations with Joan, you decide that she will follow an LCD with the outlined changes in her daily diet composition. She is excited about using the Web site to track her diet changes, and feels motivated to improve her health status through diet modification.

The key to resolving this case revolves around comparing the analysis of Joan's diet with the weight loss diet alternatives in order to find a program that Joan can adhere to. The best choice is one that allows her to make small but significant changes in her current behavior.

turn back to page 130

patient can change during the process. This change can occur as a result of weight loss or as a result of the dietary changes themselves. In the first 2 weeks, patients will usually lose weight quickly, due to water loss from the reduction in sodium intake and the mobilization of glycogen. After this phase a 1% weekly weight loss is safe; however, if weight is lost too quickly, lean tissue, including heart muscle may be lost (Burroughs & Nonas, 2005).

In patients who have diabetes or metabolic syndrome, very low fat diets should be avoided if the individual has high triglycerides or low high-density lipoprotein levels (Lichtenstein et al., 2006). Diets very low in carbohydrates have been shown to cause an elevation in low-density lipoprotein cholesterol in some cases, possibly due to an increased proportion of fat in the diet. Monitoring of lipids every 4 to 6 weeks is recommended, to ensure that these values do not worsen with dietary changes (Burroughs & Nonas, 2005).

In patients with early renal problems high levels of dietary protein intake can have an adverse effect. Replacing meat with vegetable and dairy alternatives may slow loss of kidney function, and decreased intake of sodium is also recommended. (Lichtenstein et al., 2006). If the diet consists of more than 85 grams of protein per day, creatinine and urinary protein status should be monitored (Burroughs & Nonas,

2005). In advanced renal failure, dietary modification of protein, potassium, and phosphorus is also required (Lichtenstein et al., 2006).

Patients with type 2 diabetes, who are taking hypoglycemic medication during reduced-calorie diets can experience rapid drops in blood glucose levels. Medication dosing may require continual adjustments. It may be beneficial to keep the blood glucose slightly elevated during the initial phases of weight loss as the body adjusts to the change in diet, rather than risk repeated episodes of hypoglycemia. Repeated episodes will also cause the patient to either overeat to compensate or use food in response to hypoglycemia, neither of which will help with dietary changes. The more appropriate adjustment is to lower dosages of hypoglycemic medications to prevent the incidences of hypoglycemia. Monitoring of glucose is a core skill needed by a patient with diabetes in order to safely make modifications, and the ability to self-monitor and the equipment needed to do so should be established before dietary changes are made (Burroughs & Nonas, 2005).

Individual medications may also be affected by diet composition. Green, leafy vegetables can change the coagulation profile of patients on warfarin. Reduction of sodium is of benefit to blood pressure control, and monthly monitoring of this parameter is recommended as well. Hypertensive medications may need to be reduced after even a 5% to 10% weight reduction. Patients should always be cautioned to make these changes in collaboration with their health care providers.

All patients should be monitored for signs of cholelithiasis because the disease may have been silently present but may manifest when weight loss begins with symptoms of abdominal pain, particularly in the right upper quadrant of the abdomen. This complication is brought on by cholesterol type gallstones produced by the body without compensatory increase in bile acids or phospholipids (Burroughs & Nonas, 2005).

Elderly patients have decreased caloric intake needs related to their slowed metabolism and decreased levels of physical activity. They are also at high risk for chronic disease and are often on multiple medications, requiring careful monitoring of weight loss attempts. Supplements are more frequently needed to maintain vitamin and mineral levels and prevent related anemia and osteoporosis.

SUMMARY

Dietary modification is the first step in any weight reduction program. There are many approaches to dietary modification, some of which rely solely on caloric restriction whereas others modify the diet components. Current recommendations are to combine both approaches through a program of daily caloric reduction using a balanced deficit diet. This approach allows for much individual modification related to food choices within the suggested guidelines.

A target weight loss of 1 to 2 lb per week for most individuals is suitable; however, this number may vary with individual needs. Commercial programs have little research to support advertised weight loss claims, but they may prove useful to some individuals. Careful ongoing monitoring of higher risk individuals is necessary throughout the weight loss process.

EXAM QUESTIONS

CHAPTER 9
Questions 34-37

Note: Choose the one option that BEST answers each question.

34. The energy content of a very-low-calorie diet is

    a. less than 800 kcal/day.
    b. less than 1,000 kcal/day.
    c. less than 1,200 kcal/day.
    d. between 800 and 1,200 kcal/day.

35. A balanced approach to dietary composition as recommended by the therapeutic lifestyle changes diet includes which of the following amounts of daily caloric intake?

    a. Dietary fat is less than 10% overall.
    b. Protein intake is 30% or more of the diet.
    c. Carbohydrates are 50% to 60% of daily intake.
    d. Protein, fat, and fiber each comprise 30% of the total.

36. One of the problems with the commercial weight loss industry is that

    a. their programs are so successful the industry does not have time to conduct any research.
    b. historically, the industry has not disclosed information about true costs, staff qualifications, and risks associated with treatment.
    c. their programs are so successful; the industry cannot keep up with consumer demand.
    d. the industry is struggling financially, and therefore does not have the resources to conduct any research on effectiveness.

37. Patients with type 2 diabetes may need closer monitoring during diet modifications because

    a. most diets will increase fasting glucose levels due to food restrictions.
    b. hypoglycemia can occur, but can be managed easily by increasing quantities of food.
    c. medication reduction may be required to prevent incidences of hypoglycemia.
    d. weight loss can significantly worsen glucose control.

REFERENCES

Burroughs, V. & Nona, C. (2006). Managing patient risks during weight loss. *Obesity Management.*

Expert Panel on Detection, Evaluation, and Treatment of High Blood Cholesterol in Adults. (2001). *Third report of the National Cholesterol Education (NCEP) Expert Panel on Detection, Evaluation, and Treatment of High Blood Cholesterol in Adults (Adult Treatment Panel III): Executive Summary.* Bethesda, MD: U.S. Department of Health and Human Services.

Expert Panel on the Identification, Evaluation, and Treatment of Overweight and Obesity in Adults. (2002). *The practical guide: Identification, evaluation and treatment of overweight and obesity in adults.* Bethesda, MD: National Heart, Lung, and Blood Institute Obesity Initiative.

Heber, D. (2002). Meal replacements in the treatment of obesity In C.G. Fairburn & K.D. Brownell (Eds.), *Eating disorders and obesity.* (2nd ed., pp. 529-33). New York: The Guilford Press.

Hyman, F.N., Sempos, E., Saltsman, J., & Glinsmann, W.H. (1993). Evidence for success of caloric restriction in weight loss and control: Summary of data from industry. *Annals of Internal Medicine, 119,* 681-687.

Lichtenstein, A.H., Appel, L.J., Brands, M., Carnethon, M., Daniels, S., Franch, H.A., et al. (2006). Diet and lifestyle recommendations revision 2006: A scientific statement from the American Heart Association Nutrition Committee. *Circulation, 114,* 82-96.

National Institutes of Health Technology Assessment Conference Panel. (1993). Methods for voluntary weight loss and control. *Annals of Internal Medicine, 119,* 764-770.

Partnership for Healthy Weight Management. (2008). *Voluntary guidelines for providers of weight loss products or services.* Retrieved November 16, 2009, from http://www.ftc .gov/bcp/edu/pubs/business/adv/bus38.shtm

Plodkowski, R.A. & St. Jeor, S.T. (2003). Medical nutrition therapy for the treatment of obesity. *Endocrinology Metabolism Clinics of North America, 32*(4), 934-965.

St. Jeor, S.T., Howard, B.V., Prewitt, E.T., Bovee, V., Bazzarre, T., & Eckel, R.H. for the AHA Nutrition Committee. (2001). Dietary protein and weight reduction: A statement for healthcare professionals from the Nutritional Committee of the Council on Nutrition, Physical Activity and Metabolism of the American Heart Association. *Circulation, 1004,* 1869-74.

Tsai, A.G. & Wadden, T.A. (2005). Systematic review: An evaluation of major commercial weight loss programs in the United States. *Annals of Internal Medicine, 142,* 56-66.

Tsai, A.G. & Wadden, T.A. (2006). The evolution of very-low-calorie diets: An update and meta-analysis. *Obesity, 14,* 1283-1293.

CHAPTER 10

PHYSICAL ACTIVITY RECOMMENDATIONS

CHAPTER OBJECTIVE

After completing this chapter the learner will be able to identify necessary components of a successful exercise program for the obese patient.

LEARNING OBJECTIVES

After completing this chapter the learner will be able to

1. explain how to set the frequency, duration, and intensity of an exercise prescription for individual patients who are obese.

2. compare the lifestyle approach method of increasing physical activity to structured exercise programs.

3. describe safe practices for starting an exercise program.

4. identify an individual patient's barriers to exercise and employ strategies to help the patient overcome these barriers.

INTRODUCTION

Exercise or physical activity is a key to successful weight loss and reduced weight maintenance. Obese individuals do not have a high exercise capacity, and may be at higher risk for exercise-related injuries than the normal weight person. A safe exercise program for the obese person is one that meets certain criteria, in which the physiological adaptations to exercise will be achieved at the same time that patient safety is maintained. It is important that the nurse understand these criteria, so that the exercise progression of the obese patient can be designed and modified. Furthermore, the nurse can promote a lifestyle of physical activity for obese patients by helping them to overcome barriers and monitor their exercise behaviors.

PHYSICAL ACTIVITY BENEFIT IN WEIGHT REDUCTION

Physical activity is associated with improved weight loss outcomes, and can have an independent effect on risk factors such as hypertension, hyperlipidemia, and hyperinsulinemia. Although physical activity alone has a minimal effect on weight loss, it should be a part of the overall behavior modification because it plays a crucial role in weight maintenance (Jakicic, 2003). Studies have now shown that low physical fitness is an even greater predictor of increased mortality rates than obesity (Blair & Holder, 2002). Physical activity recommendations can be divided into structured exercise programs, and lifestyle activity. Both components can be utilized to help individuals achieve improved fitness. Lifestyle exercise works particularly well with children and adolescents (Goldfield

& Epstein, 2002). Early implementation of this concept can help prevent obesity in this group.

Physical activity can also affect resting energy expenditure. It is well known that calorie reduction dieting causes a reduction in resting energy expenditure. This decrease is not a permanent change but occurs during weight loss, and appears to return to baseline after the active weight loss period (Klein & Romijn, 2008). Numerous studies have evaluated the effects of aerobic exercise and strength training in preventing this reduction. These studies have had contradictory results.

A meta-analysis of the research on the effect of exercise on resting metabolic rate (RMR) during restrictive dieting was performed several years ago (Ballor & Poehlman, 1995). The uniqueness of this review was that the investigators corrected changes seen in RMR for corresponding changes in body weight, and found that RMR was only reduced by 2% when restrictive dieting was coupled with exercise. These data show that exercise maintains RMR during restrictive dieting, and that the changes in RMR induced by restrictive dieting and exercise are proportional to the amount of lean tissue lost.

Whether exercise completely offsets the diet-induced reduction or only partially offsets the diet-induced reduction in RMR may depend on the severity and duration of the diet restrictions; type, duration, and intensity of exercise; and the magnitude of changes in body composition. Nevertheless, all obese patients should be encouraged to incorporate exercise into their weight management program. At this point, it would be more important to help the obese patient adopt an active lifestyle than to worry about the intricacies of how the exercise and diet prescriptions interact.

THE BASICS OF EXERCISE PRESCRIPTION

The four exercise guidelines to be considered when designing an exercise program are: type

or mode of exercise, frequency of exercise, duration of exercise, and intensity of exercise. The healthiest type of exercise for obese persons is cardiovascular exercise, otherwise known as aerobic exercise. Although other types of exercise have positive effects on health, aerobic exercise has proven to be the safest and have the greatest impact on health and disease risk reduction for the obese (American College of Sports Medicine, 2006).

Type of Exercise

Aerobic exercise is any type of exercise that uses oxygen in the production of energy to support the exercise. Because oxygen is transported to the exercising muscles through the cardiovascular system, aerobic exercise is also termed cardiovascular exercise. Similarly, increasing one's capacity for aerobic exercise also strengthens their cardiovascular system and reduces cardiovascular disease risk. We define an aerobic exercise as one that is continuous, rhythmic, and uses the large muscle groups (e.g., walking, running, cycling).

Walking is a form of aerobic exercise that can be done by most obese patients. It does not require expensive equipment, and can be done in a variety of locations. Depending on the severity of obesity, walking may be an activity that has been drastically reduced. Joint pain, back pain, and cardiorespiratory health risks may limit the ability of the patient to perform this activity. Other forms of aerobic activity can be utilized, such as swimming or water exercise, when these limitations are present. Although strength-building exercises and flexibility exercises add little to the weight loss effects, they may improve joint and muscle functionality, allowing the patient to participate more fully in aerobic activity.

Frequency of Exercise

The next step is to determine how often to exercise, or "frequency." The American Heart Association Guidelines for Diet and Lifestyle Recommendations (2006) for physical activity are to achieve 30 minutes or more per day most days of the week, for a total of 150 minutes per week. Other organizations have recommended from 60 to 90 minutes daily; however, a growing body of literature supports 45 to 60 minutes per day most days of the week is the most effective for improving weight loss and preventing weight regain (Jakicic, 2003). If the obese patient is not currently exercising, 1 to 2 days each week for the first few weeks may be a more manageable frequency for a structured exercise program. Each patient will determine how often he or she wants to exercise for a weight management program. Using the lifestyle approach, additional activity can then be built into the day as well.

Duration of Exercise

The third aerobic exercise guideline to be considered is duration. This refers to how long each exercise session needs to last in order to be effective. The minimal duration for improvement in aerobic fitness is 20 minutes, but this number will again vary among patients.

The lifestyle approach may involve intermittent exercise periods of shorter duration several times per day, which will meet the overall duration of daily exercise goal. This approach is helpful in those individuals who have physical limitations who cannot achieve the aerobic guidelines.

Intensity of Exercise

The final exercise parameter is more difficult to define than the previous three. The intensity of exercise refers to how hard one needs to work during the exercise bout. In order to achieve the maximal benefits of an aerobic exercise program, the patient needs to exercise at an intensity between 50% and 80% of the patient's maximal aerobic capacity. The best indicator we have outside the laboratory for estimating aerobic intensity during exercise is heart rate. The relationship between heart rate and oxygen consumption (or aerobic intensity during exercise) is valid only if the exercise is aerobic in nature.

Heart rate is variable among individuals depending upon age, size, sex, and fitness level. It is necessary to rely upon an individualized approach to determine the desirable heart rate for monitoring exercise intensity. This approach was devised by Dr. M.J. Karvonen and is described in the *Guidelines for Exercise Testing and Prescription* by the American College of Sports Medicine (2006). Dr. Karvonen's formula was used to construct Table 10-1. In this table you will find the individualized exercise heart rate that will bring the obese patient into the proper intensity while exercising. In order to determine a patient's exercise heart rate in the table, you need to know their resting heart rate. The table can then be used to obtain the exercise heart rate, or target heart rate goal.

It is difficult to measure the pulse while actually exercising. Therefore, in order to get the best estimate of heart rate during exercise, stop exercise and immediately take the pulse for 10 seconds, then check this number against the predetermined exercise heart rate. This procedure should be followed every 5 to 10 minutes during the exercise session (alternatively a heart rate monitor can be used if available). If this measured rate was at or above the predetermined exercise heart rate, the exercise should be continued without any changes. If this measured rate was below the predetermined exercise heart rate, the intensity can be increased by walking faster, running harder, playing more intensely, etc. After a few minutes at this new intensity, the pulse should be checked again to see if it has reached the target exercise heart rate. Exercise intensity throughout each exercise session should be monitored in this manner.

As obese patients increase their fitness levels, they can exercise at a higher intensity than prescribed in Table 10-1. However, if the exercise intensity is raised, make sure the duration of exercise is not compromised. Ensure that the patient is exercising for at least 20 minutes per exercise bout. On the other hand,

TABLE 10-1: TEN SECOND EXERCISE HEART RATE TARGET FOR AEROBIC EXERCISE IN OBESE PATIENTS* (1 OF 2)

RHR per Minute	Age in Years					
	18-22	23-34	35-46	47-58	59-69	70+
55	21	21	20	19	18	17
56	22	21	20	19	18	17
57	22	21	20	19	18	17
58	22	21	20	19	18	17
59	22	21	20	19	18	17
60	22	21	20	19	18	17
61	22	22	21	20	19	17
62	22	22	21	20	19	18
63	22	22	21	20	19	18
64	22	22	21	20	19	18
65	22	22	21	20	19	18
66	22	22	21	20	19	18
67	22	22	21	20	19	18
68	22	22	21	20	19	18
69	22	22	21	20	19	18
70	23	22	21	20	19	18
71	23	22	21	20	19	18
72	23	22	21	20	19	18
73	23	23	22	21	20	19
74	23	23	22	21	20	19
75	23	23	22	21	20	19
76	23	23	22	21	20	19
77	23	23	22	21	20	19
78	23	23	22	21	20	19
79	23	23	22	21	20	19
80	23	23	22	21	20	19
81	23	23	22	21	20	19
82	24	23	22	21	20	19
83	24	23	22	21	20	19
84	24	23	22	21	20	19
85	24	24	23	22	21	20
86	24	24	23	22	21	20
87	24	24	23	22	21	20
88	24	24	23	22	21	20

TABLE 10-1: TEN SECOND EXERCISE HEART RATE (EHR) TARGET FOR AEROBIC EXERCISE IN OBESE PATIENTS* (2 OF 2)						
RHR per Minute	**Age in Years**					
	18-22	**23-34**	**35-46**	**47-58**	**59-69**	**70+**
89	24	24	23	22	21	20
90	24	24	23	22	21	20
91	24	24	23	22	21	20
92	24	24	23	22	21	20
93	24	24	23	22	21	20
94	25	24	23	22	21	20
95	25	24	23	22	21	20
96	25	24	23	22	21	20
97	25	25	24	23	22	21
98	25	25	24	23	22	21
99	25	25	24	23	22	21
100	25	25	24	23	22	21

*The resting heart rate (RHR) should be measured as the baseline for 1 minute, then the targeted heart rate calculated by selecting the corresponding RHR on the left side of the chart, and the patient's age across the top of the chart. This number indicates the 10-second pulse count, which when multiplied by 6 gives the exercise heart rate target in beats per minute.

if the patient is very unfit to begin with, then the goal of the exercise program may be to increase the duration at which the person can comfortably walk, without striving for a specific heart rate. Also, short walks can be taken several times a day in order for the patient to build up to the point where he or she can exercise for 20 minutes continuously.

The key to monitoring exercise intensity with heart rate is that the exercise must meet all the guidelines for aerobic exercise. Just having an elevated heart rate over an extended period of time does not suffice. For example, if somebody was hiding behind a corner and suddenly jumped out to startle you, your heart rate would go through the roof, but this change in heart rate does not mean that you are having an exercise training effect. As another example, strength-training exercise is not aerobic in nature, even though the heart rate may be elevated. Rather, strength-training exercises improve muscular strength and enhance bone density.

Components of the Exercise Session

Every exercise session should be divided into three phases: the **warm-up, conditioning,** and **cooldown.** The focus of attention thus far has been on the conditioning phase of the exercise session that is governed by the guidelines established for type, frequency, duration, and intensity. During conditioning, the heart rate is elevated, blood pressure increases, and metabolic rate rises to meet the demand for energy. These physiological responses to exercise are a form of stress. Generally, this *exercise stress,* so to speak, is good for the body. The adaptation or adjustment to this *exercise stress* is what increases fitness levels and exercise capacity. However, abrupt changes in these physiological parameters that we call exercise stress may result in injury or provoke a disease response. A warm-up and a cooldown before and after the conditioning phase of the exercise will help the body gradually enter and exit this exercise stress zone. This gradual adjustment to exercise stress tremendously reduces any possible risks of exercise (American College of Sports Medicine, 2006).

The purpose of the warm-up period before exercise is to slowly increase the aerobic energy production so it approaches the level prescribed for intensity under the aerobic exercise guidelines. The best way to increase aerobic energy production during the warm-up is to do a light version of the aerobic type of exercise chosen, such as a slow walk or slow jog. Have the patient start out slow and gradually work up to a level close to the prescribed exercise heart rate over a period of about 3 to 5 minutes. A good indication of whether the patient has warmed up properly is the onset of perspiration. This means that the body temperature has risen slightly, the muscles are warm, and the patient is ready to start the conditioning part of the exercise session. The patient should go directly from the warm-up into the conditioning phase while following the guidelines previously established for aerobic exercise training.

When the patient has completed the conditioning phase, gradually have them cool down by either reducing the intensity of the exercise used for conditioning or walking slowly. Do not have them stand still or jump into a cold shower. These acts will decrease circulation and may be hazardous. A proper cooldown should take about 5 minutes and possibly longer if the patient is just starting an exercise program. The best reference to determine if cooldown is complete is heart rate. Take the patient's heart rate as is done during the conditioning period. If the heart rate is down to 17 for a 10-second pulse count (100 beats/minute) or within 20 beats/minute of the resting heart rate, the cooldown is complete (Brown, Miller, & Eason, 2006). Case Study 10-1 gives an example of the process of determining an exercise prescription.

Case Study 10-1: The Exercise Prescription

You are a nurse who works in a rehabilitation center. The center provides exercise programs for patients recovering from accidents, injuries, and disease-related complications. Many of the patients in the rehabilitation center are overweight or obese. Josef is a patient who has lost 60 lb through bariatric surgery. He has recovered from the surgery and is ready to begin an exercise program. Josef does not have any comorbidities. Prescribe an exercise program for Josef that will help him maintain his weight loss.

Scenario

The rehabilitation center where you work does not have sophisticated equipment for graded exercise testing. However, you can perform simple fitness tests and monitor heart rate and blood pressure during exercise. In order to design an exercise program for Josef, you will need to determine how he will meet the criteria for aerobic exercise training:

- mode or type of exercise,
- frequency of exercise sessions,
- duration of exercise sessions, and
- intensity of exercise.

The resolution to this case study revolves around your ability to match Josef's interests and personal demographics with the criteria for aerobic exercise training. You will need to find his exercise interests, what is available to him, his schedule, age, and resting heart rate. Then, with his help, you will set the parameters for his exercise program.

continued on next page

Resolution Process

The first step in designing an aerobic exercise program for Josef is to determine what mode or type of exercise will interest him, and fill the requirements for cardiovascular training. You speak with Josef about the possibilities and explain to him that the exercise needs to be continuous, rhythmic, and use the large muscle groups. Examples of suitable exercises are walking, jogging, hiking, running, swimming, rowing, stepping, stairmaster, elliptical, and cycling. Years ago Josef played basketball, and he asks you if playing basketball would be good for him. You explain that basketball can be a good aerobic exercise, but that for the time being he should focus on building up his aerobic capacity through a less intense and less demanding activity. When he becomes accustomed to regular exercise he might begin to play basketball. In response to your basketball explanation, he asks about golf. You explain that golf is a walking sport, but the intensity of golf would not be high enough to meet the "intensity" factor for developing aerobic exercise. However, you encourage him to play golf if he desires because it will help with his flexibility and keep him physically active, even though golf may not improve his aerobic capacity. Lastly, Josef tells you he has a stationary cycle in his basement, and he is interested in trying the elliptical at the rehabilitation center. He decides that for now he will focus on the elliptical and stationary cycling.

You explain to Josef that in order to maintain his weight loss he will need to exercise most days of the week. He decides that he will come to the rehabilitation center three times a week, right after work. He will exercise at home twice a week. While at the rehabilitation center, he will use the elliptical and maybe the stationary bike. At home, Josef will use his stationary bike. Thus far you have agreed that Josef's mode or type of exercise will be elliptical and stationary cycle and that his frequency of exercise sessions will be five times a week.

Next, you want to set the duration of his exercise sessions. Because Josef has not exercised for a long time, you want to begin with a duration that is achievable. The minimal recommendation for aerobic exercise session duration is 20 minutes. You and Josef decide that a 20-minute exercise session duration will be his goal for the first 2 weeks. Then he will increase the session time to 25 minutes for the next month. At that point, he will increase his exercise duration to 30 minutes a day, and keep that for a month. After he has been exercising for 30 minutes per session for a month you and he will sit down together and reassess his exercise program.

The last component of the exercise prescription is intensity. In order to set Josef's intensity, you need to know his age and resting heart rate. Josef is 45 years old. Because you and he have been sitting and talking for the past 25 minutes, you grab a heart rate monitor and check his resting heart rate. At the same time, you show Josef how to use the heart rate monitor so he will be able to monitor his heart rate when exercising. Josef has a resting heart rate of 85 beats/minute. According to Josef's age and resting heart rate, his target heart rate for aerobic exercise training is 138 beats/minute (Table 10-1). You explain to Josef that he can use a heart rate monitor to check his heart rate during exercise at the rehabilitation center, but that at home he will have to feel his pulse and check his heart rate with a watch (because he does not own a heart rate monitor). To obtain this measurement, Josef should stop cycling, palpate his pulse, and count the beats for 10 seconds. You subsequently teach Josef how to count his pulse. Josef's target 10-second pulse count is 23. So, Josef's exercise intensity is set by a target heart rate of 138 beats/minute, which translates into a 10-second pulse count of 23.

The last thing you discuss with Josef is warm-up and cooldown needs. You suggest that Josef do a 3 to 4 minute warm-up on the elliptical and stationary bike at a machine setting that is about one half of what he would use for his workout. Then after 3 to 4 minutes of warm-up, he can change the machine setting to what brings him into the target heart rate range you have set for him. He will continue at this intensity for the exercise session duration. He will monitor his heart rate throughout the exercise session to make sure he is at target heart rate. After his workout, Josef will set the machine setting to the lowest possible and continue exercising until his heart rate drops to 105 beats/minute or a 10-second pulse count of 17. *continued on next page*

Now that you are finished designing the exercise program for Josef, you and he step over to the elliptical and you bring him through his first exercise session. During this first session, you illustrate how to do all the things he was taught to do. You also help him find the proper exercise intensity that will bring his heart rate up to the predetermined rate. Remember that the target exercise heart rate you predetermined for Josef is only the minimal exercise heart rate level. Josef can exercise at a higher heart rate if he can maintain that intensity for the session duration he set for himself. At the end of the exercise session, you bring Josef through his cooldown. Now Josef is ready to continue his exercise plan and monitor himself at home.

If the exercise program or exercise prescription for the obese patient is meaningful or valuable, the patient is more likely to adhere to it. The nurse can do several things to make the exercise prescription meaningful to the patient.

- Have the patient participate in the construction of the prescription.
- Make the prescription understandable to the patient.
- Relate the exercise program to things of physical, emotional, social, or spiritual importance.
- Discuss the pros and cons of exercise.
- Debunk any myths about exercise.
- Design a monitoring system for exercise participation.
- Design a reward system for exercise participation.

Lifestyle Approaches to Exercise

Helping the patient to incorporate exercise into their lifestyle can greatly improve adherence and participation in a physical activity program. The goal is to achieve 30 minutes of moderate-intensity exercise or activity over the course of the day. It adopts a broader definition for physical activity, and includes steps such as taking the stairs instead of the elevator, parking farther away from the door, and reducing purely sedentary activities.

Self-monitoring and goal setting are used to facilitate the process. Pedometers, or step counters, have become a popular method of increasing activity in the daily routine. One popular approach uses a goal of 10,000 steps per day. For many sedentary people, this is an increase of about 3,000 to 4,000 steps per day, or the equivalent of walking approximately 3 miles (Jakicic, 2003). The Internet provides many tools for patients to monitor physical activity. Below is a sampling of programs available to encourage increased physical activity:

America on the Move
www.americaonthemove.org
This site is free and provides "virtual trails," where participants can log their daily steps or walking time compared to an identified world trail, and learn interesting information about the specific trail as they do so.

Choose to Move Program
www.choosetomove.org/learn_more.html
A 12-week program for women that uses a progressive behavior modification with one topic weekly to motivate and initiate the physical activity program.

The President's Challenge
www.presidentschallenge.org
This site offers different levels for participants (beginners to advanced), and further divides groups by age. Motivation includes earning rewards/recognition.

American Heart Association's Start!
Walking Program
www.startwalkingnow.org
This program offers links to local Start! Walking paths and provides other tools to monitor activity.

MOVE!
www.move.med.va.gov
This Web site is designed for veterans and is used in conjunction with the Veterans Affairs health care system. The site has many useful

handouts that can be downloaded free of charge for use with patients who are veterans.

Safety Issues

We have discussed the need to warm up and cool down to prevent injury related to physical activity. In addition, patients should be advised to:

- Drink water before, during, and after exercise to prevent dehydration.

- Wear comfortable, good fitting socks and shoes suitable for physical activity.

Other safety considerations pertaining to exercise outside of a structured environment include:

- Carry identification, emergency contact information and illness information; carry a cell phone if you have one. Let someone know where you are going and how long you'll be gone.

- Dress to be seen. Wear bright-colored clothing. In poor light, wear safety reflective materials designed for improving your visibility to drivers.

- Use a familiar route, be active in public places, and avoid isolated trails, paths, and poorly lit areas.

During the summer months patients will probably have to deal with a hot and possibly humid environment. Heat injury is not an all-or-none occurrence, but includes a series of stages that must be recognized and remedied before progression to the most serious stage, heatstroke, occurs. If at any time during exercise the patient feels the onset of heat stress (dizziness, extreme fatigue, nausea, headache, or elevated body temperature), stop the exercise session, get the patient out of the hot environment as soon as possible, have the patient drink plenty of cool water or a sports drink, and continue to replenish body fluids abundantly over the next 24 hours. Contact the patient's physician or health care provider either immediately or before the next exercise session and discuss the episode.

Patients can prevent heat injury and continue to exercise in a hot environment by following the guidelines listed below.

- Exercise during the cooler part of the day, usually morning or evening.

- Gradually increase exposure to heat and humidity. Allow 2 to 3 weeks to acclimate. During the acclimation period, reduce the duration and intensity of exercise.

- Drink plenty of fluids before, during, and after exercise – even if not thirsty.

- Expose as much skin surface as possible (or wear a modern fabric that assists in cooling). Evaporation of sweat from the skin removes heat from the body. Remember to use a sunscreen on the exposed areas.

- Be aware that humidity affects evaporation. The higher the humidity, the slower the rate of evaporation and less efficient the body becomes at dissipating heat.

- Be aware of the heat index before exercising. The heat index is an indicator of how temperature and humidity interact to increase the true heat stress on the body.

- Exercise indoors if possible. If the patient belongs to a health club, YMCA, spa, etc., use the air-conditioned facilities as much as possible during hot summer days. Most clubs, spas, and YMCAs also charge a daily fee for visitors and nonmembers. So if the patient is not a regular member, he or she may consider paying a daily fee for a day or two until the heat wave passes. If the patient is a walker, he or she may want to go to the shopping mall for a workout.

Cold weather can also cause problems for exercise. Tips for safe physical activity in cold winter climates include:

- Dress properly, layering materials close to the skin that will wick sweat away from the body and dry quickly, with a second layer for warmth (wool or cotton), and the outer layer to keep cold air and moisture out.

- Use warm socks to insulate the feet and mittens to keep fingers warmer. Always wear a hat or cap.

- Drink water before starting exercise; dehydration is possible even in cold weather.

- Cold is a stress on the body, so modification of activity may be needed.

IDENTIFYING AND OVERCOMING BARRIERS TO EXERCISE

Most people recognize that regular exercise is necessary for weight maintenance and for optimal health and well-being. Nonetheless, only 30% of those attempting weight loss meet the National Institutes of Health guidelines for exercise of 300 minutes a week, and merely 19% meet the Institute of Medicine exercise recommendations of 420 minutes a week (Krugar, Carlson, & Kohl, 2007). Obviously, there must be some barrier(s) that prevent people from exercising in a manner that they know will improve their health. Commonly identified barriers to regular exercise include a fear of being injured; lack of time for exercise; an inability to monitor progress; a lack of motivation, encouragement, support, or companionship; and a lack of safe a exercise environment. In order for obese patients to incorporate exercise into their lifestyle they must overcome their individual barriers to exercise.

The first step in overcoming barriers to exercise is to identify those barriers. When a person's barriers to exercise are identified, the person can design a realistic strategy to overcome or minimize those barriers. The checklist in Table 10-2 can be used to help the obese patient identify barriers to exercise. Patients may have several barriers to exercise, in which case it is generally beneficial to focus first on the barrier that the patient perceives to be the biggest problem and then help the patient to design

strategies to overcome or minimize each one of the barriers. It may be helpful to have the patient identify things that worked in the past to help overcome barriers to exercise. For example, a patient may state that he or she does not have time to exercise. A possible strategy would be to sit down Sunday evening with a weekly planner and schedule exercise times for the coming week. It is often helpful for the nurse to assist the patient in not seeing things in "black and white," or not thinking of exercise as "all or nothing." Correcting distorted thinking patterns such as these can easily help patients identify exercise barriers and realistic strategies for overcoming them.

Case Study 10-2 presents an example of helping a patient overcome exercise barriers.

TABLE 10-2: IDENTIFYING INDIVIDUAL BARRIERS TO EXERCISE

Please check all those that apply:

_____ I don't have enough time to exercise.

_____ I don't have any place to exercise.

_____ I don't know how to exercise.

_____ I am embarrassed when I exercise.

_____ I am afraid of getting injured when exercising.

_____ I am not motivated to exercise.

_____ I don't know how to monitor the progression of my exercise training.

_____ I don't have any social support to exercise.

_____ I have a medical condition that prevents me from exercising.

_____ I don't enjoy exercise.

_____ I had a bad experience with exercise in the past.

_____ I don't have a partner to exercise with.

_____ Other reason not listed above:

_____

_____ Other reason not listed above:

_____

Case Study 10-2: Overcoming Barriers To Exercise

You are a nurse who works in an outpatient cardiovascular rehabilitation program where many of the patients suffer from obesity. The program runs an adult fitness program through the community recreation center. You are the nurse on duty for the adult fitness program Monday, Wednesday, and Friday from 7:00 a.m. until 11:00 a.m. Larry is a patient who has not participated in the program for several weeks. He arrives at the facility today at about 8:30 a.m. After checking in, Larry begins his exercise session.

Scenario

The first part of Larry's exercise session consists of walking around the indoor track at your facility. Larry knows how to monitor his heart rate during exercise, and knows that the intensity of exercise becomes too great if he cannot maintain a conversation while walking. You catch up with Larry on the track. What type of conversation will you have with Larry?

Nurse: Hi Larry. Glad to see you made it today.

Larry: Yeah… I finally got my butt in here.

Nurse: Doesn't sound like you are real happy with yourself. Something wrong?

Larry: No, not in particular. Just a little discouraged about this whole exercise thing.

Nurse: Care to explain?

Larry: I don't know. Just not motivated I guess.

Nurse: Have you been exercising at home at all?

Larry: Not really.

Nurse: So, you have not been exercising much at all since we saw you several weeks ago, right?

Larry: Yes, sounds pitiful, doesn't it?

Nurse: No, not pitiful. It just sounds a little confusing because I know you always feel better after you exercise.

Larry: Yeah, you're right. So, what stops me from being regular?

Nurse: Let's see if we can figure that out. What got you in here today?

Larry: Oh…I think I just needed somebody to talk to. Not, to dump on, just to have some conversation.

Nurse: So, you like coming here to exercise because it gives you a chance to talk to people?

Larry: Yes, I think so. But…that doesn't make sense. If I need somebody to talk to, and I get that coming here, then why don't I come regularly?

Nurse: I don't know. Maybe something is stopping you. What or how are you feeling when you want to come in to exercise but don't?

Larry: Depressed. Ever since my wife died, I have days where I just don't feel like doing anything, even though I know it will make me feel better if I do.

Nurse: Ever talk to someone about your depression?

Larry: No, and I am too old to go to counseling and all that. Plus, it's not like I am seriously depressed.

Nurse: Well, you might consider talking to someone about it. I can help you find someone if you decide you want some help. In the meantime, let's see what we can do to overcome this exercise barrier of depression. You say that you come here to talk to people and that you feel better after exercising. Why don't we design a strategy where you can get your need to talk with people met here at the facility?

Larry: How are we going to do that?

Nurse: I have an idea. You already know how to exercise, and you keep a log of your exercise sessions. Why don't we add something new to your exercise log?

Larry: What?

continued on next page

Nurse: A people count.

Larry: A people count? What the heck is that?

Nurse: We can have you count the number of people you talk to here at the facility.

Larry: What am I going to talk to them about?

Nurse: I don't know. That's for you to figure out. Talk to them about anything. Ask them how their program is going. Ask them how they like their running shoes. Just get them talking. And you know what?

Larry: What?

Nurse: I bet after a while, they will be coming up to you and starting to talk.

Larry: Maybe you are right. I could set up a system of people counting, and then reward myself once I reach a goal.

Nurse: That's the spirit. Let's work together on designing your system after you finish your workout. I have to go now and check on some of the other patients.

Resolution Process

Notice how the nurse helped Larry identify his barrier to exercise? Notice how she worked with him to design a strategy to overcome his barrier? The nurse showed empathy and asked some probing questions. A good place to start discovering exercise barriers for any patient is to ask what "gets them" to exercise, and what "stops them" from exercising.

MONITORING HOME-BASED EXERCISE BEHAVIORS

Most patients will participate in a home-based exercise program. If the exercise prescription is structured within the patient's capacity, routine exercise will present the patient with minimal risk. Nonetheless, home exercise should be monitored in some way. The most common technique is to keep an exercise log. The exercise log can contain information about the exercise bout in terms of dates and time spent exercising, heart rate during exercise, feelings of perceived exertion, type of exercise performed, emotional state of being, and motivation toward exercise.

The health professional can use the exercise monitoring information in a few ways. First, the information can be used to evaluate the patient's motivations and barriers to exercise. Insights into the patient's motivations, feelings, emotional state, and perceptions can help the professional identify potential exercise barriers. The log can also be used to help identify patterns of compliant and non-compliant behaviors. It may be that there are certain links or certain common factors that cause the patient to be more or less compliant with the exercise program.

The exercise monitoring information can also be used as a reward system. Patients can be rewarded for exercise behaviors that are tallied through the exercise monitoring technique selected. For example, recording the number of hours and minutes exercised each day can be used to reward one's self with a body massage after accumulating a predetermined number of hours exercising.

SUMMARY

Regular exercise is critical to the health of the obese patient. Aerobic exercise or cardiovascular exercise is the most effective type of exercise training for obesity treatment. Four criteria must be met in order for aerobic exercise to be effective. The exercise must be rhythmic, continuous, and work the large muscle groups; be performed at least three times per week; be performed for at least 20 minutes a session; and be performed at 50% to 80% of maximal capacity. The intensity of exercise can be monitored by pulse rate, but only if the exercise is rhythmic, continuous, and working the large muscles. Methods used to obtain the recommended daily activity of 30 to 60 minutes daily of moderate activity include the use of an exercise prescription and the lifestyle approach. Each exercise session should be preceded by a warm-up and followed by a cool-down to insure a safe transition from resting metabolic rate to exercise metabolic rate and back again.

Even the best planned exercise program will fail if the patient does not adhere to the program. Exercise adherence can be enhanced if the patient sees exercise as personally meaningful. Adherence is also enhanced when specific physical, emotional, and environmental barriers to exercise are identified and strategies are designed to overcome these barriers. The nurse or other health professional is in a unique position to help the obese patient reap the benefits of exercise.

EXAM QUESTIONS

CHAPTER 10
Questions 38-41

Note: Choose the one option that BEST answers each question.

38. The four components that are integral to the exercise prescription in obesity are

    a. intensity, speed, likes, and dislikes.

    b. type of exercise, frequency, duration, and intensity.

    c. aerobic, anaerobic, abdominal strength, and flexibility.

    d. heart rate, blood pressure, perceived exertion, and energy expenditure

39. The lifestyle approach differs from the exercise prescription by

    a. using a warm-up, conditioning phase, and cooldown process.

    b. building the recommended physical activity into the daily regimen.

    c. finding the type of exercise that best suits the patient.

    d. requiring all daily physical activity in a single session.

40. Patients can prevent heat injury and continue to exercise in a hot environment if they

    a. drink plenty of fluids before, during and after exercise; exercise early or late in the day; and stay aware of the heat index.

    b. exercise more intensely for a shorter time, wear minimal clothing to avoid overheating, drink a sport drink.

    c. drink a sport drink if thirsty, exercise in the sun to acclimatize to the heat, and cool down in the shade.

    d. eliminate the warm-up from the exercise session because it is already hot outside.

41. A 52-year-old obese patient tells you she does not enjoy exercise because she goes to the health club alone and ends up in an aerobic exercise class where all the participants are young, slim and trim, and wear provocative exercise clothing. She says no one else there is like her. She sees herself as fat, ugly, and unfit. The most apparent barrier this patient has toward exercise is

    a. health clubs.

    b. gender issues.

    c. lack of time to work out.

    d. lack of a supportive environment.

REFERENCES

American College of Sports Medicine. (2006). *ACSM's guidelines for exercise testing and prescription* (7th ed., pp. 133-173). Philadelphia: Lippincott, Williams & Wilkins.

Ballor, D.L. & Poehlman, E.T. (1995). A meta-analysis of the effects of exercise and/or dietary restriction on resting metabolic rate. *Eur. J. Appl. Physiol, 71*, 535-542.

Blair, S.N. & Holder, S. (2002). Exercise in the management of obesity, In C.G. Fairburn & K.D. Brownell, (Eds.), *Eating disorders and obesity* (2nd ed., pp. 518-23). New York: The Guilford Press.

Brown, S.P., Miller, W.C., & Eason, J.M. (2006). *Exercise physiology: Basis of human movement in health and disease.* Baltimore: Lippincott Williams & Wilkins.

Goldfield G.S. & Epstein L.H. (2002). Management of obesity in children. In C.G. Fairburn & K.D. Brownell, (Eds.), *Eating disorders and obesity* (2nd ed., pp. 573-77). New York: The Guilford Press.

Jakicic, J.M. (2003). Exercise in the treatment of obesity. *Endocrinology Metabolism Clinics of North America, 32*(4), 967-80.

Klein, S. & Romijn, J.A. (2008). Obesity. In H.M. Kronenberg, S. Melmen, K.S. Polonsky, & P.R. Larsen (Eds.), *Williams textbook of endocrinology* (11th ed., p. 1567). Philadelphia: Saunders.

Kruger, J., Carlson, S.A., & Kohl, H.W. (2007). Fitness facilities for adults: Differences in perceived access and usage. *American Journal of Preventive Medicine, 32*, 500-505.

Lichtenstein, A.H., Appel, L.J., Brands, M., Carnethon, M., Daniels, S., Franch, H.A., et al. (2006). Diet and lifestyle recommendations revision 2006: A scientific statement from the American Heart Association Nutrition Committee. *Circulation, 114*; 82-96.

CHAPTER 11

NONDIETING PHILOSOPHIES FOR OBESITY MANAGEMENT

CHAPTER OBJECTIVE

After completing this chapter the learner will be able to describe different non-dieting philosophies for obesity management.

LEARNING OBJECTIVES

After completing this chapter, the learner will be able to

1. discuss the principles underlying nondieting philosophies for obesity management.

2. explain how the Healthy At Every Size philosophy and the nondiet approach for obesity management can be applied to individuals of all sizes.

3. list measures of success for obesity treatment other than body weight or size.

INTRODUCTION

Health care professionals have treated the obese patient through caloric restriction and exercise for decades. Despite these efforts, the prevalence of obesity has risen dramatically since the 1960s. This apparent ineffectiveness of traditional diet and exercise programming to reduce obesity has inspired some professionals to challenge the further use of restrictive dieting and exercise for the sole purpose of weight control and to suggest various forms of nondieting approaches to health promotion in the obese. In this chapter, we will examine how nondieting philosophies for obesity management can be incorporated into the overall treatment plan for the obese patient.

NONDIETING APPROACHES

Assumptions

During the past two decades, traditional dieting approaches have come under fire. The search for alternative approaches is founded on three basic premises:

1. dieting is ineffective in achieving sustained weight loss,

2. dieting is physically and psychologically harmful, and

3. basic assumptions about the cause of obesity (predominantly behavioral) are incorrect.

(Foster, 2002)

Proponents of the nondieting movement point to the fact that sustained weight loss has not been achieved by traditional dieting, and that these attempts have caused harm, including increases in binge eating, depression, social isolation, food and weight preoccupation, and more. Traditional dieting is also seen as a cultural reinforcement of societal views of obesity, in particular the long-standing belief that being overweight is unhealthy (Foster & McGuckin, 2002).

Program Goals and Methods

Many nondieting approaches have been developed that use a variety of methodologies to achieve their goals. These programs generally seek to:

- increase awareness of dieting's ill effects,

- promote education about the biological basis of body weight,

- encourage use of internal cues of hunger and fullness to guide eating behavior rather than external cues such as calorie counting,

- improve self-esteem and body image through self awareness, and

- increase physical activity.

Participants in nondieting programs are often asked to review their history of dieting, in particular any negative experiences or consequences that they have had. Biological information is used to "debunk" the notion that every individual can or should be the same size. Programs universally recommend increases in physical activity, many times in types of activities that may not have been recommended by traditional dieting programs (Foster, 2002).

Techniques guiding eating behavior vary the most among nondiet programs. They address the process of eating (the "how to") and the product of eating (the "what to eat") aspects. Most programs encourage a shift from the "dieting mentality" and subsequent preoccupation with food to more awareness of internal signals such as hunger and fullness. Programs vary widely on how this premise is implemented. Some use tools such as food logs, whereas others view this approach as "dieting behavior" and therefore unhelpful. All nondiet approaches promote avoidance of "diet behaviors," such as obtaining frequent weights, skipping meals, or self-deprivation. The actual food content recommendations among programs is yet more variable, with the continuum ranging from an "everything is allowed" on one end of the spectrum to nutritional prescriptions with reductions in some elements, such as fat and refined sugars (Foster & McGuckin, 2002).

A universal premise in all nondiet approaches is that of improving self-esteem and body image through self-acceptance. The Healthy at Every Size (HAES) paradigm described in the next section is an example of this approach.

Healthy at Every Size Philosophy

The HAES philosophy purports that dieting and weight obsessions are contributing to the obesity epidemic, and that our societal obsession with thinness does not allow for diversity in body shapes (Miller & Jacob, 2001). Under the HAES paradigm, the obese individual is encouraged to stop dieting and exercising for the sole purpose of losing weight. Instead, the patient is encouraged to develop skills to recognize what his or her body wants and needs. Quality of life and improved health are the goals of treatment, rather than reaching some predetermined body weight or body mass index (BMI) (Miller & Jacob, 2001). HAES affirms that an appropriate healthy weight for anybody cannot be determined by an ideal weight chart, a BMI value, or body fat percentage. HAES defines healthy weight as the weight at which a person settles at as they move toward a lifestyle that includes eating in an unrestricted manner, wherein the person is guided by internal cues and participating in enjoyable, reasonable, and sustainable levels of physical activity (Robison, 2005). HAES supports a holistic view of health for the obese patient – a view promoting feeling good about oneself, eating healthfully in a natural and relaxed way, and being comfortably active. The three tenants of the HAES philosophy are:

- self-acceptance,

- normalized eating, and

- enjoyable physical activity.

The overall goal of the HAES philosophy is to help individuals improve the quality of their lives, regardless of weight status.

ANALYSIS OF THE NONDIET APPROACH

Scientific Support

One of the basic premises of the nondiet approach is that the health status of the obese patient can be improved without significant weight loss. Many of the early studies regarding the nondiet approach were descriptive in nature and provided little in the way of comparison to traditional approaches. The following discussion highlights some of these results.

Exercise and Fitness

Normalization of body weight or body fat content through exercise is not necessary to improve health of obese individuals with metabolic disorders that are thought to be weight related. Studies have shown that fitness, rather than fatness, is the determinant for disease and mortality (Flagel, Graubard, Williamson, & Gail, 2005; Sui et al., 2007). Although it is not well understood how fitness and fatness interplay as determinants of health and disease, it is well established in the literature that regular exercise participation will improve the health of all people, regardless of size (American College of Sports Medicine, 2006; Brown, Moore, Korytowski, McCole, & Hagberg, 1997; Lamarche et al., 1992).

Research shows that obese people can improve their fitness level without losing weight (Blake, Miller, & Brown, 2000). Subjects for this study were 46 obese (BMI = 36, % fat = 38) and 43 lean (BMI = 22, % fat = 24) sedentary women who participated in a 14-week exercise program. Both groups of women performed the same amount of exercise and adherence to the exercise program was identical for both groups. Neither of the groups lost weight or had a change in body composition. However, both groups improved similarly in aerobic fitness, muscular strength, muscular endurance, and flexibility. The data from this study show that obese women respond to exercise training just as well as lean women, and that weight loss is not necessary for improved fitness.

Effectiveness of the HAES Treatment for Obesity

Only recently have obesity researchers evaluated the effectiveness of obesity interventions that employ a nondiet HAES paradigm. These studies, based on the HAES philosophy, measured variables such as self-esteem, depression, body image acceptance, quality of life, and anxiety- and eating-related psychopathology, such as restraint and binge eating, to determine HAES intervention effectiveness. All of these studies, measuring the effectiveness of HAES-based treatment programs, showed significant improvements in psychological states, psychological well-being, and quality of life (Miller & Jacob, 2001).

With evidence mainly rooted in psychological outcome studies, HAES supporters are open to attack from those who base effectiveness on medical measures, such as weight, blood pressure, blood lipids, and glucose control. Most of the few HAES studies that measured body weight as well as psychological variables showed small decreases in weight during intervention, with continued weight loss post-treatment. The most notable of these studies compared the HAES method of treatment to a traditional weight loss method and found that the HAES method induced a 3-kg weight loss during treatment, an additional 2-kg loss at 3 months post-treatment, and another 3-kg from 3 to 6 months post-treatment (Sbrocco, Nedegaard, Stone, & Lewis, 1999). By comparison, the traditional weight loss group lost 5-kg during treatment, but regained 1-kg at 12 months post-treatment. What is also interesting is that the HAES group, the group that was encouraged to eat an unrestricted amount of healthy foods, was consuming a significantly lower number of kilocalories post-treatment than the traditional weight loss group that was encouraged to consume 1,200 kcal/day.

Another nondieting HAES study showed that the HAES intervention caused improvements in cholesterol and triglyceride levels comparable to what was seen with a traditional weight loss program (Bacon et al., 2002).

Despite these reported effects, the overall scientific evidence in support of the nondiet approach is limited. A comprehensive review by Foster and McGuckin (2002) summarizes the results: Nondieting approaches favorably affect self-esteem and have been shown to have a small but significant effect on physiological variables such as changes in lipid levels and blood pressure. They have, however, shown little or no effect on weight overall. As with research related to traditional dieting, small sample sizes, short interventions periods, and incomplete follow-up hamper the gathering of data to support this concept universally.

Strengths of the Nondiet Approach

The greatest strength of the nondiet approach is clearly the affirmation of self-worth of the individual at every weight. This movement has undoubtedly helped to increase the recognition of the cultural bias faced by the overweight individual. By recognizing this barrier to effective treatment, which exists in our culture in general and in health care specifically, we can begin to find solutions to overcome it.

The focus on the ineffectiveness of traditional dieting by nondiet approaches has shone a spotlight on what clearly does not work. As a result, many of the ideas of the nondiet movement are now being absorbed into traditional therapy, such as approaching dietary and lifestyle modifications as lifetime changes rather than "temporary fixes."

Challenges for the Nondiet Approach

The biggest criticism of the nondiet philosophy surrounds the lack of support for its founding assumptions: "dieting is harmful; dieting leads to binge eating; weight is not a factor in disease." There is no evidence to support these premises, and

in the case of the third premise, evidence clearly exists that is contrary to this belief.

A blending of approaches may yet evolve, and concepts such as which individuals may benefit from this nontraditional approach remain to be sorted out. Scientific evidence needs to be provided that can show if individuals who are at risk for eating disorders, those who have dieted and given up, or those who have never dieted might be better served by this approach. Controlled clinical studies using medical and psychosocial outcomes would be beneficial in this endeavor.

AN EXAMPLE OF A NONDIET DIET

There are many types and forms of nondieting interventions and there are various philosophies as to what is considered a diet and what is considered a nondiet. To provide the reader of this book with an approach is a reliable and valid form of nondieting, this author will now describe a program that he and coworkers developed. This program is a conservative, behavioral, self-monitoring program that focuses equally upon the weight loss therapy components of diet and exercise, without severe restrictions in energy (kilocalorie) intake (Miller, Wallace, Lindeman, & Dyer, 1991). An explanation of the development of this methodology is also included.

Development of The Non-Diet Diet©

The core program of the Non-Diet Diet (NDD) began with the development of a system of self-evaluation tools using the NDD score sheet (Figure 11-1). Participants were asked to respond to behavioral statements that rate fat, carbohydrate, and sugar intake; water consumption; exercise; and eating behaviors. This scoring system was found to be highly reliable and valid (Miller et al., 1991). Body fat loss while using this monitoring tool for a 3-month period was strongly related (r=0.83,) to

FIGURE 11-1: THE NON-DIET DIET SCORE SHEET FOR MONITORING WEIGHT LOSS BEHAVIOR (1 OF 2)

Participant Name:		Date:						
Cardiovascular Exercise/Physical Activity:	**Points**							
1 point per minute of exercise at my target heart rate – no points for less than 20 continuous minutes, and/or 1 point per every 2 minutes of moderate physical activity. 50 points maximal.	0-50							
Subtotal	**50**							
Fat Consumption:								
I did not eat foods that were cooked in oil or fried in grease.	3							
I did not add butter or oil based products to my food.	3							
All my dairy products were non-fat or low-fat.	2							
My meats were very lean red meats or fish and poultry without the skin.	2							
Subtotal	**10**							
Refined Carbohydrate Consumption:								
I did not eat refined sugar products (jelly, jam, honey, syrup, candy, etc.).	4							
I did not eat sweet bakery goods (cookies, donuts, Twinkies, cake, etc.).	4							
I reduced the portion size of my sugar and sweet bakery products.	2							
Subtotal	**10**							
Natural Carbohydrate Consumption:								
¾ of my grain products were whole grains.	5							
My snacks were fruits, vegetables, or whole grain products. (No snacks = 5 points)	5							
Subtotal	**10**							
Water Consumption:								
I drank 6 or more glasses of water.	10							
I drank 4 to 5 glasses of water.	7							
I drank 2 to 3 glasses of water.	3							
I drank 2 or less glasses of other drinks.	0							
I drank 3 to 4 glasses of other drinks.	-5							
I drank 5 or more glasses of other drinks.	-8							
Subtotal	**10**							

continued on next page

FIGURE 11-1: THE NON-DIET DIET SCORE SHEET FOR MONITORING WEIGHT LOSS BEHAVIOR (2 OF 2)

Behavior:	Points								
I was satisfied, but not stuffed, after all my meals and snacks today.	4								
I had at least three meals or snacks today.	3								
I ate or snacked only when hungry.	3								
Subtotal	10								
Week Average Daily Total	100								

Copyright © 1986, 1993, 1997, 2007 – Wayne C. Miller, PhD.

each individual scoring category as well as total NDD scores (Miller et al., 1991). Thus, a valid behavior-monitoring tool for obesity management that did not use severe calorie restriction was developed.

Realizing that most attempts at weight loss are not face-to-face interactions with health care professionals, but low-cost alternatives that are primarily self-administered, the feasibility of self-administration of the NDD system was next researched. The first study along these lines recruited obese men and women to participate in a self-taught, self-administered NDD program (Miller, Eggert, Wallace, Lindeman, & Jastremski, 1993). Subjects received a workbook (Miller, 1991) detailing the NDD approach to weight control and were sent home to learn it for themselves. Participation in the weight loss program was completely independent of external monitoring from health care professionals for 6 months. At the end of 6 months, the subjects had lost an average of 8.1 kg of body weight, reduced their fat intake from 36% of kcal to 28%, increased carbohydrate intake from 46% of kcal to 50%, and increased their dietary fiber from 20 to 27 grams per day. Furthermore, exercise frequency went from 1.5 to 3.8 days/week (Miller, Eggert, et al., 1993). All of these behavioral changes reflect those changes necessary to reduce the disease risks and symptoms associated with the comorbidities of obesity.

In a second study, using the same type of experimental protocol with obese subjects follow-

ing the self-administered NDD, results showed participants again lost weight and showed similar dietary changes manifest in the first study (Miller, Wallace, et al., 1993). In addition, subjects in the second study saw a decrease in cardiovascular disease risk as illustrated by the following data. Blood cholesterol dropped from 210 to 191 mg/dL. Triglycerides dropped from 141 to 113 mg/dL while the ratio of total cholesterol to high-density lipoprotein cholesterol decreased significantly. Furthermore, resting systolic blood pressure dropped from 134 to 121 mm Hg while diastolic pressure dropped from 89 to 82 mm Hg. Concurrently, resting heart rate decreased from 86 to 73 beats/minute. These data suggest that the NDD behavior-monitoring system was a significant asset in helping obese adults teach themselves diet and exercise behaviors that not only reduce adiposity but also enhance cardiovascular health.

Non-Diet Diet Scoring.

The NDD is a simple 100-point scoring system, where points are awarded for participating in healthy eating and exercise behaviors that lead toward attainment of a healthy weight. This 100-point scoring system for monitoring healthy eating and exercise behaviors has several advantages over a traditional program for weight control that focuses on creating an energy deficit by either decreasing caloric intake and/or increasing energy expenditure. First of all, the NDD system is based on behaviors. Success in the program is not dependent upon the amount of weight lost, but upon the establishment of healthy behaviors. Secondly, the NDD is not "pass/fail." Traditionally, if a patient was on a diet consisting of 1,200 kcal per day and consumed 1,201 kcal, the patient would have failed for the day. Failure is discouraging, and after a few days of continued failure the patient would probably discontinue the diet and be unsuccessful. In contrast, everyone is familiar with a 100-point grading system. If, while on the NDD, a patient happens to score only 75 points or so out of 100 on one day, the patient is not a failure. The patient is still successful because 75 on a 100-point scale is still a passing score.

Another advantage of the NDD system is that it is easy to learn. There are no tables and charts filled with calorie counts or food exchanges that a person has to continually use. A person does not have to measure food portions either. Just one simple score sheet that takes less than 30 seconds to complete is required. The biggest advantage of the NDD is that it is not a diet. Therefore, patients do not always feel hungry or that they are punishing themselves with starvation.

Preview the NDD score sheet. Note that points on the score sheet are divided equally between eating and exercise behaviors. Exercise, which is usually aerobic (requiring oxygen) in nature, carries a maximum of 50 points. The eating behavior part of the NDD is divided equally into five categories valuing 10 points each. These five categories of eating behavior stress eating patterns that will bring the diet in harmony with the Department of Agriculture's food guide pyramid. Daily scoring and monitoring of weight control behaviors with the NDD score sheet is not difficult. A brief explanation of NDD scoring follows.

Daily scoring on the exercise section of the NDD score sheet is fairly simple. Points can be earned in one of two ways. The first way exercise points can be gained on the score sheet is for exercise that follows the established guidelines for aer-

obic exercise (American College of Sports Medicine, 2006). Under these guidelines, aerobic exercises such as walking, jogging, running, swimming, cycling, hiking, and others must be sustained for at least 20 minutes at an intensity of at least 40% of maximal capacity to realize a training effect. Under the guidelines, the minimal duration for aerobic exercise is 20 minutes. Therefore, no points are awarded until a continuous 20 minutes of exercise is achieved.

The second way points can be earned under the Exercise scoring section of the NDD is for participating in any activities of a moderate intensity. Recent research has shown us that many people can derive health benefits from moderate activity that does not necessarily meet the aerobic exercise guidelines we have previously emphasized. For example, some recreational activities, such as gardening and golf, which are not traditionally considered aerobic, may improve health in persons who would otherwise get no activity at all. Therefore, exercise points on the NDD score sheet can also be earned for moderate activity. One point is awarded for every 2 minutes of moderate activity accumulated during the day.

Daily scoring in the fat consumption section of the NDD score sheet is done by responding to four simple behavioral statements. A "Yes" or positive response to a statement will earn the points related to the behavior associated with that particular statement. A "No" or negative response will not earn any points. There is no credit given for partial compliance to the behavior associated with a particular statement.

One can easily see that the behaviors within this scoring section are designed to help patients reduce the amount of fat in their diet. A positive response here does not necessarily restrict food intake or limit the kinds of foods patients eat; but it will take some of the extra fat out of their diets. This is done by encouraging the consumption of familiar foods that have been prepared without adding extra fat. For example, if a person were to have chicken for dinner tonight, how would it be prepared? Would the person bake it, fry it, microwave it, broil it, grill it, or boil it? If the person fried it, then he or she would not get the three points for a positive response to the first statement about fried foods because frying chicken in oil or grease adds unnecessary fat to the food. If the person decided to bake the chicken, then they would gain three points for a positive behavior in this area of the fat consumption category. In this way, the patient is not restricted from eating chicken, just directed to alter the method of preparation.

The statement about butter- and oil-based products refers to spreads, oils, gravies, sauces, salad dressings, and the like. Be aware that reduced-fat products may still contain an enormous amount of fat, so read the label to find the true fat content. Nonfat substitutes, however, are acceptable. The use of butter, margarine, and almost all spreads will be scored against the patient unless they can determine that these foods are fat-free. Contrastingly, nonfat cooking sprays and artificial butter flakes will not count against the patient.

For the third behavioral statement, dairy products include milk, cheese, eggs, cream, yogurt, etc. The guidance here is to consume that which has the lowest amount of fat. Milk can be purchased as whole milk, 3.3%; low-fat milk, 2%; low-fat, 1%; low-fat, ½%; and skim. Encourage the patients to gradually work their way down to the lowest fat content they can go without eliminating milk from their diet (vegans, of course should use a milk substitute). Do the same for all dairy products. Patients may feel comfortable with skim milk, but absolutely detest nonfat cottage cheese. Go ahead and have them consume the low-fat cottage cheese if they like it and they will still earn the points.

The last behavioral statement in this scoring category deals with meat, fish, and poultry. Red meat, particularly beef, has a high fat content. However, red meat, like most other meats, has a high iron and protein content. It is desirable then, to reduce the amount of fat one consumes in meats by eating only very lean meat products. Any meat product that is 95% fat-free is acceptable. At 95% fat-free, about 30% of the calories in the meat are fat calories, not 5%, because 95% fat-free refers to the weight of the product not the calories. It is easy to evaluate packaged meats, but fresh meats are more difficult. Have patients consult with their butchers or the meat personnel at their food store for help with fresh meats. Meat substitutes or meat fillers are all acceptable. Vegetarian patients will score the full points on the score sheet for this area even if they do not consume any meat.

All sugars are carbohydrates and contribute to the nutritive value of food. Refined sugars or added sugars generally contain very little vitamins and minerals, but contribute substantially to food calories. Like the fat consumption scoring section, the refined carbohydrate consumption scoring section consists of behavioral statements geared at reducing the amount of extra sugars in the diet. Similarly, a "Yes" or positive behavioral response will earn the points associated with that particular behavioral statement, whereas, a "No" or negative response will not earn any points. The purpose of the first statement in this category is to help patients curtail the amount of refined sugars they add to their diet while limiting the amount of nonnutritious calories they consume. Some of the most common refined sugar products are listed in the behavior statement itself, but this list is not all inclusive. Food products that would count against a person under this behavior statement are those foods that are virtually all refined sugar. In addition to those foods listed on the score sheet, foods such as pudding, custard, jelly, marshmallows, and chocolate candy are easily classified as refined sugars. Scoring becomes a little difficult when patients have to evaluate foods that contain a substantial amount of refined sugar, but still have a high nutritive value. Breakfast cereals are particularly difficult to evaluate. Refined sugars contribute to over

50% of the calories in some breakfast cereals, but on the other hand, these cereals are usually fortified with vitamins and minerals. So, patients will have to make a judgment call on these types of foods. Are they primarily getting refined sugar or other nutrients from the food they are evaluating?

The second statement in the refined carbohydrate scoring section deals with bakery goods. This statement obviously refers to those bakery goods that are packed with refined sugar and not to whole grain breads, muffins, rolls, etc. Behaviors in accordance with this and the previous statement about refined sugar are quite restrictive. In an effort to help patients negotiate behaviors in the refined carbohydrate consumption scoring section, the third behavioral statement on reduced portions is included. Positive behavior here will give patients credit for reducing the portions of refined carbohydrates in their diet without eliminating sweets altogether. On the other hand, if patients eliminate the refined sugar in their diet completely (as defined by the first two statements in this scoring section) they automatically gain the two points for the third statement. Consuming no refined sugar products must be either an automatic reduction when compared to their customary intake; or if they routinely avoid refined sugar already, the behavior itself is in line with nutritious eating, which deserves full credit.

The natural carbohydrate consumption portion of the NDD deals with carbohydrates that are not highly processed or refined. There are two behavioral statements in this scoring section, each valued at five points. The first behavior to monitor is the consumption of whole grain products. If a patient estimates that three quarters of the grain products consumed during the day were whole grains, the patient gets five points for a positive behavior. The patient does not need to calculate, count grams, weigh food portions, or count food exchanges in order to determine their score in this area. A rough estimate will suffice.

The intent of the second behavioral statement in this scoring category is to encourage snacking on natural carbohydrates and not refined sugar products. If a patient is hungry, a patient should snack on a fruit, vegetable, or whole grain product rather than a refined sugar product. Notice that patients also earn five points if they do not snack. The purpose of this clause is to urge people to snack only when hungry. Patients will get the maximum of five points for this behavior by either snacking on fruits, vegetables, or grain products or by not snacking at all.

Self-evaluation in the water consumption scoring section of the NDD score sheet is similar to the other scoring sections in that there are points associated with specific behavioral statements. The purpose of this section is to help patients monitor their fluid intake as well as reduce their consumption of high-calorie drinks. Although the term water is used here, fluid intake is not restricted to only water. The word water in this sense is used to describe **any nonsugared, nonalcoholic drink.** Under this definition, beverages such as diet sodas, coffee and tea without sugar, natural fruit and vegetable juices, and diet powdered drinks are considered water. Because milk is rich in vitamins and minerals and does not contain refined sugar, it also can be counted for positive behavior scoring. Of course low-fat milk or skim milk is the preference.

The purpose of this scoring section would be defeated if a person could drink six glasses of water early in the day to get 10 points, and then consume unlimited amounts of sugared-drinks or alcohol later in the day without penalty. Thus, as patients make the transition from consuming water to other beverages they begin to be penalized. There is no penalty for consuming two or fewer glasses of other drinks during the day, but with three or more other drinks patients start losing points. Thus, the maximum points awarded for this scoring section is 10, with a possible maximum penalty of eight.

The behaviors encouraged in the behavior scoring section assist patients in learning to internally control the amount of food they eat. Notice that the first two behavioral statements actually promote eating rather than dieting; whereas the third statement discourages eating without hunger. The 10 possible points to be earned in the behavior scoring section of the NDD score sheet bring the total dietary behavioral points to 50. These dietary points added to the 50 possible exercise points make a grand total of 100 points for NDD daily scoring. By this time, you should have recognized that healthy weight management is the culmination of multiple behaviors rather than just one (eating too many calories). Thus, another positive aspect of the NDD scoring system is that patients are rewarded or penalized for multiple behaviors that affect healthy weight management.

Case Study 11-1 presents an example of a health behavior assessment with the non-diet diet.

Case Study 11-1: Health Behavior Assessment With The Non-Diet Diet

You are a nurse practitioner at a bariatric center. Julie is a patient who has selected a nondieting program to help her control her weight and improve her general health. She has been participating in the program for 2 months, and has lost 6 lb. She came to the clinic today to attend the weekly health promotion classes offered to all patients. The attached Non-Diet Diet score sheet is the record of her exercise and nutrition behaviors for the past week. Please counsel Julie on what she has done well and where she can improve.

Resolution Process

The resolution to Julie's case comes from a thorough review of her Non-Diet Diet score sheet for the week. The scores in each of the scoring categories reveal the patterns of Julie's behavior as well as how well she is doing in each of the behavior focus areas.

The overall average daily score for Julie this week is a 56, which is not a high enough score for most people to be successful at losing weight. (Most people start having success at an average above 60 points per day.) After checking the overall daily average score for the week, you look at each scoring category. Julie was not physically active at all on two days during the week, and only a little active on a third day (10 points). The goal would be that Julie be physically active on all days of the week, but not necessarily requiring that she achieve 50 exercise points each day. If Julie could achieve 30 points for exercise each day, she could raise her total average score by almost 10 points a day. This higher score would bring her into the low successful range.

Julie's scores for all of the eating categories are good, except for the refined carbohydrate consumption scores. These daily scores are generally low. Further investigation shows that Julie also scores many of her zeros in the refined carbohydrate consumption category, and that many of these zeros are because she eats sweet bakery goods. Future behavior focus should be placed on helping Julie reduce her consumption of bakery goods.

Running down the length of the column scores, two things become apparent. First, Julie's highest score was the first day of the weekly record (85 points). This was also the day after her last visit to the clinic. So, it seems like she is highly motivated after her weekly clinic visits. This suggests continued support may be necessary for Julie to be successful. Second, the last day of the week was Julie's worst day (19 points). You should probe for more information on why this day's performance was so poor. It may be that Julie had a special event (e.g., party, wedding, holiday) where she let go of all restraints. Future plans would be to help her use moderation on these types of days.

The positive aspects of Julie's score sheet are that she is doing well in fat consumption, natural carbohydrate consumption, water consumption, and behavior. If you ignore scores for the last day of the week in these categories, Julie did fairly well. She should be commended for this accomplishment.

Julie is maintaining a lifestyle that is somewhat active, but she can increase her physical activity level and become more consistent in being physically active each day. Her eating behaviors are somewhat erratic, but she is doing well in most eating behaviors. Julie's problem area is eating too many refined carbohydrates in the form of baked goods. The focus for improvement should be on daily consistency in exercise, reducing baked good consumption, and day-to-day consistency throughout.

Julie's Non-Diet Diet Score Sheet

Participant Name: Julie		Date:						
Cardiovascular Exercise/Physical Activity:	**Points**	3/18	3/19	3/20	3/21	3/22	3/23	3/24
1 point per minute of exercise at my target heart rate – no points for less than 20 continuous minutes, and/or 1 point per every 2 minutes of moderate physical activity. 50 points maximal.	0-50							
Subtotal	**50**	**35**	**0**	**35**	**40**	**25**	**0**	**10**
Fat Consumption:								
I did not eat foods that were cooked in oil or fried in grease.	3	3	3	3	0	3	3	0
I did not add butter or oil based products to my food.	3	3	0	3	3	0	3	0
All my dairy products were non-fat or low-fat.	2	2	2	2	2	2	2	2
My meats were very lean red meats or fish and poultry without the skin.	2	2	2	0	2	2	2	0
Subtotal	**10**	**10**	**7**	**8**	**7**	**7**	**10**	**2**
Refined Carbohydrate Consumption:								
I did not eat refined sugar products (jelly, jam, honey, syrup, candy, etc.).	4	4	4	4	0	0	0	4
I did not eat sweet bakery goods (cookies, donuts, Twinkies, cake, etc.).	4	4	0	0	0	4	0	0
I reduced the portion size of my sugar and sweet bakery products.	2	2	2	0	2	0	2	0
Subtotal	**10**	**10**	**6**	**4**	**2**	**4**	**2**	**4**
Natural Carbohydrate Consumption:								
¾ of my grain products were whole grains.	5	5	5	0	5	5	5	0
My snacks were fruits, vegetables, or whole grain products. (No snacks = 5 points)	5	5	5	5	5	5	5	0
Subtotal	**10**	**10**	**10**	**5**	**10**	**10**	**10**	**0**
Water Consumption:								
I drank 6 or more glasses of water.	10	10	10	10			10	
I drank 4 to 5 glasses of water.	7					7		
I drank 2 to 3 glasses of water.	3				3			
I drank 2 or less glasses of other drinks.	0							0
I drank 3 to 4 glasses of other drinks.	-5							
I drank 5 or more glasses of other drinks.	-8							
Subtotal	**10**	**10**	**10**	**10**	**3**	**7**	**10**	**0**

continued on next page

Behavior:	Points							
I was satisfied, but not stuffed, after all my meals and snacks today.	4	4	4	4	0	4	4	0
I had at least 3 meals or snacks today.	3	3	3	3	3	3	3	3
I ate or snacked only when hungry.	3	3	3	3	0	3	3	0
Subtotal	10	10	10	10	3	10	10	3
Week Average	56	Daily Total	100	85	43	72	65	63	42	19

SUMMARY

The HAES philosophy contends that part of the obesity problem is caused by our obsession with weight and dieting. The continued use of restrictive dieting and exercise solely to lose weight is unproductive because these methods for weight loss do not demonstrate long-term success. The HAES approach encompasses all aspects of health for the obese patient, and affirms that obese patients can become healthy without losing substantial amounts of weight. Nondieting eating plans fall within the realm of the HAES philosophy in that they encourage healthy eating without restriction and deprivation. Improvements in weight, mental health, disease risk, and eating pathologies have been demonstrated with HAES and nondieting treatment plans.

The nondiet approach is a relatively new approach to health promotion for obese patients that many health professionals have adopted. It represents an exciting development in the field of obesity management. Further study is needed to determine how best to utilize the principles, and to provide individuals with choices about how to manage their health and weight. The principles outlined help overweight individuals "believe that weight is just one factor that describes them – it does not define them" (Foster, 2002).

EXAM QUESTIONS

CHAPTER 11
Questions 42-44

Note: Choose the option that BEST answers each question.

42. The three tenants of the Health At Every Size (HAES) paradigm for obesity treatment includes

    a. self-control, dieting, and weight loss.

    b. self-acceptance, normalized eating, and enjoyable physical activity.

    c. size matters most, normal weight ensures normal health, and diet for health.

    d. every size can lose weight, exercise, and dietary restraint.

43. The principle used by the nondieting approach to design programs to address weight-related health issues is

    a. weight gain is purely a product of the individual's environment.

    b. regular exercise is an important component of improving health.

    c. psychotherapy is the preferred treatment strategy for weight loss.

    d. weight loss is the ultimate goal of the treatment plan.

44. The Non-Diet Diet program and its score sheet is a nondieting obesity treatment method that

    a. rewards patients for good behavior and punishes them for bad behavior.

    b. views success as the establishment of health behaviors not weight loss.

    c. encourages dietary restriction and restraint.

    d. encourages extreme changes in lifestyle to achieve rapid weight loss.

REFERENCES

American College of Sports Medicine. (2006). *ACSM's guidelines for exercise testing and prescription* (7th ed., pp. 133-173). Philadelphia: Lippincott Williams & Wilkins.

Bacon, L., Keim, N.L., Van Loan, M.D., Derricote, M., Gale, B., Kazaks, A., et al. (2002). Evaluating a 'non-diet' wellness intervention for improvement of metabolic fitness, psychological well-being and eating and activity behaviors. *International Journal of Obesity, 26,* 854-865.

Blake, A., Miller, W.C., & Brown, D.A. (2000). Adiposity does not hinder the fitness response to exercise training in obese women. *Journal of Sports Medicine and Physical Fitness, 40,* 170-177.

Brown, M.D., Moore, G.E., Korytkowski, M.T., McCole, S.D., & Hagberg, J.M. (1997). Improvement in insulin sensitivity by short-term exercise training in hypertensive African-American women. *Hypertension, 30,* 1549-1553.

Flagel, L.H., Graubard, B.I., Williamson, D.F., & Gail, M.H. (2005). Excess deaths associated with underweight, overweight, and obesity. *Journal of the American Medical Association, 293,* 1861-1867.

Foster, G.D. (2002). Nondieting approaches, In C.G. Fairburn & K.D. Brownell (Eds.), *Eating disorders and obesity* (2nd ed., pp. 604-8). New York: The Guilford Press.

Foster, G.D. & McGuckin, B.G. (2002). Nondieting approaches: Principles, practices and evidence. In T.A. Wadden & A.J. Stunkard, (Eds.), *Handbook of obesity treatment* (2nd ed., pp. 494-509). New York, NY: Guilford Press.

Lamarche, B., Despres, J.P., Pouliot, M.C., Moorjani, S., Lupien P.L., Theriault, G., et al. (1992). Is body fat loss a determinant factor in the improvement of carbohydrate and lipid metabolism following aerobic exercise training in obese women? *Metabolism, 41,* 1249-1256.

Miller, W.C. (1991). *The Non-diet diet: A simple 100-point scoring system for weight loss without counting calories.* Englewood, CO: Morton Publishing Company.

Miller, W.C., Eggert, K.E., Wallace, J.P., Lindeman, A.K., & Jastremski, C. (1993). Successful weight loss in a self-taught, self-administered program. *International Journal of Sports Medicine, 7,* 401-405.

Miller, W.C. & Jacob, A.V. (2001). The health at every size paradigm for obesity treatment: The scientific evidence. *Obesity Reviews, 2,* 37-45.

Miller, W.C., Wallace, J., Lindeman, L.K., & Dyer, D.L. (1991). The Non-diet diet: A 100-point scoring system for monitoring weight loss behavior. *Journal of American Dietetic Association, 91,* 973-975.

Miller, W.C., Wallace, J.P., Eggert, K.E., & Lindeman, A.K. (1993). Cardiovascular risk reduction in a self-taught, self-administered weight-loss program called the Non-diet diet. *Medicine, Exercise, Nutrition and Health, 2,* 218-223.

Robison, J. (2005). Health at every size: Antidote for the obesity epidemic. *Health At Every Size Journal, 19,* 3-10.

Sbrocco, T., Nedegaard, R.C., Stone, J.M., & Lewis, E. (1999). Behavioral choice treatment promotes continuing weight loss: Preliminary results of a cognitive-behavioral decision-based treatment for obesity. *Journal of Consulting and Clinical Psychology, 67,* 260-266.

Sui, X., LaMonte, J.J., Laditka, J.N., Hardin, J.W., Chase, N., Hooker, S.P., et al. (2007). Cardiorespiratory fitness and adiposity as mortality predictors in older adults. *Journal of the American Medical Association, 298,* 2507-2516.

CHAPTER 12

PHARMACOTHERAPY

CHAPTER OBJECTIVE

After completing this chapter the learner will be able to describe the clinical application of pharmacotherapy for weight control.

LEARNING OBJECTIVES

After completing this chapter, the learner will be able to

1. define the three categories of prescription medications for weight loss.

2. explain the mechanism of action behind appetite suppressants, thermogenics, and lipid partitioners for the treatment of obesity.

3. discuss the effectiveness and side effects of sibutramine, orlistat, and phentermine in the treatment of obesity.

4. describe the off-label use of medications for weight control.

5. evaluate the efficacy of some common over-the-counter remedies for weight control.

INTRODUCTION

Obesity is a chronic condition that often requires long-term treatment to promote and maintain weight loss. All levels of obesity will benefit from diet therapy, increased physical activity, and behavior modification programs. Patients with more severe obesity, or those who have not responded to these measures may need the additional intervention of pharmacotherapy. Guidelines from the National Heart, Lung and Blood Institute (NHLBI, 1998) recommend considering pharmacotherapy for obese patients with a body mass index (BMI) of 30 or greater, and for overweight patients with a BMI of 27 to 29.9 that is accompanied by comorbid disease or a waist circumference greater than 35 inches for women and greater than 40 inches for men.

It seems logical that prescription drugs and over-the-counter remedies would be valuable resources in the treatment of obesity; however, historically the use of drugs and dietary supplements for the treatment of obesity has been controversial. This chapter will present a review of the use and effectiveness for current pharmacological treatments for obesity and emerging treatments in development.

PRESCRIPTION/ NONPRESCRIPTION OBESITY DRUGS

The search for pharmacological agents to treat obesity started in the first half of the 20th century. The Food and Drug Administration (FDA) has approved and retracted several anti-obesity drugs over the past several decades. Adverse effects of some of these products forced their recall and left many people and health care professionals concerned about using drugs for the treatment of obesity. When obesity is viewed as a chronic disease, where the regulation of energy balance is dysfunctional, the use of medications for the treatment of obesity is similar to the commonly accepted pharmacological treatment of hypertension and diabetes.

The NHBLI guidelines also state that FDA-approved drugs must be used with lifestyle modifications that include dietary intervention, behavior therapy, and increased physical activity. Under these guidelines, one might look at drug therapy for obesity the same way as one would for treatment for diabetes and cardiovascular disease – medication + behavior therapy + diet change + exercise.

The three categories of drugs that have received FDA approval for the treatment of obesity are:

- appetite suppressants,
- thermogenics, and
- lipid-partitioners.

Appetite suppressants target neurotransmitters so that the body is tricked into believing that it is not hungry. This effect is achieved by increasing levels of serotonin and/or norepinephrine. Thermogenics act by increasing metabolism or energy expenditure, whereas lipid-partitioners inhibit the digestion and absorption of fat. Of all the FDA-approved anti-obesity drugs, three are commonly found in clinical use: sibutramine (Meridia), orlistat (Xenical), and phentermine.

Sibutramine

Sibutramine was approved by the FDA in 1997 for short- and long-term use (up to 2 years). Sibutramine is an appetite suppressant and a thermogenic. It inhibits the reuptake of serotonin and norepinephrine. The serotonin effects of sibutramine are localized to the brain, and therefore, sibutramine does not produce the negative side effects that the combination drug fenfluramine-phentermine (Fen-phen) had on the heart.

Several research studies have shown that sibutramine is effective in obesity treatment. However, most of the research trials included a calorie-reduced diet along with the drug treatment. So, the effects of the drug itself on weight control are hard to distinguish. One study tested the drug without confounding the trial with dietary modifications (Hansen, Toubro, Stock, Macdonald, & Astrup, 1999). In this study, 32 obese patients (BMI = 34) took sibutramine for 8 weeks. The average weight loss for the drug group was 2.4 kg (5.3 lb) and only 0.3 kg (0.66 lb) for the placebo group. This amounts to about one-half pound per week due to the drug.

Most of the other studies show that sibutramine produces a 5% to 10% weight loss when combined with dietary intervention. These studies generally last only 4 to 12 weeks, and the lost body weight tends to return after drug treatment stops. Even when drug treatment was extended for 1 year beyond the treatment phase, patients regained 50% of their lost weight (Kaplan, 2005).

The normal dose for sibutramine is 10 to 15 mg/day, taken orally. A dose-response study was done by Knoll Pharmaceuticals (manufacturer of Meridia), in which obese patients were placed into a double-blind, placebo-controlled design (Hanotin, Thomas, Jones, Leutenegger, & Drouin, 1998). Similar to other studies, the 12-week trial also provided diet and behavior modification advice to the patients. The mean group weight loss at the end of the study for the treated groups were 2.4 kg (5.3 lb) for the 5 mg/day dose, 5.1 kg (11.2 lb) for the 10 mg/day dose, and 4.9 kg (10.8 lb) for the 15 mg/day dose. The incidence and type of adverse events and the rate of withdrawal were not significantly different among the four groups. No changes in blood pressure were found, but heart rate increased 4 beats/minute in the patients who received the 10-mg or 15-mg dose.

The most common side effects associated with sibutramine include headache, dry mouth, anorexia, insomnia, and constipation (Palamara, Mongul, Peterson, & Frishman, 2006). Increased heart rate and blood pressure are possible side effects, but not very common. Contraindications for use include: any type of cardiovascular disease, stroke, liver or kidney impairment, uncontrolled hypertension, or taking any serotonergic drugs. On October 8, 2010, the manufacturer of sibutramine (Meridia) voluntarily withdrew the commonly prescribed drug from the U.S. market because clinical trial data indicated an increased risk of heart attack and stroke.

Orlistat

Orlistat (Xenical or the nonprescription form Alli) was approved by the FDA in 1999 for short- and long-term use (up to 2 years). Orlistat is classified as a lipase partitioner, and works by inhibiting pancreatic lipase, an enzyme that breaks down triglycerides in the intestine. When triglycerides cannot be broken down into their constituents (glycerol and 3 fatty acids) the would-be absorbable free fatty acids cannot be digested and are excreted in the feces. Only trace amounts of orlistat are absorbed in the system. Therefore, the primary effect of orlistat is local lipase inhibition within the gastrointestinal tract after taking an oral dose. Orlistat is eliminated in the feces.

The standard prescription dose for orlistat is 120 mg three times daily before meals. The nonprescription dose for orlistat is 60 mg, one-half the prescription dose. The prescription dose prevents approximately 30% of dietary fat from being absorbed, whereas about 25% of fat is blocked from absorption at the standard nonprescription dose. Higher doses do not produce more potent effects. Orlistat is the only over-the-counter diet drug that is approved by the FDA, and there are no generic formulations.

Orlistat was first evaluated in a 2-year randomized, double-blind, placebo-controlled trial with 880 subjects in 18 clinics (Palamara et al., 2006). The first year of the study consisted of drug treatment at the 120 mg per day dose in combination with dietary intervention. Then the drug treatment group was divided into a 120 mg group and 60 mg group for a 1-year maintenance period. Orlistat caused a 2.9 kg weight loss above the placebo during the treatment phase. This amounts to only one tenth of a pound a week difference in weight loss between the drug and placebo. During the maintenance period, the 120 mg group regained 35% of lost weight, the 60 mg group regained 51%, and the placebo group regained 63%. Other studies demonstrate that a typical 1-year trial on orlistat will produce a 5% weight loss in one third to one half of the patients, and a 10% weight loss in less than one quarter of the patients (Palamara et al., 2006).

The most common side effects associated with orlistat are oily loose stools, incontinence, frequent or urgent bowel movements, abdominal pain, and flatulence. A study administering psyllium with orlistat found a reduction by more than 50% of adverse gastrointestinal side effects (Waitman & Aronne, 2005). The manufacturer advises patients to consume a low-fat diet in order to reduce the side effects. Absorption of fat-soluble vitamins and other fat-soluble nutrients is inhibited by orlistat. Taking a multivitamin that contains vitamins A, D, E, and K, with beta-carotene is recommended. Contraindications for orlistat use include malabsorption syndrome, pregnancy, breast-feeding, and reduced gallbladder function.

Phentermine

Phentermine was approved by the FDA for short-term use (4 to 12 weeks) 50 years ago (1959). It is classified as an appetite suppressant and a thermogenic that has similar actions as other drugs in the amphetamine drug class. Phentermine's mechanism of action is to stimulate the release of catecholamines (dopamine, epinephrine, and norepinephrine). It is thought that the release of these catecholamines represses hunger signals by placing the body in the state of alarm (fight-or-flight). Stimulation of the central nervous system by phentermine-induced catecholamine release increases metabolism.

The standard dose for phentermine is a 30 mg tablet, taken at breakfast or within 2 hours after breakfast. The early morning dose of phentermine is suggested because of its stimulatory affects that can cause insomnia. Blood levels peak between 1 and 4 hours and absorption is complete in 4 to 6 hours. As with amphetamines, people can develop a tolerance to phentermine. Tolerance can be avoided by taking the drug for 5 days and then skipping 2 days.

Because phentermine was approved by the FDA in 1959, randomized controlled clinical trials have been conducted to evaluate its effectiveness in producing weight loss. In the mid 1990s, the combination of fenfluramine-phentermine became popular. Several studies were performed on the drug combination. In 1997, fenfluramine-phentermine was taken off the market because of its cause of heart valve disease. The problem in the mixture originated from the fenfluramine. Phentermine itself is still on the list of FDA-approved drugs.

The most common side effects associated with phentermine include elevated heart rate, increased blood pressure, irritability, insomnia, and addiction. Contraindications to phentermine use include cardiovascular disease, hypertension, overactive thyroid, and history of substance abuse.

Case Study 12-1 describes how to select appropriate drug therapy for a patient.

Case Study 12-1: Choosing A Pharmacotherapeutic Weight Loss Agent

You are a nurse practitioner at a women's health clinic. Judy is an obese patient with a body mass index of 32 who wants to lose weight, but she has struggled historically on calorie-restricted diets. Judy is also hypertensive, but her blood pressure is generally under control with medication. Judy has seen the clinic dietitian and brings the diet analysis report to you. Decide upon a drug treatment plan that would best suit Judy.

Intervention/Solution

The diet analysis for Judy reveals that Judy's dietary intake is approximately 2,200 kcal, only 10% above what her predicted intake should be for weight maintenance at her current weight. However, Judy's intake consists of a diet that is 42% fat, 14% protein, and 44% carbohydrate. Your decision is to place Judy on a modified diet and prescribe orlistat at a dose of 120 mg three times daily with meals.

Resolution

There are only three common prescription drugs for weight loss: orlistat, sibutramine, and phentermine. Some possible side effects of phentermine and orlistat are increased heart rate and blood pressure. Because Judy is hypertensive, you prefer not to prescribe a medication that may raise her blood pressure, so your first choice is orlistat. The second factor behind your decision to prescribe orlistat is that Judy is not overeating to a great extent. Her energy intake is 2,200 kcal/day, only 10% above predicted. However, she is consuming a high-fat diet. Because Judy has had difficulty in the past with restrictive dieting, you think that by moderately reducing her dietary fat intake and using orlistat, Judy should be able to reduce her absorbed fat calories enough to produce weight loss.

Side effects of orlistat often cause patients to discontinue the drug, so you advise Judy about the likely effects and how to decrease their severity by reducing her dietary fat intake. You also advise her to take a multivitamin with fat-soluble vitamins (A, D, E, and K), and to make sure she takes the vitamin 2 hours apart from the orlistat. She is also instructed not to take the orlistat if she skips or misses a meal.

If you have the dietitian prescribe a 1,800 kcal diet for Judy, her energy intake would be 180 kcal/day under what is predicted for weight maintenance. If the 1,800 kcal diet is prescribed at a fat content of 30%, this would bring Judy's diet to the recommended composition as well. Orlistat should block 30% of the fat calories from being absorbed, which in this case would be an additional 180 kcal per day. So, with only a

continued on next page

minor restriction in Judy's intake and a change in diet composition, Judy has a diet deficit of 360 kcal per day. This would amount to a weight loss of 1 lb every 10 days.

This may not seem like much, but if Judy walked 2 miles every day for exercise, she could easily lose 1 lb a week. In addition to diet modification, you develop a plan with Judy to increase her daily physical activity. You also recommend that she attend the weekly weight loss group meetings, which she agrees to do. Your therapeutic treatment plan now includes all recommended components of a weight reduction plan for Judy's body mass index.

FUTURE PHARMACOTHERAPY DIRECTIONS

With the recent expansion of knowledge of molecular biology and the genetic aspects of obesity, opportunities for drug treatment development are evolving. One category of drugs are those that work to interrupt the neurohormonal process signaling hunger, interfering with such hormone production as ghrelin. Other areas of research include drugs to stimulate thermogenesis and increase resting energy expenditure. Still other research is looking at meds to stimulate or mimic the actions of satiety hormones, such as cholecystokinin or leptin. And yet other efforts are looking at understanding where particular deficits may occur in the individual genetic makeup, therefore allowing more targeted pharmacotherapy.

Combination therapy is another field of development, with the advantage that therapies may be developed that alternate regimens and reduce potential adverse affects of a single regimen. This area will probably yield new treatment results most rapidly because it may utilize agents that have already shown promise in clinical trials (Heska & Heymsfield, 2002).

Off-Label Drug Use

The FDA requires numerous clinical trials to prove a drug's safety and effectiveness in treating a specific disease or condition. When the FDA becomes satisfied that the claims regarding the effectiveness and safety of a drug have been met, the FDA and manufacturer compose what is written on the drug label. The FDA then approves the drug for use in treating the specific disease or condition. When the drug receives FDA approval, the FDA allows the physician to use judgment in how to prescribe the drug. The FDA does not attempt to practice medicine. If a physician prescribes a drug for use other than what was determined in the FDA approval process, this is called prescribing the drug off-label. It is completely legal to prescribe a drug off-label. The decision of whether or not to do so is left to the judgment of the prescriber. Consequently, some drugs have been prescribed for the off-label use of weight control because in other uses one of the side effects was weight loss.

Diabetic Medications

Metformin is an agent that has been approved by the FDA for management of type 2 diabetes. When used in trials for the treatment for diabetes, it produced significant weight loss. Metformin reduces food intake in diabetic and nondiabetic patients. The drug is well tolerated and the side effects are primarily nausea, diarrhea, vomiting, and flatulence. Use in patients with renal impairment, liver disease, pulmonary disorders, or congestive heart failure is contraindicated. However, it is interesting that many obese patients with diabetes also have these comorbid conditions. Metformin is currently being evaluated for long-term weight management in patients who have hyperinsulinemia (high plasma levels of insulin often related to insulin resistance).

Pramlintide (Symlin) is an FDA-approved drug used in the treatment of patients with diabetes who also use insulin. Patients on pramlintide tend to lose weight, compared to the usual weight gain associated with insulin use (Palamara et al., 2006). Pramlintide is a parenteral medication, which in one study produced higher weight loss in African Americans (Greenway & Bray, 2006) Further evaluation for use in obesity treatment is needed.

Epileptic and Central Nervous System Medications

Zonisamide is an antiepileptic drug that has some potential for weight management. A 16-week study resulted in a 6% weight loss due to the drug compared to a 1% loss for the placebo (Gadde, Franciscy, Wagner, Ranga, & Krishnan, 2003). Zonisamide may cause appetite suppression by increasing serotonin and dopamine levels. Some possible side effects include headache, dizziness, nausea, irritability, and fatigue.

Topiramate (Topamax) drug is an antileptic agent for seizure disorders that has been found to reduce body weight in patients with epilepsy, bipolar disorder, and binge eating disorder (Waitman & Aronne, 2005). In a randomized, double-blind trial, weight loss at 24 weeks was found to be from 5% to 6.3% depending on the dosage. Side effects are related to central or peripheral nervous system effects, such as paresthesia, somnolence, and difficulty with memory and concentration.

Atomoxetine (Strattera) is an approved drug for attention deficit hyperactivity disorder. When tested on obese subjects for 12 weeks, a 3.9% higher weight loss than placebo was achieved (Greenway & Bray, 2006).

Antidepressant Medication

Bupropion (Wellbutrin) is one of the most common drugs approved by the FDA for use in depression. Results from antidepressant trials showed that many patients lost weight and did not regain the weight after conclusion of treatment. Clinical trials for the drug have shown it to be effective in producing a 5% weight loss (Palamara et al., 2006). In a dose response trial, the weight-loss effect of bupro-

pion was significant, and dose dependent (Anderson et al., 2002). At 24 weeks the placebo group lost 5% of body weight, the 300 mg/day group lost 7.2% and the 400 mg/day group lost 10.1%. After 24 weeks follow-up, the 300 mg/day group maintained a weight loss of 7.5%, whereas the 400 mg/day group maintained a 10.1% loss. Possible side effects include insomnia, anxiety, abdominal pain, dizziness, constipation, tremors, and dry mouth. However, the most common side effect in the weight loss study was insomnia. These results seem promising and suggest that obese patients with depression be prescribed bupropion.

DIETARY SUPPLEMENTS

All other weight-loss remedies sold over-the-counter are classified as dietary supplements. Dietary supplements do not need to pass through a rigorous clinical trial period, as do prescription medications. There are few scientific results showing effective weight loss. This lack of testing for dietary supplements makes it easy for marketers to sell their wares in stores and over the Internet without much regulation. Some of the most common over-the-counter remedies or dietary supplements are described below. There are three general categories: fiber supplements, minerals and metabolites, and herbal therapies.

Fiber

Chitosan – A dietary supplement made from a starch found in the skeleton of shrimp, crab, and other shellfish, chitosan cannot be digested and absorbed. The chemical makeup of chitosan allows it to bind to fatty foods, facilitating weight loss by inhibiting fat absorption in the intestine. The limited amount of research on chitosan shows that the supplement does not induce weight loss.

Glucomannan – This fiber supplement is a water-soluble polysaccharide used in food products as an emulsifier and thickener. Several health claims are associated with glucomannan, including benefits for constipation, cholesterol, obesity, acne, and diabetes. However, most of these claims have not been substantiated, and the Federal Trade Commission has reprimanded several companies for their false advertising claims. Glucomannan absorbs water in the gut and may decrease digestive transit time. These digestive actions of glucomman are what marketers promote as its mechanism of action in weight loss treatment. The weight loss benefits of glucomman are not proven, and the supplement may cause choking, due to its swelling when combined with fluid.

Minerals and Metabolites

Chromium and Chromium Picolinate – These substances are thought to enhance the effect of insulin and, therefore, help with the metabolism of carbohydrates and fat. A few studies show small statistically significant changes in weight with chromium picolinate, but other studies show no effect. Chromium supplementation can cause sterility, skeleton weakness, and DNA mutations in animals, but these side effects have not been confirmed in humans. Some evidence exists that this mineral may have an effect in preventing weight regain rather than assisting in weight loss (Bray & Ryan, 2006).

Herbal Dietary Supplements

St. John's Wort: – This substance is an herbal remedy that has been used for years to treat depression. Research shows that St. John's wort is effective in treating mild depression, but ineffective in treating moderate-to-severe depression. The side effects from St. John's wort are less than with traditional antidepressants and include digestive symptoms, dizziness, and tiredness. There is no research to suggest that St. John's wort induces weight loss. However, St. John's wort may be a mediating factor in weight loss behavior, meaning that if St. John's wort is successful in treating a person's

depression, the person may then participate in more healthful eating and activity behaviors.

Ephedra sinica (Ma huang) – This substance is an evergreen that grows in central Asia. The central ingredient is ephedrine. It is a widely used supplement for weight loss, and studies have shown significantly greater weight loss than with placebo. Because of its cardiac stimulatory effects, it has the potential to be harmful to patients. This effect appears to be dose related (Bray & Ryan, 2006).

Hoodia – The source of this herbal substance is a cactus that grows in Africa. The herb is thought to decrease appetite and thirst. Early investigation shows decreased caloric intake in a short trial among 19 obese males, with a low side effect profile. Because this cactus is rare in the wild and cultivation is difficult, it is uncertain whether supplements actually contain the active ingredient or whether supplements will have the same effects seen in early trials (Bray & Ryan, 2006).

Guarana – Although not strictly an herbal product, guarana is a plant substance made from the seeds of a plant native to Brazil. Guarana is a stimulant, and contains 3% to 5% caffeine. The weight loss claims for guarana come from its stimulatory and diuretic effects. However, there is no research to support these claims. Moreover, guarana can cause side effects of nausea, dizziness, and anxiousness.

SUMMARY

Obesity is a chronic condition that may be managed with long-term pharmacological treatment. Only three categories of drugs have received FDA approval for the treatment of obesity:

- appetite suppressants,
- thermogenics, and
- lipid-partitioners.

Appetite suppressants increase levels of serotonin and/or norepinephrine to suppress hunger.

Thermogenics act by increasing metabolism or energy expenditure, and lipid-partitioners inhibit the digestion and absorption of fat. Of all the FDA-approved anti-obesity drugs, only three are commonly prescribed:

- sibutramine (Meridia),

- orlistat (Xenical), and

- phentermine.

Several nonprescription or over-the-counter remedies are promoted as weight loss aids, but research does not support these claims. Development of new pharmacotherapy measures has expanded rapidly in the past decade, with innovative approaches on the horizon.

EXAM QUESTIONS

CHAPTER 12
Questions 45-49

Note: Choose the option that BEST answers each question.

45. The three categories of drugs that received Food and Drug Administration (FDA) approval for obesity treatment are

    a. starch blockers, appetite suppressants, glucose uptake inhibitors.

    b. diuretics, starch blockers, lipid-partitioners.

    c. thermogenics, metabolic stimulators, carbohydrate blockers.

    d. appetite suppressants, thermogenics, lipid-partitioners.

46. Sibutramine is an appetite suppressant that blocks the reuptake of which two neurotransmitters in the brain?

    a. epinephrine and acetylcholine

    b. acetylcholine and calcium

    c. serotonin and norepinephrine

    d. norepinephrine and cortisol

47. The most common side effects of phentermine are

    a. insomnia, hyperactivity, attention deficit disorder.

    b. elevated heart rate, increased blood pressure, irritability.

    c. hypotension, dry mouth, nausea.

    d. nausea, irritable bowel, diarrhea.

48. Prescribing a drug for weight loss "off-label" means the physician has prescribed a drug

    a. for an indication other than the intended use determined in the FDA approval process.

    b. for when some side effects occur that were not listed on the label.

    c. that is a generic brand of the trade drug.

    d. when the drug never received any FDA approval.

49. Dietary supplements and over-the-counter remedies for weight loss

    a. are regulated closely by the FDA.

    b. are safe to take because they produce very few adverse effects.

    c. have few scientific results showing effective weight loss.

    d. are effective with or without dietary modification.

REFERENCES

Anderson, J.W., Greenway, F.L., Fujioka, K., Gadde, K.M., McKenney, J., & O'Neil, P.M. (2002). Bupriopion SR enhances weight loss: A 48 week double-blind, placebo-controlled trial. *Obesity Research, 10,* 633-641.

Bray, G.A. & Ryan, D.H. (2006). Supplements used in weight management. *Obesity Management, 2*(5), 186-189.

Gadde, K.M., Franciscy, D.M., Wagner II, H.R., Ranga, K., & Krishnan, R. (2003). Sonisamide for weight loss in obese adults: A randomized controlled trial. *Journal of the American Medical Association, 289,* 1820-25.

Greenway, F.L. & Bray, G.A. (2006). Obesity medications: Where are we headed? *Obesity Management, 2*(5), 181-185.

Hanotin, C., Thomas, F., Jones, S.P., Leutenegger, E., & Drouin, P. (1998). Efficacy and tolerability of sibutramine in obese patients: A dose-ranging study. *International Journal of Obesity and Related Metabolic Disorders, 22,* 32-8.

Hansen, D.L., Toubro, S., Stock, M.J., Macdonald, I.A., & Astrup, A. (1999). The effect of sibutramine on energy expenditure and appetite during chronic treatment without dietary restriction. *International Journal of Obesity and Related Metabolic Disorders, 23,* 1016- 1024.

Heshka, S. & Heymsfield, S.B. (2002). Pharmacological treatments on the horizon. In C.G. Fairburn & K.D. Brownell (Eds.), *Eating disorders and obesity* (2nd ed., pp. 557-61), New York: The Guilford Press.

Kaplan, L. (2005). Pharmacological therapies for obesity. *Gastroenterology Clinics of North America, 34,* 91-104.

Palamara K.L., Mogul, H.R., Peterson, S.J., & Frishman, W.H. (2006). Obesity: New perspectives and pharmacotherapies. *Cardiology in Review, 14,* 238-258.

National Heart, Lung and Blood Institute; National Institutes of Health. (1998). Clinical guidelines on the identification, evaluation, and treatment of overweight and obesity in adults: The evidence report. *Obesity Research, 6*(suppl), 51S-209S.

Waitman, J.A. & Aronne, L.J. (2005) Pharmacotherapy of obesity. *Obesity Management, 1*(1), 15-19.

CHAPTER 13

BARIATRIC SURGERY

CHAPTER OBJECTIVE

After completing this chapter the learner will be able to describe bariatric surgery as an effective treatment option for severe obesity.

LEARNING OBJECTIVES

After studying this chapter, the learner will be able to

1. state the eligibility criteria for bariatric surgery.

2. list the most common types of bariatric surgery.

3. describe the effectiveness of the most common types of bariatric surgery.

4. list possible complications associated with bariatric surgery.

INTRODUCTION

Severe obesity, classified as morbid obesity, is becoming a widespread condition with considerable morbidity and mortality. Morbid obesity is classified as a body mass index (BMI) of 40 or more, or 35 or more with significant comorbidity (hypertension, diabetes, sleep apnea, or cardiac disease). Conventional weight loss treatments, such as very-low-calorie diets, intensive lifestyle modification, and pharmacotherapy are often not successful in producing long-term results in this population. As a result, there is an accumulating agreement that bariatric sur-

gery is the most effective and enduring treatment for severe obesity. The number of surgical procedures for weight loss has increased from approximately 20,000 a year during the first few years of the 1980s to over 120,000 a year for the past few years (Ellison & Ellison, 2007; Tessier & Eagon, 2008). The American Society of Metabolic and Bariatric Surgery (ASMBS) estimates that 220,000 patients with morbid obesity in the United States underwent bariatric surgery in 2008.

ELIGIBILITY FOR BARIATRIC SURGERY

The National Institutes of Health (NIH) held a development consensus conference that established initial guidelines for bariatric surgery in 1992. The original guidelines set standards for the use of bariatric surgery as a means of treating severe obesity, and identified the criteria for eligibility. Since that time, surgical techniques have evolved, and new procedures have been developed. In 2004, a consensus conference of experts in the field of bariatric surgery and other related disciplines convened to review the most current research on bariatric surgery. An updated set of guidelines was released that represents the current state of available surgical care and treatment options (Buchwald, 2005). Table 13-1 outlines the guidelines from the 2004 report.

TABLE 13-1: 2004 CONSENSUS GUIDELINES FOR BARIATRIC SURGERY
1. Bariatric surgery is the most effective therapy available for morbid obesity and can result in improvement or complete resolution of obesity comorbidities.
2. There are currently four types of procedures that can be used to achieve sustained weight loss: • gastric bypass • laparoscopic adjustable gastric banding • vertical banded gastroplasty • biliopancreatic diversion and duodenal switch.
3. Both open and laparoscopic bariatric operations are effective therapies.
4. Bariatric surgery candidates should have attempted to lose weight by nonoperative means prior to seeking surgery but should not be required to have completed formal nonoperative obesity therapy as a precondition for the operation.
5. The bariatric surgery patient is best evaluated and subsequently cared for by a multidisciplinary team.
6. Bariatric surgery candidates should have a comprehensive medical evaluation before the operation; management by specialty disciplines may be indicated.
7. Bariatric surgery should be considered in morbidly obese adolescents; however, it should only be performed in experienced centers.
8. Extending bariatric surgery to patients with Class I obesity (body mass index [BMI] 30 to 34.9 kg/m^2), who have a comorbid condition that can be cured or markedly improved by substantial and sustained weight loss,may be warranted and requires additional data and long-term risk and benefit analyses.
9. Bariatric surgery can be cost effective before the fourth year of follow-up.
10. Bariatric surgery offers opportunities for research to provide a better understanding of the factors involved in the regulation of food intake, pathophysiology of obesity, metabolic and clinical effects of sustained weight loss, and best treatment options for obese persons.

Adapted from: Buchwald, H. (2005). Consensus conference statement: Bariatric surgery for morbid obesity: Health implications for patients, health professionals, and third-party payers. *Journal of the American College of Surgeons, 200*, 593-604.

SURGICAL TECHNIQUES

Bariatric surgical procedures for weight loss consist of modifying the gastrointestinal tract in order to reduce energy intake and absorption. Surgical techniques for weight loss are divided into three categories:

• restrictive procedures,

• malabsorptive procedures, and

• combined restrictive and malabsorptive procedures.

Restrictive bariatric procedures reduce the storage capacity of the stomach. The goal is to reduce food intake while producing early satiety with a full, smaller-sized stomach. Malabsorptive procedures shorten the functional length of the small intestine, causing a decreased surface area for the absorption of nutrients. The diminished capacity of the small intestine to absorb nutrients causes a negative energy balance that induces weight loss. In general, restrictive procedures are simpler to perform and are accompanied by fewer complications than malabsorptive procedures. The combined approach uses a reduced functional stomach size with bypass of a lesser section of small intestine, providing restriction and malabsorption with less risk of nutritional deficiency than a purely malabsorptive procedure.

Gastric Banding

Gastric banding, or the more common procedure known as laparoscopic adjustable gastric banding (LAGB), is a restrictive procedure that does not alter the patient's food absorption. One of the common early attempts at reducing caloric intake using a band to restrict the stomach was done with a procedure called the vertical banded gastroplasty (VBG). A section of stomach was divided by stapling it in a vertical direction, and then applying a nonadjustable band to provide a restricted outlet at the bottom of the section. This band restricted food intake but involved no modification of the intestine. Over time, however, the stapled division often failed, causing the ability to eat additional food, resulting in weight regain. This surgery was fairly successful in initial weight loss, and had a lower risk profile for surgical complications and long-term nutritional deficiencies than the malabsorptive procedures. As surgical technique developed, better options for banding were developed, and this procedure has been largely abandoned in favor of adjustable gastric banding. The health care professional may still encounter patients who have undergone VBG because many of them have experienced weight regain due to eventual failure of the surgery.

The modern successor to the VBG is LAGB (Figure 13-1). The procedure involves implanting an adjustable silicon band around the proximal area of the stomach, which portions the stomach into two sections – a smaller reservoir the size of an egg that empties into the bottom portion of the unmodified stomach. The inflatable band is connected to an injection port attached to the abdominal wall under the surface of the skin. Adjustments in the band restriction are made by injecting saline into the port, which inflates the silicon band, causing greater stomach restriction. Gastric banding is not only adjustable, but also reversible, though reversal of the procedure will usually result in weight regain, just as the failure of the VBG in earlier

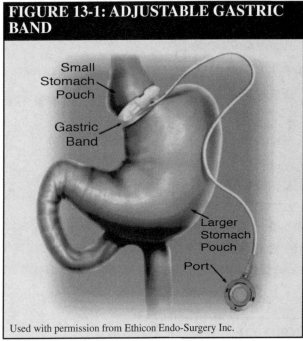

FIGURE 13-1: ADJUSTABLE GASTRIC BAND

Small Stomach Pouch

Gastric Band

Larger Stomach Pouch

Port

Used with permission from Ethicon Endo-Surgery Inc.

patients. The patient is required to eat very small meals, which provide volume restriction and satiety due to fullness of the small stomach.

Sleeve Gastrectomy

During this procedure, the surgeon creates a small sleeve-shaped stomach by excising a large portion of the stomach (Figure 13-2). The remaining stomach sleeve (20% to 40% of original size) is about the size of a banana and is larger than the stomach pouch created by gastric banding. There is no modification to the intestine, and the sleeve gastrectomy is considered a purely restrictive surgery. Its advantage is felt to be due to the exclusion of the portion of stomach that produces ghrelin, one of the powerful hunger stimulating neurohormones.

In larger patients with BMIs greater than 60, the sleeve gastrectomy is combined with a second surgical procedure, either a gastric bypass or duodenal switch (see below). In such cases, the sleeve gastrectomy is performed first, and the patient is given 12 to 18 months to recover. During the recovery period, the patient will lose a substantial amount of weight that decreases the risk of the second procedure. Sleeve gastrectomy is not reversible.

FIGURE 13-2: SLEEVE GASTRECTOMY

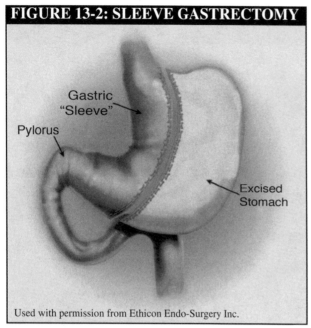

Used with permission from Ethicon Endo-Surgery Inc.

Roux-en-Y Gastric Bypass

This procedure is restrictive and malabsorptive (Figure 13-3). A small stomach pouch is created by using a stapling device to partition the stomach. Then the small intestine is separated into two sections, and the distal portion of the small intestine is attached to the newly-created stomach pouch. Food passes directly from the stomach into the distal portion of the small intestine, bypassing a significant portion of the small intestine (the duodenum) to reduce nutrient absorption. The proximal portion of the small intestine is re-connected to the distal portion of the small intestine at a place more distal than where the stomach pouch is connected. The bile and pancreatic juices from the liver and pancreas flow into the common channel, and allow the food to be completely digested.

This surgery has been the "gold standard" of weight loss surgery for many years, and it is felt by many experts to be the optimal method of more permanent weight loss (Griffen, 2007). Since the late 1990s, the laparoscopic approach has gained popularity over the open midline incision, making the surgery less invasive. It should be noted that patients with very high BMIs (greater than 65) are less often candidates for any laparoscopic surgery due to body habitus.

FIGURE 13-3: ROUX-EN-Y GASTRIC BYPASS

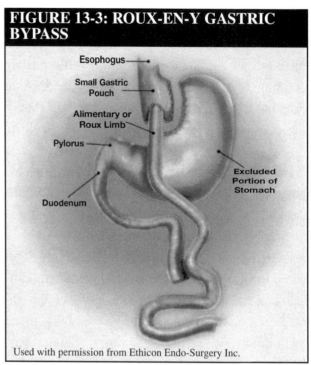

Used with permission from Ethicon Endo-Surgery Inc.

Biliopancreatic Diversion with Duodenal Switch

This procedure, also referred to as BPD/DS, is restrictive and malabsorptive; however, the major weight loss results from the degree of malabsorption provided by the bypassed intestine (Figure 13-4). A gastrectomy is performed in a similar manner as in the sleeve gastrectomy. The surgeon then attaches the distal section of the small intestine to the stomach sleeve. Weight loss is a product of the restriction of the stomach and the diversion of food, bile, and pancreatic digestive juices to the distal portion of the small intestine. Only a small portion of intestine (100 cm) is then involved in nutrient absorption. The method of weight loss with this surgery is fat malabsorption, and a resulting side effect is foul smelling, frequent stools associated with steatorrhea (fatty diarrhea).

EFFECTIVENESS OF BARIATRIC SURGERY

Bariatric surgery seems to be more successful than medical treatment for morbid obesity. The majority of bariatric surgery patients lose more than

FIGURE 13-4: BILIOPANCREATIC DIVISION

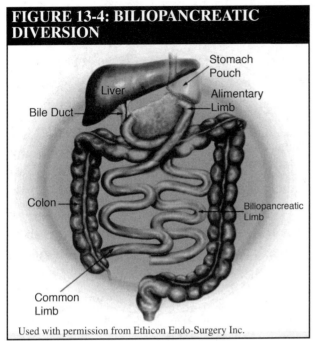

Used with permission from Ethicon Endo-Surgery Inc.

50% of their excess weight in the first year. A meta-analysis revealed that the average percentage of excess weight loss maintained after 2 years was 61% for all bariatric procedures, and ranged from 47% for gastric banding to 70% for BPD (Buchwald et al., 2004). Other reviews report that absolute weight loss ranges from approximately 30 kg (66 lb) for adjustable gastric banding to 53 kg (116.6 lb) for BPD of weight loss at 10 years ranges from 20 kg (44 lb) to 30 kg (66 lb) (Elder & Wolfe, 2007).

Long-term results for the Roux-en-Y gastric bypass procedure are 50% to 60% of excess weight lost over a 5-year period, with an absolute weight loss of about 40 kg (88 lb) at 1 and 3 years. Sleeve gastrectomy causes a weight loss of 30% to 50% of excess weight during the first year, which amounts to 35 kg (77 lb) to 45 kg (99 lb). The amount of weight loss is augmented if the sleeve gastrectomy is followed by a gastric bypass or duodenal switch.

In addition to the weight loss, bariatric surgery produces many other health benefits. Bariatric surgery can increase blood glucose control and even help people recover from type 2 diabetes. Hypercholesterolemia and hypertriglyceridemia improve after all types of bariatric surgical proce-

dures. Other benefits of bariatric surgery include a reduction in the prevalence of hypertension and obstructive sleep apnea, improvements in polycystic ovary syndrome, and an improvement on psychological functioning. All of these health benefits lead to an improvement in the quality of life for the severely obese patient. However, it must be noted that 10% to 40% of all bariatric surgery patients cannot maintain a substantial amount of weight loss or the corresponding health benefits (Elder & Wolfe, 2007).

What has become clear to all in the field of bariatric surgery over the past several decades is the need to incorporate the procedure into a multidisciplinary approach to weight loss. Surgical revision should not be considered the solution to obesity. It should be a "tool" to help the morbidly obese individual make the necessary lifestyle changes. These changes include healthy eating habits, increased physical activity, and behavior modification of behaviors that contribute to weight gain. The ideal bariatric surgery program will incorporate this concept into their approach. The ASMBS has established the Center of Excellence program for Bariatric Surgery, which requires that a bariatric surgical program have all of these components in place.

Some might advocate that if these components were utilized effectively by patients, there would be no need for surgery. Indeed there are occasional cases in which successful weight loss has occurred in morbidly obese patients without the use of surgical modification of the digestive system. In reality, the majority of patients do not turn to weight loss surgery until they have exhausted all conventional methods of weight loss. As we have seen throughout the chapters in this book, weight loss is a complex process, and it may be that yet undiscovered factors help cause this approach to be the most effective for the most severely obese patients.

COMPLICATIONS AND SIDE EFFECTS

Complications of bariatric surgery are dependent on the specific type of procedure done. Intraoperative complications are most commonly related to the technicality of the surgery, with gastric bypass and BPD surgeries requiring more proficiency. The ASMBS has long advocated that surgeries be performed by appropriately trained or supervised surgeons, and established recommendations for credentialing of surgeons performing bariatric surgery (ASMBS, 2005). These guidelines have been incorporated into requirements of both the ASMBS and American College of Surgeons Centers of Excellence for Bariatric Surgery in recent years.

The most serious early complications that occur in the perioperative period include pulmonary emboli and anastomotic leak. All bariatric patients are at risk for pulmonary emboli because venous stasis and decreased physical activity are risk factors commonly seen in morbidly obese patients. Central abdominal obesity contributes to the decreased venous return from the lower extremities as well. Aggressive measures such as thromboembolism prophylaxis and early ambulation are taken to prevent this complication.

A gastric leak can occur in any of the stapling procedures; however, it is seen most commonly in BPD/DS procedures, which are the most difficult technically (Sugarman, Shikora, & Schauer, 2007). A leak occurs when a staple line does not hold properly, leaking stomach or intestinal contents into the abdominal cavity. Peritonitis then develops, causing a systemic reaction. Early detection and correction is key in preventing prolonged morbidity and mortality. Centers that perform higher numbers of surgeries are more proficient at early detection of this complication (Gleysteen, 2007). Other perioperative complications include bleeding and wound infections, which are seen less commonly. Increased risk is seen with higher BMIs and more technical surgery (Sugarman, Shikora, & Schauer, 2007).

Later complications can occur related to the type of surgery. With the LAGB, slippage or erosion can occur, as well as problems with the port itself. Slippage rates have been reported up to 25% (Sugarman, Shikora, & Schauer, 2007), and may require reoperation. Complications for the other surgeries include anastomotic stricture, bowel obstruction, and marginal or anastomotic ulceration. The frequency of occurrence of each of these problems varies among procedures and among individual surgeons, and it is affected by the type of technique used for the surgery. A frank discussion of the potential risks with each patient is an essential part of the surgical preparatory process.

Nutritional deficiencies can occur, and are more often seen with malabsorptive procedures, particularly the BPD/DS or the Roux-en-Y gastric bypass. It should be noted that guidelines are in place for each surgery to help prevent nutritional deficiencies. When these instructions are followed and proper monitoring is maintained, nutritional deficiencies are less frequent. The ASMBS Allied Health Nutritional Guidelines for the Surgical Weight Loss Patient (Allied Health Sciences Section Ad Hoc Nutrition Committee et al., 2008) provide a comprehensive review and recommendations for all types of bariatric surgery.

Vomiting is often thought to be a common side effect of surgery; however, it occurs most frequently during the first months after surgery when the patient is not accustomed to the decreased stomach size. It can occur with all bariatric surgeries, until the patient begins to understand the actual size of the "new" stomach. "Dumping syndrome" is a complication seen with malabsorptive procedures that results in sweating, dizziness, rapid heart rate and occasionally, diarrhea (DiRocco, Halverson, Planer, Walser, & Cunningham, 2007). This effect usually occurs after the patient has eaten a meal rich in simple carbohydrates or with a high glycemic index. The exact mechanism for this occurrence is debated, but it will occur in about 50% of patients, and can provide a deterrent to eating the offending food.

Because all bariatric procedures reduce the amount of food absorbed, the possibility of nutrient deficiencies exists. The most susceptible nutrients vary with the type of procedure. Supplementation is recommended postoperatively, and if guidelines are followed, most deficiencies are avoided. Iron supplementation can easily protect against iron deficiency. The BPD/DS patient is susceptible to fat-soluble vitamin, calcium, B_{12}, and iron deficiencies. Gastric bypass patients most commonly manifest iron and B_{12} deficiency, whereas LAGB patients show lower incidence of all nutritional deficits but may develop deficiency related to their diet and other health issues (Sugarman, Shikora, & Schauer, 2007). Protein deficiency is not commonly seen in the majority of procedures but is a higher risk in BPD/DS due to the malabsorptive component. Most programs recommend a daily intake of 60 to 80 grams of protein per day, with 90 grams per day suggested for BPD/DS patients (Allied Health Sciences Section Ad Hoc Nutrition Committee et al., 2008). Much research is now devoted to the study and prevention of nutritional deficiencies in all types of bariatric surgery.

SELECTION OF A BARIATRIC PROCEDURE

Selection of the most appropriate surgical procedure for a morbidly obese patient is best done in consultation between the bariatric surgeon and the individual patient. Selection of an experienced surgeon is key to minimizing risks and complications. A multidisciplinary team approach that involves nutritional counseling, behavioral guidance, and close postoperative monitoring is desirable. Providing safe bariatric care is a goal of both the ASMBS and the American College of Surgeons Center of Excellence for Bariatric Surgery. More information about these programs, including a listing of qualified surgeons and centers can be found on their bariatric center Web sites: http://www.surgical review.org and http://www.acsbscn.org/Public/index.aspx. Case Study 13-1 discusses bariatric procedure options for an individual patient.

Case Study 13-1: Candidate For Bariatric Surgery

You are a nurse at a university weight loss center. The center provides an entire range of weight loss treatments, including behavior modification, psychological counseling, very-low-calorie diets, pharmacological therapy, nutrition therapy, and bariatric surgery. Joseph has been in and out of treatment for more than 15 years. He is discouraged about his lack of success and has come to you to discuss the possibility for bariatric surgery. How will you counsel him?

Intervention/Solution

Joseph is a 45-year-old man who weighs 361 lb and is 6' tall. He has attended the clinic on and off for the past 15 years. His lowest weight achieved was 300 lb after a protein-sparing-modified fast, but he quickly gained that weight back. Most of the time Joseph fluctuates between 350 and 370 lb. Joseph has type 2 diabetes and is also hypertensive.

Resolution Process

Joseph meets the eligibility criteria for bariatric surgery. At his current weight, Joseph has a body mass index (BMI) of 49. Even at Joseph's lowest recorded weight, his BMI was 41. Joseph also has a history of failed weight loss attempts. These attempts are documented in his medical file over the past 15 years. Joseph's diabetes and hypertension put him at high risk. Your clinic offers full services for obesity intervention. Therefore, Joseph is eligible for bariatric surgery and he has the medical support team for the surgery

continued on next page

and follow-up. You conclude that Joseph is a good candidate for bariatric surgery and discuss his options for surgery.

There are four possible surgical procedures that the clinic could offer Joseph: gastric banding, sleeve gastrectomy, Roux-en-Y gastric bypass, and biliopancreatic diversion with duodenal switch (BPD/DS). You advise Joseph that the type of surgery to be performed will be a decision he will make with his bariatric surgeon based on his BMI, preference, body configuration, previous surgical history, and individual medical issues.

As you discuss the potential surgeries, the expected weight loss, and the long term effects with Joseph, you ask him what his goals for weight loss surgery are. Joseph wants foremost to better control his diabetes; he is "afraid of becoming dependent" on insulin, which occurred with his father and mother. He is also concerned about further deterioration to his health, particularly with heart disease. His weight loss goal is to lose "about 150 pounds" with a target goal weight of 200. This loss would equal about 75% of current excess body weight.

Joseph rules out adjustable gastric banding because he does not feel comfortable having a device embedded in his abdomen. Because Joseph has diabetes, any of the three remaining surgeries would be beneficial in improving his glucose status. You review the surgeries with Joseph and discuss the potential long-term effects of each. The side effect of persistent long-term diarrhea with the BPD does not appeal to Joseph, because he travels a great deal with his job and feels this would not be tolerable for him. You rule out the BPD as a desired option. Joseph is interested in the sleeve gastrectomy, but he likes the proven record of the gastric bypass. You concur that these are both viable options and refer him to the surgeon for further discussion regarding his individual history. Joseph and the surgeon decide together that the gastric bypass would provide the best proven option for control of his diabetes and would provide greater weight loss overall, allowing him to potentially reach his goal of 200 pounds.

Your role in the discussion process has been to help Joseph clarify what his specific goals in undergoing bariatric surgery are and to help him find the surgery that will best meet his expectations. You also help him gain a realistic perspective of life after surgery and what he can expect. Patients often approach the option of surgery with unrealistic goals, which will need to be adjusted through the sharing of current data about surgical practices.

SUMMARY

Conventional medical treatments for severe obesity are largely unsuccessful, making bariatric surgery the most effective approach in this population. Patients eligible for bariatric surgery need to have a BMI greater than or equal to 40 or a BMI greater than or equal to 35 with significant comorbidities (hypertension, cardiovascular disease, obstructive sleep apnea, or diabetes). Surgical techniques for weight loss are divided into three categories: malabsorptive procedures, restrictive procedures, and those that use a combined approach. Choice of surgical procedure is based on patient expectations and goals, as well as medical issues, and should be made in consultation with an appropriately trained surgeon.

Most bariatric surgery patients lose more than 50% of excess body weight in 12 months, and maintain 40% to 60% excess weight loss after 2 to 10 years. Successful maintenance of weight loss is dependent on behavior and lifestyle changes that reinforce the use of the surgery as a tool for weight loss.

EXAM QUESTIONS

CHAPTER 13
Questions 50-53

Note: Choose the option that BEST answers each question.

50. Candidates for bariatric surgery include patients with a body mass index

    a. above 30 who failed conventional weight loss treatment.

    b. above 40 or between 35 and 40 with a severe comorbidity.

    c. above 35 with or without a comorbidity.

    d. between 30 and 40, with at least two comorbidities.

51. Malabsorptive bariatric surgery is where

    a. food is restricted from entering the stomach, slowing transit through the system.

    b. food is forced to pass through the stomach quickly so it cannot be absorbed.

    c. the stomach size is reduced to provide decreased volume.

    d. the functional length of the small intestine is reduced, so less food is absorbed.

52. The success of bariatric surgery programs for weight loss in morbidly obese patients is often attributed to the fact that

    a. the surgery usually requires no dietary modification.

    b. procedures improve comorbid diseases with little weight loss.

    c. weight loss is now effortless.

    d. a comprehensive program including lifestyle modification is used.

53. The most common nutritional side effects of bariatric surgery

    a. include protein deficiency and dehydration.

    b. can be avoided if nutritional guidelines are followed.

    c. are only seen in malabsorptive procedures.

    d. are a result of persistent vomiting.

REFERENCES

Allied Health Sciences Section Ad Hoc Nutrition Committee; Aills, L., Blankenship, J., Buffington, C., Furtado, M., & Parrott, J. (2008). ASMBS allied health nutritional guidelines for the surgical weight loss patient. *Surgery for Obesity and Related Disease, Supplement, 4,* 73-108.

American Society for Metabolic and Bariatric Surgery: *Fact sheet: Metabolic and bariatric surgery.* Retrieved April 14, 2009, from http://www.asbs.org/Newsite07/media/asmbs_fs_surgery.pdf

American Society for Metabolic and Bariatric Surgery. *Guidelines for granting privileges for bariatric surgery.* Retrieved April 14, 2009, from http://www.asbs.org/Newsite07/resources/asbs_granting_privileges.htm

Buchwald, H. (2005). Consensus conference statement: Bariatric surgery for morbid obesity: Health implications for patients, health professionals, and third-party payers. *Journal of the American College of Surgeons, 200,* 593-604.

Buchwald, H., Avidor, Y., Braunwald, E., Jensen, M.D., Pories, W., Fahrbach, K., & Schoelles, K. (2004). Bariatric surgery: A systematic review and meta-analysis. *Journal of the American Medical Association, 292,* 1724-1737.

DiRocco, J.D., Halverson, J.D., Planer, J., Walser, M., & Cunningham, P.R.G. (2007). Postoperative care of the bariatric surgery patient. In H. Buchwald, G.S.M. Cowan, & W.J. Pories (Eds.), *Surgical management of obesity* (pp. 131-138). Philadelphia: Saunders.

Elder, K.A. & Wolfe, B.M. (2007). Bariatric surgery: A review of procedures and outcomes. *Gastroenterology, 132,* 2253-2271.

Ellison, S.R. & Ellison, S.D. (2007). Bariatric surgery: A review of the available procedures and complications for the emergency physician. *Journal of Emergency Medicine, 34,* 21-32.

Gleysteen, J.J. (2007). Requisite facilities for a bariatric surgical practice. In H. Buchwald, G.S.M. Cowan, & W.J. Pories (Eds.), *Surgical management of obesity* (pp. 437-440). Philadelphia: Saunders.

Griffen, Jr., W.O. (2007). Open Roux-en-y gastric bypass. In H. Buchwald, G.S.M. Cowan, & W.J. Pories (Eds.), *Surgical management of obesity* (pp. 185-190). Philadelphia: Saunders.

National Institutes of Health. (1992). Gastrointestinal surgery for severe obesity: National Institutes of Health consensus development conference statement. *American Journal of Clinical Nutrition, 55*(Suppl), 615S-619S.

Sugarman, H.J., Shikora, S.A., & Schauer, P.R. (2007). Bariatric surgery. *Obesity Management, 3*(6), 251-254.

Tessier, D.J. & Eagon, J.C. (2008). Surgical management of morbid obesity. *Current Problems in Surgery, 45,* 68-137.

CHAPTER 14

WEIGHT LOSS MAINTENANCE

CHAPTER OBJECTIVE

After completing this chapter the learner will be able to discuss behavioral factors that enhance weight loss and maintenance.

LEARNING OBJECTIVES

After reading this chapter, the learner will be able to

1. describe how much food a previously obese patient needs to consume in order to maintain a reduced body weight.

2. describe how much physical activity a previously obese patient must perform in order to maintain a reduced body weight.

3. identify several self-monitoring techniques for reduced weight maintenance in the previously obese.

4. explain how the chronic disease model is related to weight loss maintenance in the previously obese patient.

INTRODUCTION

The most critical component of any weight loss attempt is maintenance of the newly achieved weight. Many programs and products can help a person lose weight, but maintenance of weight loss is much more difficult. If the previously obese per-

son cannot maintain a reduced body weight, the health benefits of losing weight will become negligible. Because weight maintenance is a matter of balancing energy intake with energy expenditure, this chapter focuses on the behaviors necessary to achieve energy balance in the previously obese, and the factors that affect those behaviors.

REDUCED ENERGY INTAKE FOR WEIGHT MAINTENANCE

The National Weight Control Registry contains a volunteer enrollment list of adults who have successfully lost at least 30 lb and maintained that weight loss for a minimum of 1 year (Klem, Wing, McGuire, Seagle, & Hill, 1997). The first Registry report included a total of 629 women and 155 men (784 total) who maintained an average weight loss of 65 lb for an average of 5.5 years (Klem et al., 1997). Eighty-nine percent of the sample used diet and exercise to achieve weight loss. These participants in the National Registry maintained their weight loss by consuming a low-calorie diet. Men reported consuming 1,700 kcal/day, whereas women reported consuming only 1,300 kcal/day. Even with the low-calorie diet, participants were eating five times per day. Thus, they were eating small amounts of food frequently. Twenty-four percent of their daily energy intake came from fat and

56% came from carbohydrate. These individuals also reported that they consumed less than one fast-food meal a week.

A follow-up study was done on the initial Registry participants as well as new participants that entered the registry between 1997 and 2003 (Phelan, Wyatt, Hill, & Wing, 2006). The total enrollment for the follow-up study was 2,708 men and women. These participants reported consuming about 1,400 kcal/day, of which 27% of the kilocalories were from fat and 53% were from carbohydrate. Participants in both of these studies reported that they also exercised to maintain their reduced weight.

EXERCISE FOR WEIGHT MAINTENANCE

Participants in the National Weight Control Registry use a combination of dietary restraint and physical activity to maintain their reduced body weight. Men reported expending approximately 3,500 kcal/week in exercise, whereas women reported expending about 2,700 kcal/week in exercise. These counts amount to walking approximately 4 (women) to 5 (men) miles per week (one half to three fourths of a mile per day). A follow-up report, performed almost a decade later, revealed that the 2,708 National Weight Control Registrants who were successful at maintaining a 30 lb weight loss for at least 1 year were expending an average of 2,700 kcal/week in exercise (Phelan et al., 2006).

Data from the National Weight Control Registry are only estimates of energy expenditures that are derived from self-report. More accurate data have been obtained from objective measures of exercise energy expenditure. The amount of energy spent in physical activity that is required for maintaining reduced body weight in previously obese women was calculated by taking direct metabolic measurements. The metabolic measurements that were taken during a weight-stable period revealed that the women were exercising 700 kcal/day in order to maintain their reduced body weight. This translates into 80 minutes/day of moderate physical activity, 35 minutes/day of vigorous activity, or walking about 7 miles/day. The American College of Sports Medicine (2006) recommends the obese person expend 300 kcal/day in exercise in order to maintain health.

A second study that calculated the amount of physical activity energy expenditure needed to maintain body weight produced findings similar to the first study (Weinsier et al., 2002). However, the subjects in this study were normal weight women who maintained their body weight for a year. In order to maintain their normal body weight, these women spent 700 kcal/day in physical activity. It must be noted, though, that the women in these two studies were directed to follow their normal eating patterns during the study; and the dietary intake of the women in both studies was not reported. Therefore, we can only assume that if a person consumes a normal diet, they would need to expend 700 kcal in exercise each day to maintain body weight. We also can only assume that the women in these studies would have regained weight if they expended less than 700 kcal/day in exercise.

SELF-MONITORING FOR REDUCED-WEIGHT MAINTENANCE

One early study examined the behaviors of men and women who were successful at maintaining a weight loss of at least 20% of their original weight for a period of 2 years or more (Colvin & Olson, 1983). Average weight loss for the men was about 75 lb and for women was just over 50 lb Behaviors relevant to reduced body weight maintenance were similar between the sexes, with 85% of the men and 78% of the women increasing their exercise, 77% of the men and 66% of the women increasing their nutrition knowledge, and 85% of the men and 66% of the women self-monitoring. The three keys to successful reduced weight maintenance in this study were exercise, knowledge, and self-monitoring.

Several years later, another group of scientists were able to make comparison measurements among three groups of women: those who successfully lost and maintained weight (maintainers), those who lost and regained weight (relapsers), and those who never had a weight problem (normal weights; Kayman, Bruvold, & Stern, 1990). It is interesting to note that a high percentage of the maintainers devised a personal eating plan (73%), whereas only a low percentage of the relapsers had personal eating plans (39%). This means that the maintainers followed a plan that was specific to their needs, a plan that took into account their personal eating styles, a plan that catered to their likes and dislikes, and a plan that took into account their personal strengths and weaknesses with regard to healthy eating. On the other hand, the relapsers used a plan that was standardized, a plan that was based on general theory, a plan that was not designed by themselves, a plan that was not structured around their personal needs, and a plan that was intended for masses of people rather than a single individual. Such standardized or nonpersonal eating plans are what are found in many commercial weight loss programs and in many popular weight loss books.

Another interesting study finding was that a high percentage of the maintainers exercised (76%), whereas only a small percentage of the relapsers exercised (36%) (Table 14-1). When the maintainers were asked how they maintained their reduced body weight, their responses were similar to the normal weights. They monitored their weight (87% vs. 76%, respectively), exercised (83% vs. 88%), and monitored their food intake (60% vs. 50%). Again, exercise and self-monitoring came out as critical to successful reduced weight maintenance. Similar findings were discovered a couple years later when Miller and Eggert (1992) found that people who were unsuccessful at maintaining weight loss reported the reason for their failure was that they reverted back to their old eating behaviors and stopped exercising. Thus, a consistent finding is that the key to successful weight loss and reduced weight maintenance is a personalized eating plan and exercise.

It is curious to note that when the three groups, in the comparison study were asked how they coped with problems, the relapsers responded differently from the maintainers and normal weights. About 70% of the relapsers used escape and avoid-

TABLE 14-1: COMPARISON OF WEIGHT CONTROL STRATEGIES AMONG SUCCESSFUL MAINTAINERS, RELAPSERS, AND NORMAL WEIGHT ADULTS

	Relapsers	Maintainers	Normal Weights
Weight Loss Strategy			
Devised a personal eating plan	39%	73%	N/A
Exercised	36%	76%	N/A
Weight Maintenance Strategy			
Monitored body weight	N/A	87%	76%
Exercised	N/A	83%	88%
Monitoring food intake	N/A	60%	50%
Problem Coping Strategy			
Escape, avoidance (drink, pills)	70%	33%	35%
Seek social support	38%	70%	80%
Problem solving/confronting	10%	95%	60%

(Kayman, Bruvold, & Stern, 1990)

ance techniques (denial and repression) to cope with their problems, whereas only 33% of the maintainers and 35% of the normal weights coped in this way. Only 38% of the relapsers problem solved by seeking social support (talking), whereas 70% of the maintainers and 80% of the normal weights communicated to solve problems. Furthermore, only 10% of the relapsers solved problems through confrontation and problem-solving techniques, compared to 95% for the maintainers and 60% for the normal weights. The data for those successful at maintaining weight in this study are definitely in line with what the Healthy at Every Size philosophy and behavioral approaches promote for obesity treatment: healthy emotional coping, emotional expression and communication, and building a positive social environment.

More recent research has confirmed early findings. People listed in the National Weight Control Registry reported that they counted calories, restricted fat intake, counted fat grams, and restricted intake of certain foods in order to meet their weight control goals (Klem et al., 1997). A follow-up report 10 years later revealed that National Weight Control Registrants who were successful at maintaining a 30 lb weight loss for at least 1 year weighed themselves frequently (Butryn, Phelan, Hill, & Wing, 2007). Those participants who weighed themselves frequently also reported a lower fat intake and better eating restraint than those participants who were less successful at weight maintenance and weighed themselves infrequently.

More detailed information about the eating behaviors of those who are successful at reduced-weight maintenance come from the Centers for Disease Control and Prevention (Kruger, Blanck, & Gillespie, 2006). A lifestyle survey was completed by a sample of 4,345 adults that was representative of the U.S. population. Respondents who were able to lose weight and maintain that weight loss reported that they planned meals, monitored

calorie intake, monitored fat intake, and measured food on their plate. Those who were successful at maintaining weight loss were also more likely to weigh themselves daily. In addition, they exercised for more than 30 minutes a day and added physical activity into their lifestyle.

A weight loss maintenance trial is currently underway. The purpose of this trial is to compare alternative strategies for maintaining weight loss over a 30-month period. Preliminary results from the initial 20 weeks of the weight loss phase show that those adults who were the most successful at losing weight kept daily food diaries and exercised (Hollis, Gullion, Stevens, Brantley, Appel et al., 2008). In fact, those who kept daily food diaries lost approximately 8 kg during the 20-week trial compared to approximately 4 kg for those who did not keep the food diaries. Similarly, those who exercised an average of 60 minutes per day lost approximately 8 kg compared to about 5 kg for those who did not exercise. Although these results are preliminary, and come from the weight loss phase of the trial, they suggest that daily exercise and monitoring of food intake are critical to weight loss success and maintenance.

If we examine the data from these notable studies, we see that the commonality in successful reduced-weight maintenance is fourfold; exercise, healthy eating, self-monitoring, and coping skills. Exercise and healthy eating themselves are behaviors that need to be monitored, and so are coping skills. So, the four keys to weight maintenance really all consolidate into self-monitoring – self-monitoring of exercise, self-monitoring of eating behavior, and self-monitoring of emotional distress. When the patient gains the knowledge, attitudes, and skills for healthy weight management, the patient will only be successful in the long run when the newly established behaviors are maintained through self-monitoring. Case Study 14-1 provides an example of self-monitoring techniques.

Case Study 14-1: Self-Monitoring Techniques

You are a nurse practitioner for a clinic that has six physicians. Your responsibilities include overseeing patient education, rehabilitation, and chronic care. The clinic offers a weight management class that meets weekly for 15 weeks. Following the weight management class, patients have the option to continue with bi-weekly group support sessions. Patients in the group support sessions may also be in rehabilitation for other chronic conditions that are comorbid to obesity, such as cardiovascular disease, diabetes, and hypertension. Thus, the group makeup can be diverse. Also, because the group is an ongoing support group, the length of time patients have been attending the support group varies. Two new patients are entering the group today. They have just completed the 15-week weight management class and are beginning the group support for chronic care. Four other members of the group have been attending between 4 months and 3 years. Two other regular group members are absent today. The discussion topic today is "Monitoring Techniques for Healthy Weight Management." Your goal is to help the two new group members, Debbie and Laura, design some strategies for self-monitoring.

Intervention/Solution

Four group members have been in the maintenance phase for a period of 4 months to 3 years. All of them have managed to maintain 85% of their weight loss. Therefore, you decide to facilitate a discussion around what techniques they use to self-monitor.

Resolution

Nurse Practitioner: Welcome to our group today. As you can see we have two new members, Debbie and Laura. Let's take a minute and introduce ourselves to Debbie and Laura. (Group introductions follow.) It has been several months now since we have discussed strategies for healthy weight maintenance, so today we are going to revisit this topic. Because Debbie and Laura are new to our group, I think our time will be best spent if the older members of the group share their experiences of self-monitoring with the group and then we can work to help Debbie and Laura develop their own self-monitoring plans.

Brian: Well, I can start. Just over a year ago I had a cardiac event that put me into cardiac rehabilitation. At that point in time, I realized that my weight was a factor contributing to my poor cardiovascular health. So, I went to the weight management program and subsequently came into this group about 10 months ago. Since then I have done fine.

Nurse Practitioner: Thanks Brian. Can you explain what your self-monitoring strategies are and how they work for you?

Brian: Sure I can. I am not much into dieting and all that because the thought of starving myself seems so unappealing. So my initial plan was to concentrate on developing a healthy eating and exercise program. Up until a year ago, I hadn't exercised regularly since high school, and my eating was…who knows? Anyway I designed a program in the weight management class and continue it today.

Nurse Practitioner: Wonderful. Explain more how it works for you.

Brian: I found out that the key to weight loss and weight control for me is the exercise. If I just eat a reasonable diet, I am OK with the weight when I exercise regularly. It took me a few months to discover that, but once I did, I refined my plan and it works. My plan is to exercise for 40 minutes, 5 days a week. If I start slipping to only 1 or 2 days a week on exercise, I can see the weight coming back in about 2 weeks.

Nurse Practitioner: Anything else?

Brian: Yeah. I know my trigger for going off the wagon is tiredness. When I am under a lot of pressure and don't get sleep, I start cutting out the exercise and eating poorly to soothe my emotions. In order to not let this happen, I keep a sleep log as well as an exercise log. I program my exercise into my calendar, but also program my sleep into my calendar. It works!

continued on next page

Nurse Practitioner: Great Brian. Anybody else?

Karen: OK, I'll go. I came into the group 3 years ago. I had gained weight after each one of my three deliveries, but never lost it. My weight after the third baby was probably 60 pounds over what it should be. I went to the weight management class, and then came here.

Nurse Practitioner: So, what keeps you coming?

Karen: I am different from Brian. I don't mind the dieting. In fact, I like keeping track of my food intake. I write down everything I eat and count the calories. I know if I get above 1,600 calories a day, I start gaining weight.

Nurse Practitioner: Some people might find that method restrictive. How do you feel?

Karen: I felt restricted at first. But now I realize that there will be days that I eat more, or days when I feel like treating myself.

Nurse Practitioner: So, how do you navigate around those days?

Karen: I allow myself one treat day a week. Once I use it up, that's it.

Nurse Practitioner: I see…Your strategy is to carefully monitor your food intake and allow yourself a day in the week to relax.

Karen: Yep.

Nurse Practitioner: Who is next?

Reid: I sort of agree with Brian. I don't like the dieting thing. Maybe it's a guy thing.

Nurse Practitioner: You are not too far off, Reid. The research shows that, in general, men do better at weight control with exercise and women better with dieting. Anyway, go on…

Reid: I have type 2 diabetes. So, it is important that I follow a healthy diet, but that doesn't mean I have to starve myself. I went through the weight management course as well as a diabetes education course. I have been coming to this class now for 4 months.

Nurse Practitioner: Tell us what works for you Reid.

Reid: I follow the food exchange lists they gave me in the diabetes course. Obviously, I also track my blood sugar. However, I learned in diabetes education that exercise has an insulin like effect, and that people with diabetes who exercise are better off than those that don't.

Nurse Practitioner: So what are your strategies to keep exercising and eat healthy?

Reid: The way I feel. I only have lost a few pounds, but it isn't the weight that discourages me or keeps me going. I don't focus on the weight. My medication has been reduced once already, and I feel so much better than just before I was diagnosed. So, tracking my blood sugar, and keeping a log of my emotions helps me monitor my overall well-being. When my blood sugar gets too high, I feel sleepy, irritated, and anxious. My wife just says I get cranky.

Nurse Practitioner: Is your wife involved in your self-monitoring?

Reid: Yes she is. She really doesn't care about my weight either. She just knows that when my blood sugar is under control, and I am behaving healthfully, our relationship is good.

Nurse Practitioner: Interesting. How about you Rebecca?

Rebecca: I have been in the program the longest. Forty-eight months now.

Nurse Practitioner: That is commendable. I know you don't talk in public about your weight, but we all know that you have lost a significant amount of weight and maintained that loss for 48 months now.

Rebecca: Yes, I have. I never thought I would. My key to success is the Non-Diet Diet. When I came into the weight management program, I had tried every diet in the book. You name it, I tried it. Actually, when I entered the weight management program I was following my own program of eating only 900 kcal per day and walking 2 miles, three times a week, but I still could not lose weight.

continued on next page

Nurse Practitioner: I remember. You were pretty discouraged when you came to see us.

Rebecca: Yes, but thanks to you, I learned that I must have done so many bizarre things in an attempt to lose weight that my metabolism had slowed down. On the Non-Diet Diet I actually began eating 1,300 kcal a day and started to lose weight. I admit I was walking 40 to 60 minutes a day. But still…

Nurse Practitioner: What are you doing now, after 48 months?

Rebecca: I still monitor my behaviors and log my points with the Non-Diet Diet score sheet. I know exactly how many points I need to get in order to maintain my weight loss.

Nurse Practitioner: Really?

Rebecca: I'm not kidding.

Nurse Practitioner: What keeps you going? I mean, in addition to the Non-Diet Diet score sheet?

Rebecca: My weight and the feel of my clothes. I weigh myself every day. If my weight changes, I increase my points on the Non-Diet Diet score sheet. If my clothes start feeling tight, I do the same thing.

Nurse Practitioner: Now that we have heard from everybody, let's see if we can help Debbie and Laura find some self-monitoring monitoring strategies that might work for them.

It is beyond the scope of this book to include the lengthy dialogue among the group members that would have followed what was presented in the case. However, some suggestions on how to help Debbie and Laura develop their own self-monitoring strategies are given next.

The nurse practitioner should facilitate a discussion about self-monitoring among the group members. Most of the talking and "brainstorming" should come from Debbie and Laura. The other members of the group have already shared their ideas. The nurse practitioner should restrain anybody from forcing their ideas or what works for them on Debbie and Laura.

The nurse practitioner should probe to find out what Debbie and Laura like and dislike. Are they numbers people who might like keeping track of calories, fat grams, Non-Diet Diet points, etc.? Is their own philosophy in line with the Healthy at Every Size philosophy or restrictive diet and exercise? How do they feel about exercise? What barriers do they have for healthy eating and physical activity? What have been their past experiences with weight control? What type of support system do they have? What is their social environment? What are their time constraints? Are they realistic in their expectations?

All of these things and more should be brought forward before Debbie and Laura design their own weight management strategies. Then, regardless of strategies created, the strategies should be individualized, include some type of healthy eating plan, include some form of physical activity, and incorporate coping mechanisms or ways to deal with emotional distress or out of the ordinary situations. Most important is that these strategies must be measurable.

Resolution Process

Notice how the nurse practitioner helped the older group members relate their experiences. Notice how the nurse practitioner kept the dialogue focused. Notice how the nurse practitioner praised patients for success and did not judge one behavior or strategy as being better or worse than another. Notice how all of the older members had a strategic plan that included the components mentioned above and was measurable.

MONITORING EATING BEHAVIORS

Monitoring is the key to maintaining newly established eating behaviors. As with exercise, the specific technique used to monitor eating behavior is not important. The important thing is that the monitoring technique used works for the individual patient. Some patients do well counting calories. Some patients do well weighing food servings. Some patients do well using food exchange lists. Some patients are successful counting fat grams. Other patients are successful keeping food diaries. Other patients manage weight best using monitoring tools like the Non-Diet Diet score sheet.

Patients who are successful at losing weight and changing their eating behaviors generally know what monitoring tool works best for them. Therefore, they usually do not need much guidance in selecting a monitoring tool. Quite often the monitoring technique they prefer is the same or very similar to what they used to lose weight in the first place.

Patients sometimes have trouble determining how strictly they need to monitor their eating behavior during reduced weight maintenance. Most patients who used a restrictive diet to help them lose weight are afraid that if they relax their limits they will regain weight. Some experimentation may be necessary to help the patient find a comfortable eating style that will allow them enough flexibility to where they can maintain a healthy weight without always feeling restricted and deprived. Table 14-2 gives some examples of monitoring techniques that can be used for healthy weight management.

CHRONIC CARE MODEL

The chronic care model is a model of health care that requires patient, provider, and system-level interventions to manage a chronic disease or condition. In other words, the disease or condition is not cured and does not go away, but is managed and controlled with constant compliance to ongoing treatment. The goals of the model are to assure patients get evidenced-based care, to aid patients in participating in their own care, and for care to be proactive, not reactive. These goals of the chronic care model have been focused upon throughout this book. Application of the chronic care model to successful maintenance of reduced body weight can help achieve these goals, for data clearly shows that constant, long-term vigilance is necessary if one wants to maintain a healthy body weight.

Self-management is the key concept in diet, physical activity, and management of emotions. Chen and Bodenheimer (2008) outlined the following seven activities that enable the individual to partner with the health team to achieve successful self-management:

- Encouraging patients to become active participants

TABLE 14-2: HEALTHY WEIGHT MANAGEMENT MONITORING TOOLS

Monitoring tool	How the monitoring tool will be used
Food journal	I will keep a daily journal of the food I eat, including time of day. My goal is to reduce my sweet intake and not snack after 7:00 p.m.
Food labels	I will read the food labels on all the food I purchase. My goal is to consume a diet that is less than 30% of calories from fat.
Non-Diet Diet score sheet	I will maintain an average score of 45 out of a possible 50 points for eating behaviors on the Non-Diet Diet score sheet.
Food exchange list	I will follow the diet plan prescribed for me using the food exchange list for persons with diabetes.
Personal journal	I will keep a daily journal of my feelings about my food intake. I will be careful to note if I am feeling deprived because I know that when I feel deprived I want to binge.
Fruit and vegetable count	I will count the servings of fruits and vegetables I consume each day. My goal is to maintain a five-a-day plan.

- Providing information
- Teaching condition-specific skills
- Promoting healthy behaviors
- Teaching problem-solving skills
- Assisting with the emotional impact of the chronic condition
- Regular and sustained follow-up

The first two steps are started during the weight loss process, along with promotion of healthy behaviors and learning specific skills to achieve weight loss goals. Weight maintenance is involved with continuing behavior changes, and learning to problem solve new barriers that arise. The emotional impact of the long-term aspects of maintaining weight loss cannot be underestimated. It may seem harsh or unfair, in that the obese person may think that once he/she reaches the desired body weight, the job is done. The nature of the problem is lifelong, and there is no "quick fix" for the problem of obesity. However, the same message of chronic care or constant monitoring is seen with other conditions and diseases. For example, the person diagnosed with hypertension may reduce blood pressure with exercise, but if the person ceases to exercise, the risk of hypertension returning is high. Therefore, constant monitoring of blood pressure and diligence in maintaining an exercise program are necessary for the patient with hypertension to remain healthy. The same can be said if the treatment plan for hypertension were medication. Once blood pressure is under control, medication must be continued in order to maintain a healthy blood pressure. Regular follow-up is essential in sustaining self-management behaviors.

Similarly, with a chronic conditions such as type 2 diabetes, the treatment plan may consist of healthy eating and exercise and/or medication. Regardless of the approach or treatment philosophy, when blood glucose is under control, continued monitoring and care are necessary to maintain control. In conclusion, obesity is like many other chronic diseases or conditions in that successful treatment includes chronic self-monitoring. What needs to be monitored? Eating and exercise behaviors and the coping skills that made treatment successful.

SUMMARY

In order for an obesity treatment to be successful, it must demonstrate long-term effectiveness. This means that the reduced body weight must be maintained as well as the improvements in health that accompanied treatment. Previously obese adults who are successful at maintaining a reduced body weight consume 1,300 to 1,700 kcal/day and expend about 400 kcal/day, or 45 to 60 minutes a day of moderate physical activity. Those who maintain a reduced body weight without restricting energy intake expend 700 kcal/day in exercise, or 60 to 90 minutes a day of moderate activity. In addition to eating less and exercising more, those successful at weight loss maintenance develop positive coping skills and the ability to self-monitor their health-promoting behaviors. Chronic self-monitoring and care are necessary for the obese person to maintain weight loss and improved health.

EXAM QUESTIONS

CHAPTER 14
Questions 54-57

Note: Choose the option that BEST answers each question.

54. Previously obese people who are successful at maintaining a reduced body weight consume approximately how many kilocalories per day?

    a. 900 to 1,200

    b. 1,300 to 1,700

    c. 1,500 to 2,000

    d. 2,700 to 3,500

55. Studies of previously obese people who are successful at maintaining a reduced body weight without restricting their diet expend approximately how many kilocalories per day in exercise?

    a. 200 kcal/day

    b. 300 kcal/day

    c. 500 kcal/day

    d. 700 kcal/day

56. Previously obese people who are successful at maintaining a reduced body weight employ which weight maintenance skills?

    a. exercise, monitoring of food intake, coping skills

    b. exercise, coping skills, low-carbohydrate diet

    c. low-carbohydrate diet, self-talk, imagery

    d. mediterranean diet, exercise, reading food labels

57. Obesity treatment is similar to many chronic diseases in that

    a. there is no hope of cure or long-term survival.

    b. medication is the best treatment.

    c. long-term vigilance in monitoring health promoting behaviors is necessary.

    d. once the damage is done, there is no recovery.

REFERENCES

American College of Sports Medicine. (2006). *ACSM's guidelines for exercise testing and prescription* (7th ed., pp 216-220). Philadelphia: Lippincott Williams & Wilkins.

Butryn, M.L., Phelan, S., Hill, J.O., & Wing, R.R. (2007). Consistent self-monitoring of weight: A key component of successful weight loss maintenance. *Obesity, 15*, 3091-3096.

Chen, E. & Bodenheimer, T. (2008). Applying the chronic care model to the management of obesity. *Obesity Management, 4*(5), 227-231.

Colvin, R.H. & Olson, S.B. (1983). A descriptive analysis of men and women who have lost significant weight and are highly successful at maintaining the loss. *Addictive Behaviors, 8*, 287-295.

Hollis, J.F., Gullion C.M., Stevens, V.J., Brantley P.J., Appel, L.J., Ard, J.D., et al. (2008). Weight loss during the intensive intervention phase of the weight-loss maintenance trial. *American Journal of Preventive Medicine, 35*, 118-126.

Kayman, S., Bruvold. W., & Stern, J.S. (1990). Maintenance and relapse after weight loss in women: Behavioral aspects. *American Journal of Clinical Nutrition, 52*, 800-807.

Klem, M.L., Wing, R.R., McGuire, M.T., Seagle, H.M., & Hill, J.O. (1997). A descriptive study of individuals successful at long-term maintenance of substantial weight loss. *American Journal of Clinical Nutrition, 66*, 239-246.

Kruger, J., Blanck H.M., & Gillispie C. (2006). Dietary and physical activity behaviors among adults successful at weight loss maintenance. *International Journal of Behavioral Nutrition and Physical Activity, 3*, 17-26.

Miller, W.C. & Eggert, K.E. (1992). Weight loss perceptions, characteristics, and expectations of an overweight male and female population. *Medicine, Exercise, Nutrition, and Health, 1*, 42-47.

Phelan, S., Wyatt, H.R., Hill, J.O., & Wing, R.R. (2006). Are the eating and exercise habits of successful weight losers changing? *Obesity, 14*, 710-716.

Weinsier, R.L., Hunter, G.R., Desmond, R.A., Byrne, N.M., Zuckerman, P.A., & Darnell B.E. (2002). Free-living activity energy expenditure in women successful and unsuccessful at maintaining a normal body weight. *American Journal of Clinical Nutrition, 75*, 499-504.

CHAPTER 15

WEIGHT BIAS AND SENSITIVITY

Authored by
Jessie M. Moore, APRN, MSN, CEN

CHAPTER OBJECTIVE

After completing this chapter the learner will be able to discuss the issue of weight bias and the steps needed to create a sensitive health care environment.

LEARNING OBJECTIVES

After completing this chapter, the learner will be able to

1. describe the occurrence of weight bias in the general population.

2. state the incidence of weight bias in health care settings.

3. list ways to increase sensitivity for overweight and obese patients in the health care setting.

INTRODUCTION

Throughout this manuscript, we have discussed the complexity of obesity's etiology and treatment and the need to tailor the treatment approaches to the individual patient. We have discussed many barriers to behavior changes for a healthier lifestyle, including availability of resources, affordability of recommended changes, and motivational aspects of changing behavior. A comprehensive discussion of the problem is not complete without examining the role that weight bias plays in this problem and exploring ways to provide care sensitive to emo-

tional, physical, and cultural aspects of obesity. Failure to do so can result in a negative impact on the health of the obese patient. Recognition of the existence of these barriers is essential to developing strategies to overcome them.

WEIGHT BIAS IN THE GENERAL POPULATION

Weight discrimination is a common occurrence throughout the United States. Areas of identified discrimination include employment, educational settings, and health care. There is also limited evidence related to transportation, jury selection, housing, and adoption proceedings (Puhl & Brownell, 2001). A national survey of 2,290 individuals conducted between 1995 and 1996 compared incidences of perceived weight/height discrimination and compared them to other forms of discrimination, including race, gender, and age. Of note, men were found to identify such discrimination at higher body mass index (BMI) levels of 35, whereas women identified a notable increase at BMI levels of 27 or greater. The overall incidence rates were comparable to reported rates for racial discrimination. In women, it was noted as the third most common form of discrimination, after gender and age discrimination. Settings noted were institutional, such as employment settings, and interpersonal (Puhl, Andreyeva, & Brownell, 2008).

Some have suggested that stigmatization associated with obesity may be a motivating factor for the likelihood of dieting; however, studies have shown this perception to be inaccurate. Puhl, Moss-Racusin, and Schwartz, (2007) found that those individuals who believed that common stereotypes regarding obesity were true were less likely to diet and reported more episodes of binge eating behavior.

Research suggests that prejudice toward obese people develops at a young age (Gallagher, 2005). Several studies have shown that weight bias begins as early as age 4, when children can identify an individual's excess weight as the reason for their attitude. This stigmatizing attitude appears to worsen as children get older, extending into college-age peers. There is also growing evidence that parents and educators show weight bias toward children. This was identified in 1994 in a report from the National Education Association, which stated that the school setting is a common venue for stigmatization and discrimination from nursery school through college. A recent review of weight bias studies found little change in this area has occurred, despite awareness of its existence and efforts to change behavior (Puhl & Latner, 2007). Family members also contribute to weight bias behavior.

The consequences of weight bias for youths and adults alike may have psychological, academic/employment, and health outcomes. The psychological aspects include lower self-esteem, depression, body image dissatisfaction, difficulty in developing interpersonal relationships, and suicidal behaviors. Employment researchers have long shown established patterns of reduced job availability, lower pay, and discriminatory practice for obese individuals, yet there are no laws that prevent this type of discrimination (Puhl & Brownell, 2001). Direct correlation of weight bias to academic performance in children and adolescents has been more difficult, and although it is clear that weight bias may be a contributing factor, some experts believe the psychological impacts noted above may more directly affect academic problems than actual bias events (Puhl & Latner, 2007).

A new area of research regarding weight bias is that of interpersonal bias. In a survey that examined the most common sources of weight bias among obese women, family members ranked the highest, with 72% of participants experiencing weight bias from a close family member, and 60% experiencing bias from friends (Puhl & Hueur, 2009). These data suggest that the obese individual faces a continuous barrage of weight bias and stigmatization in the public and personal environment. The constant negative messaging and feedback undoubtedly contribute to the cycle of helplessness and hopelessness that many obese individuals may experience. Treatment strategies will need to evolve to help reduce these areas of conflict and to better help support the behavior of change for all obese patients.

What is most alarming is the correlation between weight bias and the development of unhealthy weight and weight behaviors, particularly in adolescents. Weight teasing has been shown to increase the incidence of disordered eating, including binge eating behavior, and to decrease the performance of physical activity. It is also being theorized that increased stress levels of weight bias behaviors can directly cause physiological changes, including increased blood pressure and cortisol and metabolic abnormalities. These issues in turn, may lead to increased levels of obesity, and especially to the development of early comorbid disease in the adolescent (Puhl & Latner, 2007). Although this area of research is in its early stages, it may prove to have a significant impact on addressing the childhood epidemic of obesity now seen in this country.

At the same time, many efforts are underway to change the treatment of the overweight individual. Founded in 1969, the National Association to Advance Fat Acceptance (NAAFA) is a human rights organization dedicated to improving the quality of life for obese individuals. One of NAAFA's chief aims is to eliminate discrimination based on body size. Many organizations that promote size acceptance and denounce dieting to lose weight have begun since NAAFA established in 1969. These organizations seem to have a common theme – to change societal attitudes toward individuals who are obese. These organizations try to accomplish this goal through various different mechanisms, but the general focus areas seem to be the same:

- Love and accept people for who they are, not according to their looks.
- End discrimination against people of larger size.
- Halt the use of dieting to lose weight.
- Health can be improved in people of all sizes.

WEIGHT BIAS IN HEALTH CARE

Significant bias occurs in health care settings. The evidence of bias can be subtle or overt and includes provider attitudes and behaviors as well as aspects of the health care environment. Weight bias has been documented in studies on dietitians, mental health care providers, nurses, medical students and physicians. In a survey of 2,449 overweight and obese women, 69% identified that they had experienced physician bias, 47% had encountered nurse bias, 37% identified bias from dietitians, and 21% from mental health professionals (Puhl & Brownell, 2006).

Research has identified more specific details about health care bias. Dietitians were found to have beliefs that obesity is due to emotional problems, pessimism about adherence to treatment plans, and negative attitudes (Berryman, Dubale, Manchester, & Mittelstaedt, 2006). Psychologists believe obese patients have more pathology, more negative attributes, more severe symptoms, and worse prognosis (Davis-Coelho, Waltz, & Davis-Coelho, 2000; Hassel, Amici, Thurston, & Gorsuch, 2001). Nurses view obese patients as

"noncompliant," "lazy," "overindulgent," or "unsuccessful." In one study, 31% of nurses indicated they would prefer not to care for obese patients (Bagley, Conklin, Isherwood, Pechiulis, & Watson, 1989; Hoppe & Ogden, 1997; Maroney & Golub, 1992). A more recent review found that little has changed in this area (Brown, 2006).

Physician attitudes use many of the same stereotypes, and care provided was affected by spending less time with obese patients, ordering fewer interventions, assigning more negative symptoms to the patient, and being reluctant to perform certain screening exams (Bertakis, 2005; Campbell, Engel, Timperio, Cooper, & Crawford, 2000; Hebl & Xu, 2001). This bias has been shown to result in a delay of care for obese patients because they may avoid health care encounters and preventive screenings. Recent research has linked this avoidance directly to patients having previous experience with health care bias involving provider attitudes and behavior and a lack of sensitivity in the health care environment (Amy, Aalborg, Lyons, & Keranen, 2006; Drury & Louis, 2002).

ELIMINATING WEIGHT BIAS IN HEALTH CARE SETTINGS

Understanding the sources of weight bias in health care settings is the first step in reducing its occurrence. Increased sensitivity to the issues faced by the obese individual is manifested by behavioral and environmental changes. Self-examination of personal bias about obesity is a key step in the process because many well-intentioned providers have subtle bias of which they are not aware. The Rudd Center for Food Policy and Obesity at Yale University has suggested the following questions for self reflection:

- Do I make assumptions based on weight regarding character, intelligence, professional success, health status, or lifestyle behaviors?

- Am I comfortable working with people of all shapes and sizes?
- Do I give appropriate feedback to encourage healthful behavior change?
- Am I sensitive to the needs and concerns of obese individuals?
- Do I treat the individual or only the condition?

An honest appraisal of one's own feelings is the first step in acknowledging and changing any subtle bias that may be present. Also incorporated into attitudes may be the provider's own weight and issues surrounding it. It is not necessary to be overweight to have empathy for the overweight or obese individual, nor does the overweight or obese provider have less credibility in addressing the issue of weight loss. It is, however, important for the provider to model desired health care behavior changes and to be comfortable in discussing weight loss with the patient (Hill, 2006).

Providing a sensitive environment is also important. The office or clinic setting is commonly the scene of subtle bias that may not be recognized. The waiting room should have armless chairs that support at least 300 lb. Exam tables should accommodate larger size patients, and step stools with handles should be available. Large-size patient gowns should be provided, and equipment such as extra large blood pressure cuffs should be available. Bathrooms should be size accessible, and safety equipment such as grab bars and floor mounted toilets should be used.

Weighing procedures tend to manifest subtle bias. Only one in eleven physician's offices have a scale that goes over 300 lb (Amy et al., 2006). Weight-sensitive weighing procedures include locating the scale in a private area, asking for permission to weigh the patient, allowing patients to face away from the scale, and asking permission to discuss any weight changes. As in all interactions, verbal and nonverbal communication should always remain nonjudgmental.

Open communication between the health care provider and the patient is critical, and has been discussed in Chapter 8. Key strategies for overcoming bias in the health care setting can be summarized as follows:

- Be aware that patients may have previously experienced bias from providers, which resulted in avoidance of care.
- Understand that being overweight is a product of many factors, some of which are outside of a patient's control.
- Self-awareness of internal bias toward obesity can help eliminate its impact.
- Providing a safe and weight-sensitive environment enhances the patient/provider relationship and effectiveness of desired interventions.

Additional tools and references, including a checklist for the office environment can be found at the Rudd Center for Food Policy and Obesity Web site, under the Weight Bias and Stigma section at http://www.yaleruddcenter.org/what_we_do.aspx?id=10

SUMMARY

Obese persons are subject to bias, prejudice, and discrimination. Weight bias has been documented in educational institutions, employment settings, health care facilities, family relationships, and society as a whole. Prejudice toward obese people is well documented among physicians, medical students, nurses, and mental health professionals; the most logical place to end prejudice and discrimination is for health care professionals to take it upon themselves to change their attitudes and behaviors toward obese patients.

EXAM QUESTIONS

CHAPTER 15
Questions 58-60

Note: Choose the option that BEST answers each question.

58. According to a large study of adult obese women, the most frequent source of weight bias experienced is

    a. the health care provider.

    b. a family member.

    c. an employer.

    d. a close friend.

59. Weight stigmatization among health care providers

    a. occurs only among those providers who are not overweight themselves.

    b. does not affect the delivery of health care to obese individuals.

    c. often results in a delay of care for the obese individual.

    d. occurs more often among lower trained health care providers.

60. Which action demonstrates sensitivity for an obese patient?

    a. documenting weight at each visit

    b. including family members in all discussions

    c. not requiring the patient to remove his or her clothing

    d. using a correctly sized blood pressure cuff

This concludes the final examination.

Please answer the evaluation questions found on page v of this workbook.

REFERENCES

Amy, N.K., Aalborg, A., Lyons, P. & Keranen, L. (2006). Barrier to routine gynecological cancer screening for White and African-American obese women. *International Journal of Obesity, 30,* 147-155.

Bagley, C.R., Conklin, D.N., Isherwood, R.T., Pechiulis, D.R., & Watson, L.A. (1989). Attitudes of nurses toward obesity and obese patients. *Perceptual and Motor Skills, 68,* 954.

Berryman, D., Dubale, G., Manchester, D., & Mittelstaedt, R. (2006). Dietetic students possess negative attitudes toward obesity similar to nondietetic students. *Journal of the American Dietetic Association, 106,* 1678-1682.

Bertakis, K.D. & Azari, R. (2005). The impact of obesity on primary care visits. *Obesity Research, 13*(9), 1615-1622.

Brown, I. (2006). Nurses' attitudes towards adult patients who are obese: Literature review. *Journal of Advanced Nursing, 53,* 221–232.

Campbell, K., Engel, H., Timperio, A., Cooper, C. & Crawford, D. (2000). Obesity management: Australian general practitioners' attitudes and practices. *Obesity Research, 8,* 459-466.

Davis-Coelho, K., Waltz, J., & Davis-Coelho, B. (2000) Awareness and prevention of bias against fat clients in psychotherapy. *Professional Psychology: Research and Practice. 31,* 682-684.

Drury, C.A.A. & Louis, M. (2002). Exploring the association between body weight, stigma of obesity, and health care avoidance. *Journal of the American Academy of Nurse Practitioners, 14*(12), 554-560.

Gallagher, S. (2005). Sensitivity. *The challenges of caring for the obese patient.* Edgemont, PA: Matrix Medical Communication.

Hassel, T.D., Amici, C.J., Thurston, N.S., & Gorsuch, R.L. (2001). Client weight as a barrier to non-biased clinical judgment. *Journal of Psychology & Christianity. 20,* 145-161.

Hebl, M.R. & Xu, J. (2001).Weighing the care: physicians' reactions to the size of a patient. *International Journal of Obesity, 25,* 1246-1252.

Hill, J.O. (2006). Does your weight affect how you address obesity in your patients? *Obesity Management, 2*(1), 1-2.

Hoppe, R., Ogden, J. (1997). Practice nurses' beliefs about obesity and weight related interventions in primary care. *International Journal of Obesity, 21,* 141-146.

Maroney, D. & Golub, S. (1992). Nurses' attitudes toward obese persons and certain ethnic groups. *Perceptual and Motor Skills, 75,* 387-391.

Puhl, R.M., Andreyeva, T., & Brownell, K.D. (2008). Perceptions of weight discrimination: Prevalence and comparison to race and gender discrimination in America. *International Journal of Obesity.* Advanced online publication March 4, 2008.

Puhl, R.M. & Brownell, K.D. (2001). Bias, discrimination and obesity. *Obesity Research, 9*(12), 788-805.

Puhl, R.M. & Brownell, K.D. (2006). Confronting and coping with weight stigma: An investigation of overweight and obese adults. *Obesity, 14*(10), 1802-1815.

Puhl, R.M. & Hueur, C. (2009). The stigma of weight of obesity: A review and update. *Obesity,* Advanced online publication January 22, 2009.

Puhl, R.M. & Latner, J.D. (2007). Stigma, obesity and the health of the nation's children. *Psychological Bulletin, 133*(4), 557-580.

Puhl, R.M., Moss-Racusin, C.A., & Schwartz, M.B. (2007). Internalization of weigh bias: Implications for binge eating and emotional well being. *Obesity, 15*(1), 19-23.

Rudd Center. (2008). *Weight bias and stigma.* Retrieved April 14, 2009, from http://yalerudd center.org/what_we_do.aspx?id=10

RESOURCES

American College of Sports Medicine (ACSM) – Professional organization that deals with exercise and its relationship to health and performance.

http://www.acsm.org/

Position stands of the ACSM on exercise in various populations, including the elderly, obese, children, and women.

http://journals.lww.com/acsm-msse/pages/collectiondetails.aspx?TopicalCollectionId=1

Behavior Change Theories and Models – Briefly describes and compares various popular behavior change theories.

http://www.csupomona.edu/~jvgrizzell/best_practices/bctheory.html#Health%20Belief%20Model

Centers for Disease Control and Prevention – Resources and information on overweight and obesity.

http://www.cdc.gov/obesity/

Obesity Society – Professional organization that focuses specifically on obesity and overweight.

http://www.obesity.org/

Society of Behavioral Medicine – Professional organization that deals with all aspects of health and behavior, including obesity.

http://www.sbm.org/

United States Department of Agriculture – Numerous resources on the food guide pyramid, with information on menu planning, 2010 dietary guidelines, pyramid for kids, pyramid for preschoolers, and tracking your progress.

http://www.mypyramid.gov/

U.S. Department of Health and Human Services and National Institutes of Health, Weight-control Information Network – Contains a wealth of information about obesity for the professional, including resources on obesity, eating disorders, nutrition, and exercise.

http://win.niddk.nih.gov/

World Health Organization – Resources and information about the prevalence of obesity worldwide, projects combating obesity, and the disease risks of obesity.

http://www.who.int/en/

GLOSSARY

adiposity: The amount of fat stored on the body, or the degree of body fatness.

bariatrics: The practice of medicine that focuses specifically on the treatment of obesity.

cardiovascular exercise: Exercise that taxes the aerobic energy system, thus stressing the heart, lungs, and circulatory system.

comorbidity: A disease that is strongly related to another disease or medical condition. Cardiovascular disease, diabetes, and hypertension are comorbidities with obesity.

glycemic index: A rating of how much a food raises blood glucoses levels in comparison to how much ingesting the same amount of pure glucose raises blood glucose. If the glucose standard is set at 100, comparison foods are considered high glycemic if their index is 70 or greater.

glycemic load: Calculated by dividing the glycemic index by 100 and then multiplying it by the grams of carbohydrate in a specific amount of food, meal or diet. The glycemic load indicates how much a certain volume of food raises blood glucose levels.

glycemic stress: large fluctuations in blood glucose levels stress the metabolic system. Foods that have a high glycemic index and/or high glycemic load cause abrupt rises in blood glucose levels, thus stressing the system that regulates blood glucose.

Health at Every Size (HAES): An obesity treatment philosophy that insists that people of all sizes can be healthy and that health is not related to body size.

hyperinsulinemia: an excessively high level of blood insulin, commonly seen in type 2 diabetes and sometimes seen in obese patients who are at risk for diabetes.

meta-analysis: A statistical technique that combines data from a number of studies to arrive at a composite conclusion. The entire sample data from one individual study is treated as a single data point within the meta-analysis. Thus, each data point within the meta-analysis represents the mean of the sample data from one study.

NAAFA: National Association to Advance Fat Acceptance: A human rights organization that fights discrimination against people based on their body size or body fatness.

National Weight Control Registry: A registry of Americans who have been successful at losing a significant amount of body weight and maintaining that weight loss.

neurotransmitter: A chemical substance or compound that is released from a nerve ending and changes the permeability of the membrane on an opposing cell, facilitating the transmission of a nerve impulse from one cell to the next.

portion size: The amount of food any given individual eats in one sitting. Portion size can vary tremendously among individuals.

reliability: A statistical term that describes how well a method, tool, or technique can reproduce data that are supposed to be identical.

self-monitoring: Any method used by an individual to monitor, measure, or evaluate his or her own behavior or condition.

serving size: The amount of food the average person eats at one time. Serving sizes are based on consumption surveys.

validity: A statistical term that describes how well a method, tool, or technique measures what it is supposed to measure.

INDEX

Page references followed by *fig* indicate an illustrated figure; followed by *t* indicate a table.

X
Xenical, 175

Y
YMCA Fitness Assessment, 63

Z
Zonisamide, 178

Western Schools® offers over 2,000 hours to suit all your interests – and requirements!

Cardiovascular
Cardiovascular Nursing: A Comprehensive Overview
Cardiovascular Pharmacology
A The 12-Lead ECG in Acute Coronary Syndromes
Women and Cardiovascular Disease

Clinical Conditions/Nursing Practice
A Advanced Assessment
Ambulatory Surgical Care
Assessment of Pain in Special Populations
Clinical Care of the Diabetic Foot
A Complete Nurses Guide to Diabetes Care
Death, Dying, & Bereavement
Diabetes Essentials for Nurses
Essentials of Patient Education
Evidence-Based Practice: What Every Nurse Needs to Know
Fibromyalgia in Women
Helping the Obese Patient Find Success
Holistic & Complementary Therapies
Home Health Nursing
Humor in Health Care: The Laughter Prescription
IV Therapy: Essentials for Safe Practice
Management of Lupus
Multiple Sclerosis: Nursing Strategies to Improve Patient Outcomes
Orthopedic Nursing: Caring for Patients with Musculoskeletal Disorders
Ostomy Management
Pain Management: Principles and Practice
A Palliative Practices: An Interdisciplinary Approach
Pharmacologic Management of Asthma
Pneumonia in Adults
Rotator Cuff Injury and Recovery
Seizures: A Basic Overview
Wound Management and Healing

Critical Care/ER/OR
Basic Trauma Nursing
Critical Care & Emergency Nursing
Fire Risk Reduction for Operative and Invasive Procedures
Hemodynamic Monitoring
A Practical Guide to Moderate Sedation/Analgesia
Traumatic Brain Injury

Geriatrics
Alzheimer's Disease: A Complete Guide for Nurses
Alzheimer's Disease and Related Disorders
Cognitive Disorders in Aging
Depression in Older Adults
Early-Stage Alzheimer's Disease
Geriatric Assessment
Healthy Aging
Nursing Care of the Older Adult
Psychosocial Issues Affecting Older Adults
Substance Abuse in Older Adults

Infectious Disease
Avian Influenza
H1N1 Flu
Hepatitis C
HIV/AIDS
Infection Prevention for Healthcare Professionals
Influenza: A Vaccine-Preventable Disease
MRSA
Pertussis: Diagnosis, Treatment, and Prevention
Tuberculosis across the Lifespan
West Nile Virus

Leadership /Law/Ethics
Ethical Issues in Children's Health Care
Ethical Practices with Older Adults
Legal Implications for Nursing Practice
Protecting Patient Safety: Preventing Medical Errors
Leadership and Management for Every Nurse
Ohio Nursing Law Affecting Daily Practice

Oncology
Cancer in Women
Cancer Nursing
Chemotherapy and Biotherapies
Lung Cancer
Skin Cancer

Pediatrics/Maternal-Child/Women's Health
A Assessment and Care of the Well Newborn
Birth Control Methods and Reproductive Choices
Childhood Obesity
Diabetes in Children
Effective Counseling Techniques for Perinatal Mood Disorders
Fetal and Neonatal Drug Exposure

Induction of Labor
Manual of School Health
Maternal-Newborn Nursing
Menopause: Nursing Care for Women throughout Mid-Life
A Obstetric and Gynecologic Emergencies
Pediatric Abusive Head Trauma
Pediatric Health & Physical Assessment
Perinatal Mood Disorders: An Overview
Pregnancy Loss
Respiratory Diseases in the Newborn
Women's Health: Contemporary Advances and Trends

Pharmacology
Anticoagulant, Antiplatelet and Thrombolytic Medications
Antidepressants
Anxiolytics and Mood Stabilizers
Cardiovascular Pharmacology
Chemotherapies and Biotherapies
A Child/Adolescent Clinical Psychopharmacology
A Clinical Psychopharmacology Made Simple
Psychopharmacology Nurses

Psychiatric/Mental Health
A ADHD in Children and Adults
ADHD throughout the Lifespan
Adoptive Families: Trends and Therapeutic Interventions
Asperger's Syndrome
Behavioral Approaches to Treating Obesity
Best Practices with LGB Youth and Their Families
A Bipolar Disorder
Bullies, Victims, and Bystanders: From Prevalence to Prevention
Caring for Patients with Mental Health Issues: Strategies for All Nurses
A Childhood Maltreatment
Childhood Trauma
Clinical Neuropsychology: Applications in Practice
A Collaborative Therapy with Multi-stressed Families
Counseling Substance Abusing or Dependent Adolescents
Depression: Prevention, Diagnosis, and Treatment
Disaster Mental Health
A Ethnicity and the Dementias
A Evidence-Based Mental Health Practice
Grief, Bereavement, and Mourning in Children and Adults
A Growing Up with Autism
Identifying and Assessing Suicide Risk in Adults
Identifying and Treating Young and Adult Children of Alcoholics
A Integrative Treatment for Borderline Personality Disorder
Intimate Partner Violence: An Overview
Major Depression in Adults: Signs, Symptoms & Treatment Strategies
A Mental Disorders in Older Adults
A Mindfulness and Psychotherapy
A Multicultural Perspectives in Working with Families
Multidimensional Health Assessment of the Older Adult
A Obsessive Compulsive Disorder
Post-Divorce Parenting: Mental Health Issues and Interventions
A Problem and Pathological Gambling
Psychiatric Nursing: Current Trends in Diagnosis
A Psychosocial Aspects of Disaster
PTSD: An Overview
A Schizophrenia
Schizophrenia: Signs, Symptoms, and Treatment Strategies
Serious Mental Illness: Comprehensive Case Management
Sexual Health Counseling
Substance Abuse
Suicide
A Trauma Therapy
A Treating Explosive Kids
A Treating Substance Use Problems in Psychotherapy Practice
A Treating Victims of Mass Disaster and Terrorism
Understanding Attachment Theory
Understanding Loss & Grief: Implications for Healthcare Professionals

Reference Books
Nursing Drug Handbook
When Your Life is Touched by Cancer
Type 1 Diabetes in Children: A Quick Reference Guide

Respiratory
Acute Respiratory Distress Syndrome: An Overview
Adult Acute Respiratory Infections
Arterial Blood Gases: A Systematic and Easy Approach
Auscultation Skills: Heart and Breath Sounds
Birth Defects Affecting the Respiratory System
Chronic Obstructive Lung Disease
Genetic and Inherited Disorders Affecting the Pulmonary System
Lung Transplantation
Pulmonary Rehabilitation
Respiratory Pharmacology
SARS: An Emerging Public Health Threat

Visit our website at www.WesternSchools.com for course descriptions and additional CE offerings!